RÉT
50

ATLA Monograph Series
edited by Dr. Kenneth E. Rowe

Judaism in German Christian Theology Since 1945:

Christianity and Israel
Considered in Terms of Mission

by

EVA FLEISCHNER

ATLA Monograph Series, No. 8

The Scarecrow Press, Inc., Metuchen, N.J.

and

The American Theological Library Association

1975

Library of Congress Cataloging in Publication Data

Fleischner, Eva, 1925-
    Judaism in German Christian theology since 1945.

    (ATLA monograph series ; no. 8)
    Bibliography: p.
    Includes index.
    1. Judaism--Relations--Christianity. 2. Chris-
tianity and other religions--Judaism. 3. Missions
to Jews--Germany. 4. Judaism (Christian theology)
I. Title. II. Series: American Theological Library Association. ATLA monograph series ; no. 8.
BM535.F56 1975   261.2   75-22374
ISBN 0-8108-0835-8

PREFACE and ACKNOWLEDGMENTS

This work is the fruit of a discovery that began several years ago. Like most important discoveries, it happened slowly, was nurtured by the encouragement of friends, and resulted in an involvement that carried me far beyond my initial interest. Of the many friends and scholars, Jews and Christians, who have shared in this work, it is possible to thank only a few by name.

Bernard Cooke, Chairman of the Marquette Theology Department until 1969, was the first to listen sympathetically to my growing concern with Judaism and the Holocaust. It was he who introduced me to Rabbi Dudley Weinberg, who in turn opened to me many doors into Jewish experience and tradition.

Other Jewish scholars have given me encouragement and advice over the years. Rabbi Irving Greenberg, of Yeshiva University, New York; Professor Michael Wyschogrod, of City University of New York, and Dropsie College; Rabbi Asher Finkel, of New York University; Rabbi Abraham Heschel, of Jewish Theological Seminary, who managed to keep my concerns at heart even during a severe illness. The list of names could be prolonged. Let me say only that, wherever I have gone, I have been received with warmth and trust by Jewish scholars and experienced an openness to me as a Christian which has probably contributed in large measure to my belief that we live on the threshold of hitherto unprecedented possibilities for mutual understanding. I owe to these men, and to some dear Jewish friends who have taken me into their homes, what beginning insights into Judaism I may have at this time.

I also wish to express my gratitude to several Christian scholars:

Msgr. John M. Oesterreicher, who has generously shared with me his vast knowledge of the field, and the resources

iii

of the Institute of Judaeo-Christian Studies.

Professor Krister Stendahl of Harvard, who has not ceased to follow my project from its inception, always ready to listen, advise and encourage. The Harvard Divinity School has given me free access to its library facilities whenever I was able to spend time in Cambridge.

A three-month stay in Germany proved most informative, not only in gathering materials, but in meeting personally many of the Christian theologians who are responsible for renewed contact between Judaism and Christianity since World War II. I wish to express special thanks to Professor K. H. Rengstorf and his staff at the Institutum Judaicum Delitzschianum in Münster, for putting at my disposal the excellent library facilities of the Institute.

Professor Helmut Gollwitzer of Berlin welcomed me warmly to his home, and shared with me his experience and rich insights gained from his long-standing involvement in Jewish-Christian dialogue. I am grateful also to Professor Hans-Joachim Kraus of Göttingen, and Heinz Krewers of Duisburg, for their valuable time and advice.

Dr. Ursula Bohn, Assistant Director of the Institut Kirche und Judentum an der Kirchlichen Hochschule, Berlin, not only assisted me with valuable bibliographical data while I was in Berlin, but has continued to send me materials and bibliography since my return to the States.

My profound thanks are due to Professor Kenneth Hagen of Marquette University, who has guided me with his incisive criticisms and suggestions and given unstintingly of his time. Without his patience, trust and encouragement this work would in all likelihood never have been completed. Without one other man, Professor Jacques Audinet, of the Institut Catholique of Paris, it might never have been begun. For he fostered my interest in Judaism at a time when I was barely aware of it as yet myself.

A grant from the Memorial Foundation of Jewish Culture has enabled me to devote full time to research and writing this past year.

All translations appearing herein, unless otherwise identified, are mine.

The completion of this study marks the beginning of my return to teaching. It is a new beginning in an area that I consider vital to the life of the Church today: helping Christians to deepen their knowledge of the Jewish experience and tradition which have so much to contribute to an understanding of Christian experience and tradition. It is only through such knowledge that all of us, Jews and Christians alike, can come to a full understanding of what it means to be people of God in this world.

Eva Fleischner

Milwaukee
November, 1971

TABLE OF CONTENTS

EDITOR'S NOTE

Since 1972 the American Theological Library Association has undertaken responsibility for a modest dissertation publishing program in the field of religious studies. Our aim in this monograph series is to publish in serviceable format and at reasonable cost two dissertations of quality each year. Titles are selected from studies in the several religious and theological disciplines nominated by graduate school deans or directors of graduate studies in religion. We are pleased to publish Eva Fleischner's fine study of the view of Judaism in German Christian theology since 1945 as number eight in our series.

Professor Eva Fleischner is a native of Vienna. Following undergraduate studies at Radcliffe College, a Fulbright scholarship enabled her to pursue medieval studies at the University of Paris. She also studied liturgics at the University of Notre Dame and theology at the Institut Supérieur de Pastorale Catéchétique. She took the doctorate at Marquette University and currently serves as Associate Professor of Religion at Montclair State College, Upper Montclair, New Jersey. Active as a lecturer, translator, author and editor as well as teacher, Professor Fleischner most recently helped organize the Holocaust Symposium at the Cathedral of St. John the Divine in New York City in June, 1974, on the theme, "Auschwitz: Beginning of a New Era?," and will edit the proceedings.

A special word of appreciation goes to Dean Krister Stendahl of Harvard Divinity School for his helpful Foreword.

Kenneth E. Rowe, Series Editor

Drew University Library
Madison, New Jersey

xi

FOREWORD

This study by Eva Fleischner is a welcome contribution toward re-opening, and--what is now even more important--keeping open and lively the quest for truth in Christian thinking about Israel and Judaism, the Synagogue and the Jewish experience.

She writes with the sense of urgency that the subject requires after the Holocaust--and after the Yom Kippur war of 1973. There are many pieces of insight scattered both in the text and in the footnotes. From them I would especially lift up her awareness that "Christians should not expect the same theological preoccupation with Christianity on the part of Jews that Christians feel toward Judaism. Christianity as a religious phenomenon concerns Jews in general very little." And also her quotation from Elie Wiesel, "I think we Jews are the question mark of mankind, and that in creating us, God chose thus to question mankind. Which is the reason, perhaps, why we seem to be the center of so many tales, often not our own" (emphasis added). This process, by which Christians have made and make tales about the Jews, is what Arthur Cohen describes when he says that the "Church cut us off ... and refashioned us as a Christian myth," and it is helpful when Eva Fleischner brings into focus the penetrating reflections by the Dutch theologian Kornelis H. Miskotte in his Das Judentum als Frage an die Kirche.

With such perspectives and sensitivities, Eva Fleischner reports and analyzes the German theological discussion after 1945, especially as it shaped up around the 1961 Kirchentag and the Lutheran World Federation consultation in Løgumkloster, Denmark (1964). She contributes to the evaluation of the complex changes and constants in German Judenmission, and she reflects on the peculiarities in the present German situation with its human guilt, the virtual absence of a Jewish presence, and the awkward tendencies of some theologians not to say what is easy or what their hearts may prompt them to say. I call those tendencies "awkward" since they

xiii

are both ugly and beautiful. Beautiful, since they are part of human integrity and an awareness of how cheap words can be when prompted by a desire to please. Ugly, since they often confuse integrity with what in recent American language has become known as stonewalling--against the risks of truth.

Having read the study now before us, I would like to offer a few observations and reflections. I think of them both as a guide to the reader, and as items on the agenda ahead of the Church. First, it becomes shockingly clear that the future of Jewish-Christian relations calls for more than good intentions. The ethical arguments are not enough. The root of Christian sins and horrors is not in a lack of love. It is in wrong loves, and the more love, imperialist or condescending, the more sin. Good intentions become then just an excuse from radical re-thinking. In the long run, wrong thinking is more dangerous than wrong-doing.

Second, as a New Testament scholar, I am aware of significant work ahead. Both in detailed exegesis and in total perceptions. Let me mention only three items:

(A) I am convinced that the only New Testament passage claimed for calling the Church by the name "Israel" rests on a wrong reading of the text. It is rather a passage in which Paul speaks of the original Israel as "the Israel of God." The passage is Galatians 6:16, and a careful reading of the Greek text must lead to the translation: "And as many as walk according to this standard [the new creation in Christ], peace be upon them--and mercy also upon the Israel of God." The Revised Standard Version has suppressed the striking and strong kai (=also) before "the Israel of God." The King James Version and the New English Bible retain it faithfully, but awkwardly. The translation given above is the only one that fits the syntax of the Greek. It also fits well into Paul's thinking according to Romans 9-11. And thus it follows that nowhere in the New Testament is the Church called expressis verbis by the name of Israel, or the New Israel.

(B) In that majestic section of Paul's (Romans 9-11) we should begin to reflect on the surprising fact that, as Paul moves toward the resolution of the mystery of Israel, he does not say, as do many Christian interpreters, that Israel will finally recognize Jesus as the Messiah. It is striking that in this whole section Paul's language has shifted from Christ-language to God-language (the last reference to Jesus or Christ is in 10:17, where some manuscripts read

"God"); this in marked contrast to common Pauline usage.
Why? That question deserves serious further attention.

(C) Furthermore, Biblical reflection on the continuity
and discontinuity between Israel and the Church should perhaps also be directed toward the glorious figure of Melchize-
dek (Psalms 110:4 and Hebrews 5:6 and passim).

A third observation would be that the Jewish-Christian
dialogue must be rightly related to the wider questions of religious pluralism and to different forms of Christian and Jewish "theology of religions." Such approaches should be con-
genial to the Jewish sentiment mentioned above, i. e., that
Judaism has no reason for being especially preoccupied with
Christianity. And it would open up the complex questions of
to what extent the perspective of Heilsgeschichte, which dominates the study now before us, could and/or should be wid-
ened or even considered partially translatable into the perspectives of wisdom and ahistorical reality. It may be that
such questions would explain and sharpen up some of the
peculiarities in the German discussion, since by and large
religious pluralism and comparative religion have made less
of an impact on German and European than on American theology.

Finally, a crucial term in Jewish-Christian relations
is the word "witness," and it is one of the focal terms in the
study before us in this book. I could foresee a development
whereby this term is exonerated and even becomes of key
value in the relations among believers across all barriers.
But such a development has one necessary condition, and
that is a big one: we Christians must learn to leave the result of our witness to God. We can learn this from Israel,
and from the Jewish experience. For Jews have learned
what it means to accept a peculiar mission as a minority,
to be "a light to the nations" (Isaiah 40:5) without expecting
the nations, the Gentiles, to become like them. By their
witness to the oneness of God, and the moral order as expressed in the Torah, they fulfill that mission, leaving it to
God in faith how such witness fits into His total plan for His
creation. It may be that the witness and the mission of the
Church and its members is meant to be of that faithful style
and order. To witness in such a manner, rather than to
make others in our image, requires faith in God, instead of
trust in self-gratifying statistics....

At that point the question of Judenmission turns around

before our eyes. The Jewish understanding of the mission and the witness of those gripped by God offers the critique and the model for a church that begins to recognize what Paul knew and what is obvious to any contemporary observer with open eyes: the Christian Church is just as peculiar a small people as are the Jews, in the midst of God's very big world, and it hardly seems to be the will of God to have the world "Christianized." But there is the salt and the light ... and perhaps there may even be the curry and the sweet fragrances of the East.... But we witness as it has by grace been given us to see. The rest is in God's hand.

Krister Stendahl

September 1974
Nantucket, Massachusetts

Twenty-five years. A quarter century.
And we pause, trying to find our bearings,
trying to understand: what and how much
did these years mean? To some a generation,
to others an eternity. A generation
perhaps without eternity.

Children condemned never to grow old,
old men doomed never to die. A solitude
engulfing entire peoples, a guilt tormenting
all humanity. A despair that found a face
but not a name. A memory cursed, yet
refusing to pass on its curse and hate.
An attempt to understand, perhaps even to
forgive. That is a generation. Ours.

(Elie Wiesel. One Generation After)

INTRODUCTION

One generation after the end of World War II men begin to dare confront one of the greatest catastrophes in the history of humanity. The systematic extermination of six million Jews has shaken the world and men's faith in progress and Western civilization. It has also led to an examination of conscience for a growing number of Christians, and to a reappraisal of Christianity's teaching with regard to Judaism. This reappraisal is taking place in many countries of the West, but also, and especially, in Germany, the very country where the tragedy took place. It is the purpose of this work to examine one of the aspects of this reappraisal: Christianity's mission toward Israel.

The relationship of Christianity to Judaism can be analyzed in a variety of ways. Studies of a historical, psychological, or sociological nature, an examination of the contacts between the two communities, all these have their contribution to make. Our purpose, however, is to pursue the question along theological lines, and to study the manner in which the Christian Churches have conceived, analyzed and legitimated their relationship to Judaism in Germany since 1945.

The specific topic of our study, Christianity's relationship to Judaism in terms of mission, is a focus for our broader concern with Judaism and its relevance for Christianity. We have taken our starting point not in the chronological order, but in the existential situation in which Christians today find themselves with regard to Judaism. This existential situation is shaped by two major historical events, related symbolically, though not causally: the Holocaust, and the establishment of the State of Israel. [1]

The Holocaust

The first major historical event which dominates the

19

existential situation of Jew and Christian is the Holocaust, the systematically planned and meticulously executed murder of one-third of the world Jewish population, which sprang from the determination of Hitler and his collaborators to be done with the "Jewish Question" once and for all. Awareness of this event cannot yet be taken for granted among Christians. Indeed, twenty-five years later the word itself, which has become a household term for Jews the world over, and symbol of one of the greatest disasters to befall them in their more than 3000 years of history, is still unknown to many Christians in its new 20th-century meaning. 2

Since this study deals specifically with German Christian theology, * it should be pointed out that no literal equivalent to "Holocaust" exists in German, which to this day frequently uses the Nazi-coined Endlösung--"Final Solution. " The name Auschwitz, however, has acquired a larger and symbolic meaning and may be considered the equivalent of Holocaust in German usage. In this context a 1970 article by the German author Günter Grass is significant:

... Adorno's saying, that no more poetry can be written since Auschwitz, has led to so many misunderstandings that we must at least attempt to qualify it by interpreting it: poems written since Auschwitz must let themselves be measured by the norm of Auschwitz.

At this point I linger, listen to the word Auschwitz, and try to measure the impact of its echo.

We are familiar with the most trivial resonance: Again Auschwitz! Still Auschwitz? Must we keep on with this? Is there no end to it?

My answer is: I hope not. I also protest against the restrained and noble-sounding response: the answer to Auschwitz can be nothing but silence, nothing but shame and inability to speak. Auschwitz was no mystery which calls forth awe and interior, discreet contemplation. Auschwitz was reality, deed of man, hence subject to scrutiny.

It is true that, since Auschwitz, the calendar does not follow a new time reckoning. Yet there has taken place in our mentality--rarely consciously, but unavoidably unconsciously--something like a new way of

---

*The reasons for this are outlined later in the Introduction.

measuring time. Since Auschwitz man sees himself differently....

What happened prior to Auschwitz is subject to different norms. Although the mechanism of destruction had always existed, it was only its perfection that made it into a category. The new, unprecedented element was not the frightful cruelty of individual people, but the anonymous effortlessness of desk work carried out conscientiously and without a flaw....

Making of Auschwitz a turning point in time has endowed the former concentration and extermination camp with symbolic meaning. Auschwitz stands representatively for Treblinka and Mauthausen, for a whole assortment of former concentration and extermination camps. This symbolization process renders more difficult the task of explaining the day-to-day mechanism of Auschwitz because, when we pronounce the name of this one place, we at the same time pronounce the key word for genocide everywhere.

... What is asked of us is to understand Auschwitz in its historical past, recognize it in the present, and not assume blindly that Auschwitz lies only behind us. [3]

Another point worth noting is the curious phenomenon of transmutation which certain Jewish terms seem to undergo rapidly in our society. The word "Holocaust" is being used more and more widely today for major disasters of various kinds, ranging from Hiroshima to the brush fires in southern California in the fall of 1970. Similarly, the word "ghetto, " an Italian word meaning that part of a city (i. e., in Italy) where Jews were required to live, is today applied to inner-city slums, frequently without a knowledge of its original meaning. It seems to us that this applied usage tends to attenuate the original powerful meaning of the term and its uniqueness and that, from a pedagogical point of view, as well as for the sake of doing justice to history, the primary meaning should be pointed out to those unacquainted with it.

The Holocaust is an event that goes beyond Jewish history. The enormity of what happened, in which all the major Western nations had a share--whether through active participation or tacit acquiescence--inscribes it once and for all in 20th-century history, at least that of the West; hence, in Christian history. *

---

*The degree to which a given country is still Christian in

It is part of our existential situation then that we belong to a generation that has known, either directly or from afar, the Holocaust. Whatever our knowledge or lack of it, [4] the Holocaust has happened in our lifetime. This applies to Western man in general, but it presents the Christian with a problem of his own; a problem which is theological or religious in nature, and a challenge to his Christianity. The Christian today is confronted with the phenomenon of the survival of the Jewish people. In the face of systematic attempt to exterminate them--an attempt surpassing all previous attempts, and carried out with all the ingenuity and resources a modern technological state could muster--the Jewish people survived. Survival of any kind would have been nothing less than extraordinary, given the physical and psychological horrors of the Holocaust. But Jewish survival was not "bare" survival. The same generation--the same decade--that witnessed the Holocaust witnessed as well the rebirth of a Jewish homeland, for the first time in almost 1900 years. That weak, decimated people are today stronger than ever.

This is the existential situation in which the Christian finds himself vis-à-vis Judaism today. Early generations of Christians who witnessed the Roman wars of A.D. 70 and 135, in which Jerusalem and the Temple were destroyed, were faced with the same puzzle: the Jewish people "should" have disappeared, but did not. The situation of those Christians, however, differed from ours in at least two respects. They were still expecting the Parousia in the near future, even though its imminence had begun to recede by the second century. They could no more envisage the continued existence of Israel for another 2000 years than they could that of the world in general. Furthermore, they attempted a theological explanation for the continued existence of the Jews, which resulted eventually in what a contemporary Jewish author has called "the teaching of contempt." It may be summed up as follows: the Jews, having rejected the Messiah, are no longer God's chosen people. They are punished for their crime--the crime of deicide--by being dispersed all over the world, doomed to perpetual homelessness and a miserable existence in keeping with their degenerate, obdurate condition. [5]

(*cont.) actual fact is unimportant; the interest is with the Christian heritage which nations of the West have in common, and of which there are more than a few vestiges left even in a post-Christian era.

The situation today is reversed on both counts. Israel's ability to survive 1900 years of persecution makes its
continued existence--in the present expanded historical per-
spective--as good as a certainty. At the same time, the influence which traditional Christian teaching has had on modern anti-Semitism, including the Holocaust, has begun to op-
en our eyes to the dangers of this teaching.[6] Thus if Christians today still seek an explanation for Israel's existence
and meaning, they are likely to seek it along very different
lines from those pursued by the primitive Church.

Anti-Semitism

Reference has been made to the impact of traditional
Christian teaching on anti-Semitism. Since it is, however,
by no means universally accepted in Christian circles,[7] an
attempt should be made briefly to try to substantiate the theory that, while Christianity cannot be held responsible for
the Holocaust, Christian teaching helped prepare the ground
for it.

However one assesses the role of Christianity in the
Nazi persecution of the Jews, only the most naive interpretation will permit the Churches to escape unscathed. Helmut
Gollwitzer points out that although Jews have been persecuted for centuries in many countries of the world, "real
anti-Judaism with all its excesses existed only in Christian
countries," and that the Passion of the Jewish people began
many centuries prior to 1933 ["Die Judenfrage--eine Christenfrage," in Christen und Juden, ed. Wolf Dieter Marsch
and Karl Thieme (Mainz: Matthias-Grünewald Verlag, 1961),
p. 287]. While individual Christian leaders on many occasions helped and protected Jews, these instances "cannot
outweigh the evil that was wrought" [p. 288].

The distinction frequently made nowadays between anti-
Judaism and racial anti-Semitism seems ultimately to beg
the question, and does not really come to grips with the
problem of Christian guilt. Hermann Greive, a contemporary German historian whose interpretation is remarkably
moderate, underlines both the difference and the link between
the two:

> ... Medieval anti-Judaism and modern anti-Semitism
> are certainly not identical. Nonetheless, Christianity

plays an important role in both.... The arian-Se-
mitic contrast is not the negation of the Christian-
Jewish contrast, but rather presupposes the latter
and assumes it... [Ideologie und Theologie. Katholizismus und Judentum in Deutschland und Oester-
reich 1918-1935 (Heidelberg: Lambert Schneider,
1969)].

He maintains that, while not everyone countenanced the Nazi
persecution of the Jews, it was nevertheless tolerated by the
majority of Christians as divine judgment--an attitude fostered by centuries of Christian teaching:

... The widespread conviction of the profound and
manifold guilt of the Jewish people prevented the rise
of a determined opposition. In the light of this conviction, the sufferings of the Jews seemed not so
much the result of human failure--including one's own
--but rather, as the execution of God's punishing justice and guiding love... [Ibid., p. 226].

Not only were Christians not exempt from this kind
of perverted theological interpretation, but they had been conditioned to it for centuries. In the words of the French
theologian Kurt Hruby, "The 'teaching of contempt' was a
theological vision that deeply vitiated the religious appreciation of God's plan for his people. This is a brutal fact that
cannot be eliminated by theological subtleties or distinctions"
["Reflections on Dialogue," Brothers in Hope, The Bridge.
Judaeo-Christian Studies, Vol. V (New York: Herder and
Herder, 1970), p. 129].

One could hardly find a more graphic illustration of
how deeply the "teaching of contempt" had taken root than
the following text by Dietrich Bonhoeffer, one of the most
courageous opponents of Nazism, and a great Christian:

The Church of Christ has never lost sight of the
thought that the 'chosen people' who nailed the redeemer of the world to the cross must bear the curse for
its action through a long history of suffering....
But the history of the suffering of this people, loved
and punished by God, stands under the sign of the final homecoming of Israel to its God. And this homecoming happens in the conversion of Israel to Christ
.... The conversion of Israel, that is to be the end
of the people's period of suffering. From here the

Christian Church sees the history of the people of Israel with trembling as God's own, free, fearful way
with his people, because God is not yet finished with
it. Each new attempt to solve 'the Jewish question'
comes to naught ... nevertheless such attempts must
be made [quoted in No Rusty Swords. Letters, Lectures and Notes 1928-1936 from the Collected Works
of Dietrich Bonhoeffer, Vol. I., ed. & introd. Edwin
H. Robertson (New York: Harper, 1965), pp. 226-
27].

It is true that Bonhoeffer wrote these lines early in the Nazi
rise to power, in 1933. Yet, despite his consistent and heroic opposition to Nazism, which ultimately cost him his
life, there is no evidence that he ever repudiated the notion
of a divine curse hanging over the Jewish people.

Among Jewish authors, not surprisingly, there is general unanimity that the traditional teaching of the Church fed
and fanned Nazi anti-Semitism directly. Here are two
sources by way of example. The first is Jules Isaac, the
respected French historian, who was probably more influential than any other single individual in persuading John XXIII
of the urgency of considering the relationship between Judaism and Christianity as part of the agenda of Vatican II.
Isaac writes:

There is a Christian anti-Semitism. Whether conscious or sub-conscious, it is perennial and virulent,
of great scope and intensity.... For even in the best
Christians, even in those who fought most courage-
ously against Nazi anti-Semitism, it is easy to distinguish traces of a kind of sub-conscious anti-Semitism.

There is no better example of this than the perpetual
distortion of Jewish history by Christian theologians.
When I read in Pax Nostra, a book published in 1936
by Father Gaston Fessard, S.J., a chapter entitled
"The Negative Mission and Destiny of the Jewish
People," I submit that this very title, referring to a
people to whom the Christians owe the Bible and the
concept of monotheism, is itself a tendentious denial
revealing subconscious prejudice. It is exposed
throughout the chapter, as the author points to 'the
murderous race ... eternally riveted at the cross-
roads where the destinies of mankind meet and inter-
sect, in order to point out to passers-by the direction

of history.' [The Teaching of Contempt, p. 24].

Our second source is the French philosopher André
Neher, who writes in L'Existence Juive [Paris: Editions
du Seuil, 1962]:

> A nearly thousand-year-old history raises up barriers,
> a history of relations between Christians and Jews in
> which I [the Jew] have constantly, without exception,
> played the role of victim in the face of the persecu-
> tor and executioner. In vain do I seek another type
> of man who, to the same degree as the Christian,
> marked me out so deliberately as the adversary to be
> insulted and brought low. I find the only parallel in
> the Nazi. He alone in history, like the Christian,
> conceived the battle against the Jew as a primordial
> task and, likewise, brought about its realization with
> perseverance and method. I can imagine how painful
> and hateful this juxtaposition of the Christian and
> Nazi, of the stakes of Toledo, Blois, Worms, and
> the crematoria of Bergen-Belsen, Maydanek, Ausch-
> witz, is to my Christian brothers. But I beg you to
> imagine, for your part, how painful and hateful it is
> also to me. All the more painful because, despite
> the undeniable fact that the anti-Semitism of Hitler
> is historically different from Christian anti-Semitism,
> it is nonetheless certain that the Christian precedent
> helped Nazism to grow, and that the collective psy-
> choses developed by Christian anti-Judaism fostered
> those of Nazi anti-Semitism [pp. 240-41; emphasis
> added].

Many believe that the Holocaust reveals, as nothing
else has done, Christianity's failure, Christianity's "un-
Christianness." A facing up to the Holocaust, which includes a facing up to the Church's part in it, is essential
for Christianity's own survival and future. A beginning toward this has been made.[8] The revelation of the Holocaust
has led not only to an examination of conscience and admission of guilt on the part of Christians,[9] but also, at least in
limited theological circles, to a new and sincere effort to re-
examine Christian teaching about Judaism, the relationship
of Christianity to Judaism, and Judaism's meaning and relevance for Christian faith today.

The State of Israel

The second major historical event which affects
Christianity's relationship with Judaism today is the rebirth
of the State of Israel. Like the Holocaust, though in a different way, it goes beyond Jewish history, and is likely to
have a far-reaching impact on the Church's view of Judaism.
The establishment of the State of Israel in 1948 was the realization of the age-old longing of the Jewish people for the
return to Zion, expressed year after year at the end of the
Seder: "Next year in Jerusalem!" For the first time since
the Roman war of A.D. 66-70, the Jewish people have a
land of their own. In the words of André Neher,

> An uninterrupted chain of prayers in the language of
> the Bible, directed toward the land of the Bible, links
> the last Jewish emigrant of the age of Titus to the
> first Russian immigrant of the age of the Czars. Be-
> tween the Israeli of the twentieth century and the He-
> brew of antiquity there is something other than the
> similarity of the Palestinian setting and countryside:
> there is the communion of destiny [quoted in Alain
> Guichard, Les Juifs (Paris: Grasset, 1969), p. 217].

There are signs that the concrete fact of Israel's existence is effecting a major change in Christianity's view of
Judaism, forcing it to abandon myths and stereotypes--such
as that of the Jew doomed forever to be a homeless wander-
er over the face of the earth--which have contributed so
heavily to religious anti-Jewish sentiment in the past and to
the Teaching of Contempt. In an interview with the World
Council of Churches in 1948 in Amsterdam, Karl Barth said
that the way in which the names of Jerusalem and other holy
places were being bandied about sounded to him like a par-
ody of their Biblical meaning. Yet two years later, in 1950,
events in Israel appeared to him, in their similarity with
Old Testament events, as a sign of God's election and love
of Israel. [10]

The evolution in Barth's view of the State of Israel
was not yet at an end. In 1962, when asked about the meaning of the State, Barth answered as follows:

> A possible explanation is that it is another and new
> sign of the electing and providentially ruling grace
> and faithfulness of God to the seed of Abraham, a

very visible sign, visible for every reader of the papers, the whole world--a sign which is not to be overlooked.... The reappearance of Israel, now as a nation in the political realm, even as a state, may well be called a miracle for all that have eyes to see. [11]

Still later, in 1967, in a discussion with students of the Mennonite School in Basel, Barth called the State of Israel "an eschatological sign," and spoke of the events in Israel since 1948 as a repetition of the Biblical account of Israel's entrance into the promised land. [12]

This is but one example of a remarkable evolution in attitude that can be traced directly to the irrefutable fact of the existence of the State of Israel. It is too soon to know where this development will lead; but already it is beginning to open up important and new dimensions in Christian theological understanding of Judaism. The State of Israel has been a shock for the non-Jew, disturbing the image of the Jew he had made for himself.

Mission to Israel--A Theological Problem

Christianity achieved its first expansion by addressing itself to Jewish communities. The apostles' proclamation to their fellow Jews consisted of announcing Jesus as the fulfillment of the promises made to the Fathers (Acts 2). Very early, however, the Christian proclamation broadened in scope, as the young Church went out to gentiles as well as Jews. Since Jesus was the Savior of all men, the Church's mission, conceived as the fulfillment of that of Israel and realized through the coming of the Messiah, must be addressed to all.

The Christian mission to the gentiles soon led to conflicts as to the form this mission was to take. The most ancient and best-known of these arose in Antioch (Acts 15), over the manner in which the gentiles should become members of the Church. Was it necessary for them to pass through the observance of the Mosaic Law--in particular, circumcision--in order to become followers of Christ? In more contemporary terms: Must the mission of the young Church to the gentiles--a universal mission--take on the forms of one particular group, the Jewish people?

This question led to the first serious crisis in the

taken place, bringing theologians from Israel to Germany, and German theologians to Israel.[16] Germans were among the founders (in 1962) of one of the most promising communities to be established in Israel, the Christian village of Nes Ammim, in the northern part of the state.* It is probably inevitable that some of the motives for this interest be seen as mixed. Yet this should not obscure or negate genuine and positive aspects of contact with the Jewish reality in Germany today, no matter their difference from those in the United States. Nor does it lessen the need for theological reflection about Israel. Such reflection, in the words of Wolfgang Wirth, is "an existential necessity for Christianity. It must take place even if no encounter is possible between Christians and Jews.... wherever Christians seek to understand themselves as Christians" ["Der ökumenische Aspekt der Begegnung mit den Juden," in Judentum und christlicher Glaube, ed C. Thoma (Klosterneuburg, 1965), p. 145].

For the Jew, however, post-Hitler Germany is above all a Germany without Jews, the one country of Europe where Judaism has not been able to regain root.[17] This is all the more tragic when one recalls the fact that Jews had lived in Germany without interruption, though not always in peace, for more than a thousand years, in contrast to other European countries where the Jewish presence had been intermittent and at times totally absent for centuries--such as in Spain after the expulsion of 1492. This presence came to an end with the Holocaust and with it the remarkable Jewish contribution to German culture and history.[18]

Despite these ambiguities the German theological scene has been chosen as the field of this study. As Reinhold Mayer points out, the contribution of German theology to the Christian-Jewish debate has special significance, since nowhere else "was the Church so threatened in her own theological existence as in Germany" [Zum Gespräch mit Israel (Stuttgart: Calwer Verlag, 1962), p. 40]. The influence of German theology (especially in the United States) is another reason for this choice. Finally, given a profound concern with the Holocaust itself, the German scene could not be bypassed, whatever possible pitfalls it may present.

---

*The settlement of American, German, Dutch and Swiss Christians seeks to contribute to the country economically and agriculturally, explicitly disavowing all missionary intent.

Church. The efforts of the Council of Jerusalem to resolve the conflict, by inviting into one and the same faith community Jews and gentiles, were doomed to failure. Positions soon became clear that the Jewish people as a whole would not join the Church, while the latter achieved rapid success among the gentiles and, beginning with the fourth century, became identified with the institutions of society.

Yet the Jewish people continued to exist, despite political and military catastrophes that "should" have brought about their disappearance. The Church was confronted with the nagging question of what to make of this people. It was an urgent and practical question, first and foremost theological in nature and involving the Church's identity. How was it to explain the coexistence of the two communities, since it perceived itself as the new and true Israel, successor and heir to the old?

The tragic and painful history that resulted from this coexistence, and from Israel's "refusal" to disappear, is better known today than ever before, as is the manner in which the Church attempted to solve the question of the meaning of the Jewish people. Unable to deny their continued existence, it explained this existence, with its accompanying sufferings and dispersion throughout the world, as a sign of God's punishment and rejection of the Jews for their failure to recognize Jesus as the Christ. Thus there evolved the Teaching of Contempt (see page 22) and the historical forms of an anti-Semitism that were to last down the centuries and come to an unprecedented climax in our own day.

The question as to Israel's meaning and relationship to the Church was not confined to the first centuries of Christianity. Its ramifications have continued to haunt the Church throughout history and it remains an urgent and vital question today. The continued existence of Israel since the coming of Jesus challenges the nature of the Church. If, once the Promise has been realized, the Children of the Promise continue to exist, what is the nature of that Promise? How is the Church to conceive the salvation brought by Christ? How is it to look upon the Children of the Promise who refuse to recognize Jesus Christ as the fulfillment of the Promise? Do they still have a place in the divine plan of salvation and, if so, what is it, and how does it affect the Church's own role in the world? What is to be Christianity's attitude toward Israel and the nature of

Christian mission toward the Jewish people? How is the Church to understand the universality of its mission, so long as one group--the Sons of Abraham, sharing the same faith in the God of Abraham--reject Christ?

These questions, which Israel's continued existence poses for the Church, ultimately touch a broader theological subject: Christian mission, its nature, and the ways in which it is to be carried out. For the Church, which sees itself as salvation community inseparable from its head, the concept of mission is linked to Christ, questions about the Church's own nature, the universality of salvation, the unity of faith. Thus, the specific focus of the present study, Christianity's mission to Israel, can serve as a catalyst for these broader questions confronting Christianity in a pluralistic age. While not the direct concern of the present work, they are part of Christianity's challenge today.

Why the German Scene?

Theological concern with Judaism is evident today in many countries of the Western world. In some respects it is perhaps at its most significant in the United States, where the proportionately large number of Jews--roughly one-half of the world Jewish population--as well as the long-standing tradition of a pluralistic society, make possible frequent and regular contact between Jews and Christians on a day-to-day basis which, not surprisingly, spills over into theological dialogue. The Jewish presence makes itself felt in the political and cultural, as well as religious aspects of American life.

The German situation, by contrast, is far more complex and ambivalent.* The trauma of the Nazi past and the extermination of six million Jews, which brought opprobrium upon Germany in the eyes of the entire world, is understandably greater for Germans than for citizens of other nations. Feelings of guilt, the desire to atone for the past--or be done with it--easily color theological thinking. This need

---

*It should be pointed out that "German" or "Germany" (in reference to the years after 1945) refers throughout to West Germany. Interest in Judaism among German Christian theologians and German Jewish-Christian dialogue are visible in the post-war years only in the Federal Republic.

not be a liability. On the contrary: when history does not make an impact on theology, the latter is in danger of losing its relevance and its claim to shape contemporary thought. The situation in Germany since the war does, however, call for a careful examination of sources, if one is to distinguish genuine theological effort from what might be called "compensatory mechanisms."

Post-Hitler Germany is ambiguous for another reason: the almost total absence of Jews. The Jewish theologian Hans-Joachim Schoeps describes what he found upon returning to Germany in 1945 from exile in Sweden:

All my investigations made it clear that nothing remained of the ancient German Judaism. The few Jewish communities that had been reconstituted in large cities were composed of old people, people who were weary and whose spirits had been blunted; nor was anything happening religiously. In the years since then this lethargic situation has hardly changed, for until now [1956] the return of Jews to Germany is limited to very modest numbers [Rückblicke (Berlin, 1956), p. 142].

Fewer than 30,000 Jews are living in Germany today, many of them elderly men and women who, having escaped the Nazi terror or survived the death camps, have settled in Germany because life there is made relatively easy for them by the government.[13] Synagogues and Jewish community centers have been rebuilt everywhere, but are largely empty.[14] The once so significant Jewish contribution to German life is a thing of the past. Hence, Jewish-Christian encounters and "dialogues" frequently have something contrived about them, and the Christian theologian's reflection about Judaism occurs largely in a vacuum, without the benefit of testing against the Jewish reality of today.[15]

Although one can hardly speak of a living Judaism in Germany today, it is paradoxically true that Judaism is "present" in other ways. For many years the question of reparations--both to individual refugees abroad, and to the State of Israel--was in the forefront of German politics. Hardly anywhere else is there to this day such a lively, consistent interest in the State of Israel. German tourists visit Israel in large numbers, and individual Germans and groups have contributed substantially to the country's economic growth. In the religious sphere also an exchange

The Period Covered

The limitation of this study to the period since 1945 is motivated by a belief that the end of World War II marked the beginning of a new era in Christianity's attitude toward Judaism, which affects the concept of mission to Israel. It is obvious, however, that the theological questions referred to on page 29 are neither posed nor resolved once and for all, but are part of the slow and gradual evolution of theology through the centuries. Thus, it will frequently be necessary to refer to the past history of Christianity's relation to Judaism. While the 19th-century background will form the substance of Chapter I, here briefly is described the more immediate historical background to our period.

The Nazi persecution of 1933 to 1945, which culminated in the Holocaust, resulted from the debacle of World War I and the overthrow of the Weimar Republic. The years 1918 to 1933 present a curious paradox. On the one hand, they witnessed a rise of nationalism that was accompanied by a growth in anti-Semitism. The racial concept of peoplehood, as propounded by Houston Stuart Chamberlain, had already come to the fore in the pre-war years. Writing in 1907, H. Rost stressed the basic opposition between the Jewish and German character, contrasting German warmth, idealism, faith, life of the spirit, etc., with Jewish sarcasm, irony, and materialism. This trend gained momentum in the turbulent years that followed Germany's defeat. Guardini describes the force and newness with which the concept of peoplehood emerged as a new and unique phenomenon. It is seen as the primeval bond between men who are one through a common country and historical evolution.

The Jews, always considered aliens and strangers, now appeared as a threat to the preservation of this sacred entity constituted by the people. Anti-Semitism erupted with a new intensity and 19th-century anti-Semitic books were reprinted and widely circulated. Jews were held responsible for the fall of the monarchy, for the destruction of which they supposedly had been working ever since the days of Bismarck. The myth of an international Jewish conspiracy to seize world power was revived. Jewish influence on the press and on cultural and economic life was depicted as a disturbing and destructive element in German life. From 1929 on, under the influence of the Depression and of Nazism's rapid rise, these trends grew ever more prominent.

While the picture was by no means simple or uniform, the main ideological concepts remained: race, blood, soil, people and peoplehood. The Jews were considered not simply members of an alien race, but "as the alien race par excellence."[19]

What constitutes the paradox referred to earlier is that during the same period and along with the rise of anti-Semitism, there was a growth in efforts at mutual understanding between Jewish and Christian German theologians; and among the latter, at least the attempt to treat their Jewish colleagues as equals.[20] The culminating point of these efforts was reached in the historic debate between Martin Buber and K. L. Schmidt in Berlin, in 1933.[21] It marked both the climax and temporary end of a growing theological rapprochement between German Jews and Christians, and was followed by the total silence of the Nazi period, lasting more than fifteen years.

After the war, discussions and encounters resumed only gradually. In the fall of 1948, in Darmstadt, the "Deutsche Evangelische Ausschuss für Dienst an Israel" organized a meeting between Jewish and Christian theologians, at which Leo Baeck spoke.[22] In the same year we find the first explicit statement--not without many ambiguities--regarding Judaism, from an official German ecclesiastical body: the "Bruderrat der Evangelischen Kirche Deutschlands."[23] The trauma of the revelation of the full horror of the Holocaust was so great that some years had to pass before German Christians could even begin to face it. Renate Maria Heydenreich characterizes these early post-war years as "a continuation of being at a loss."[24]

If one were to draw a curve of the interest in Judaism as reflected in discussions and writings since 1945, it would begin to rise around 1948, mount to a peak in the early sixties with the Kirchentag controversy (see Chapter III), and start on a downward slant in the second part of the decade.[25] It is difficult to determine whether the latter trend reflects a lessening theological concern with Judaism, or only a more limited, but greater in-depth theological effort.

An assessment of the present situation is complicated by two factors in particular. A number of theologians who were most involved with Judaism through the fifties and early sixties have moved to other concerns of human and social justice--various protest movements such as disarmament, peace, or rapprochement with Eastern Europe.[26] At the same time, while some of the post-war pioneers among Christian theologians are moving on to other concerns, a new and younger generation, some of them their students, is breaking fresh ground: men like Reinhold Mayer (Tübingen), W. F. Marquardt (Berlin), W. P. Eckert (Cologne), Adolf Exeler (Münster), Heinz Kremers (Duisburg), Martin Stöhr (Darmstadt), and Rolf Rendtorff (Heidelberg).

The second major factor affecting Christian theology vis-à-vis Judaism, in Germany as elsewhere, is the political situation in the Middle East. The rapidly growing number of theological works dealing with the questions arising from international politics there is an indication of a certain shift in emphasis,[27] and of a growing theological concern with the State of Israel.

Despite the keen interest in Israel which is evident in Germany today, one cannot ignore a new danger signal. There are signs that Israel's aggressive determination to maintain itself as a free, independent state at all costs is giving rise to a new anti-Semitism, which differs from the old mainly in that its most vocal spokesmen are members of the New Left. That Germany is no exception is vividly illustrated by the following report:

> In Germany, New Left students, in a sickening replay of the behavior of their Nazi predecessors of 1928-1933 (university students were the first stratum in Germany to back the Nazis, giving them majorities in student council elections as early as 1931), chant as they parade: 'Mach die Nahe Osten rot; schlag die Zionisten tot!' (Make the Near East Red; smash the Zionists dead!) Dieter Kunzelmann, who played a major role in the demonstrations at the Free University of Berlin during the late nineteen-sixties, and who is now in the Middle East with the fedayeen, being instructed, according to his published letters, 'in the use of explosives ... [and] the manufacture of time bombs,' has written from Amman that the German left must break down pro-Semitism that emerged out of German guilt at the holocaust, that Germany must get over 'den Judenknax' (the thing [hang up] about the Jews).[28]

SOURCES USED

Since the concern of this work is with the German scene, non-German authors whose writings are influential there--such as Swiss, French, Dutch, Austrian, Scandinavian and, more rarely, American--are freely used. Both Protestant and Roman Catholic theologians will be examined, since Christian theology in general is being dealt with.

Among Protestants, the names of Lutheran theologians occur most frequently. For the German Lutheran Church has not only taken the lead in theological reflection about Israel and in contact between Christians and Jews after the war, but also still actively endorses and engages in missionary work to Jews.[29]

The Roman Catholic Church, on the other hand, has no official missionary policy or organization toward Israel. This partially explains the fact that relatively few Catholic authors are mentioned in the present work. There is probably a more basic reason for their conspicuous absence: German Catholic theological scholarship in general has only begun to catch up with Protestant theology, in the area of Judaism as elsewhere. To our knowledge only Hans Küng, among Germany's major Catholic theologians, has dealt with Jewish problems. The subject is totally absent from the works of J. Metz and W. Kasper, and occupies a minimal place in the writings and thought of Karl Rahner.[30]

The names that occur in this book do not all belong to well-known theologians. The number of German theologians concerned with the question of Israel and the Church is limited to begin with; those who deal with the missionary question are fewer still. (Neither Helmut Gollwitzer, nor his student W. F. Marquardt, for example, is concerned with this question as such, yet both contribute greatly to the theology of Israel in general.) The criteria used in the selection of sources are their theological import, their usefulness in revealing certain mentalities and attitudes, and/or their impact on or reflection of public opinion. The starting point, then, has not been a list of Germany's most renowned theologians, but those writings which shed some light on Christianity's mission to Israel. Some famous names are conspicuous by their absence.

A further principle of selection is the inclusion of

Jewish authors in cases where their views provide a contrast
to or new perspective for Christian theology. Since there is
no longer a living Judaism in Germany, American and other
European Jews are mentioned, some of whom, such as the
French scholar André Neher, are not widely known in Germany, yet are well versed in the German situation. While
the concern of this study is not with dialogue as such--the
term is increasingly overused today and tends to obscure the
real issues--but with theological understanding, an acquaint-
ance with Jewish thought, whether in the form of face-to-
face discussion, reading, or preferably both, is essential.
The subject of dialogue will therefore recur frequently. One
underlying conviction is that Jewish self-understanding, and
the way in which the Jew sees himself in relation to the
Christian, are by and large a closed book for the Christian,
and in no way influence his theologizing about Israel. Unless
this situation changes, and he learns to listen to the Jew and
take him seriously, there can be no question of new insight
and understanding on the part of the Christian and he will
continue to formulate views and theological statements about
Judaism and Jews in which the latter utterly fail to recognize themselves. While the differences between Judaism and
Christianity may well be too great ever to permit harmony
and convergence,[31] the Christian must be willing to have even
his most cherished concepts challenged by exposing himself to
Jewish views.[32]

TERMINOLOGY

ISRAEL and JUDAISM. Although both terms are used interchangeably to some extent,[33] "Israel" has been deliberately
retained in the title of this study, as well as in many instances in the text, to designate the totality of the Jewish
people. It is true that, since 1948, "Israel" has become the
name of a political state, so that its more general use may
at times cause some confusion. No other term, however, is
as ancient, rich in theological resonance, or represents as
fully the complex phenomenon of Jewish peoplehood: a phenomenon in which religious, cultural, historical and political
elements are blended and cannot ultimately be separated.[34]
As Leonhard Goppelt points out,

> Present-day Israel is, theologically speaking, not just
> one people among others, and not just one religion
> among the non-Christian religions. But neither is Is-
> rael one confession alongside other Christian

confessions, so that the relationship to Israel could
be said to be a part of the 'ecumenical problem.'
Judaism and the Jews can still today be correctly
designated only by the unique term 'Israel' ["Israel
and the Church..., Lutheran World X, No. 4 (Oct.
1963), p. 370].

The use of the term "Israel" and its application by
Christians to post-Biblical and contemporary Judaism may
be of special significance today, and play a role that is both
revealing and educational. For the Church has seen itself
as the new Israel from the beginning of its history, a per-
ception which, the teaching of Romans 9-11 notwithstanding,
by and large led it to dismiss the "old" Israel as outdated
and cast aside. Hence the use of the term today may reflect a growing willingness by Christians to admit that Israel is still "Israel." At the same time, it can foster this
awareness in those who still identify Israel either with the
Old Testament Jews, or with the Church. A text from the
1967 Bristol Report issued under the auspices of the World
Council of Churches is indicative of this attitude:

The words 'Israel' and 'Jews' can have different
meanings both in Biblical and current usage. In order to avoid misunderstandings, we have used the
term 'Israel' in this Report only with reference to the
people of Old and New Testament times.... Whenever we speak of the [Jewish] people of post-Biblical
times, we prefer to use the concepts 'Jews' and
'Judaism,' designating by the latter the Jews of the
whole world collectively [quoted by Anker Gjerding
"Dokumentation," Das Zeugnis der Kirche für die Jud-
en, ed. R. Dobbert (Berlin: Lutherisches Verlagshaus, 1968), p. 84f].

Many agree with R. Mayer [Zum Gespräch mit Israel,
p. 36] that it is particularly important that post-Biblical
Judaism retain "the title of honor, 'Israel'." Otherwise,
Christians are likely to continue to see Judaism since the
time of Jesus as little more than a fossil, and to apply the
concept Israel either to the Jewish people prior to Jesus, or
to the Christian Church. While the Church's view of itself
as the "new" Israel is implicit in the discussions of the
People of God (see, for example, Chapter VI), in this study
the term is not used with regard to the Church.[35]

GERMAN and GERMANY. The Federal Republic of

Germany (West Germany) is meant exclusively by these terms in all references to the post-war years.

THE "JEWISH QUESTION" ("Judenfrage"). The term itself is not new; it seems to have become part of common usage through Marx's controversy with Bruno Bauer.[36] Under the Nazis, however, it took on a far more sinister meaning, becoming a synonym for the "Jewish problem" of which Hitler sought to rid Germany and the world. The term has, consequently, remained highly ambiguous. Nevertheless, it has seemed useful to us to retain it here and there, despite some hesitation. For it is frequently used in post-Hitler Germany by a number of prominent theologians sympathetic to Judaism,[37] with reference to the theological question of Christianity's relationship to Judaism in all its varied aspects, a question as old as the Church itself. When the term is used pejoratively, it has been set within quotation marks.

SYNAGOGUE. During the centuries of hostility between Judaism and Christianity, this term tended to be used by Christians to designate Judaism in its most unfavorable light: not only no longer "Israel," but rejected, cursed, blind, obdurate. This is graphically illustrated by the two famous figures of the Cathedral of Strasbourg (ca. 1250). On one side of the portal stands the Church, a figure queenly and proud in bearing, a crown on her head, a victory standard in her hand. Across from her stands the Synagogue, dejected, with broken sword, the scroll of the Law hanging limply from her hand. She is blindfolded.

Somewhat surprisingly, this term also, like the "Jewish Question," seems to have lost its pejorative sense in post-war Germany and is not infrequently used either neutrally or positively, as an equivalent for Judaism, or even Israel. It will therefore occasionally occur in this text.

JUDENMISSION. This is, strictly speaking, a German technical term which designates the specific form of missionary work carried on among Jews by the German Lutherans beginning in the 18th century. In the present work, however, it is often used--mostly for brevity's sake--in the broader sense of Christianity's attitude and work with regard to the conversion of Jews in general. (The word occurs so frequently in the text it has not been treated as a foreign term.)

CHRISTIANITY and THE CHURCH. The two terms are used interchangeably throughout. Unless a particular denomination is explicitly specified, "Church" refers to Christianity and the various Christian churches in general.

Part One

Mission: Conversion as Goal

Chapter I

"JUDENMISSION" IN THE 19TH
AND EARLY 20TH CENTURIES

The question of Christianity's mission toward Israel is
as old as the Church. One can speak of an initial period of
"success," insofar as Jews were the first to believe in
Christ, so that Christianity in its original form was a Jewish Christianity. Before long, however, it became clear that
Israel as a people would not accept Christ, while Christianity
achieved rapid success among the gentiles. Hostility between
the two communities increased and their destinies were severed in the A.D. 66-70 Roman War. In place of Paul's passionate longing and zeal, which made him willing "to be
anathema from Christ if I might save some of them" (Rom.
9:3),[1] we find a growing enmity and, as the Church became
identified with the Roman empire, the use of force against
the Jews.

During the Middle Ages the Church's attitude to the
Jews generally took one of two forms: either outright hostility and persecution, or active efforts toward conversion. Nor
were these mutually exclusive. For the common phenomenon
of forcing Jews to accept baptism as an alternative to death
or expulsion was a consequence of the Church's condemnation
of Judaism: the Jew could be saved only by ceasing to be a
Jew and becoming a Christian.

It is true that medieval theologians and popes repeatedly condemned enforced baptism.[2] Yet in actual fact the
practice was widespread, both during and after the Crusades.
Thus in Strasbourg, more than 2000 Jews were burned at the
stake in 1349; only those who accepted baptism were spared,
and children were snatched from the flames and baptized

41

against their parents' will.[3] Even when the sword and stake
were abandoned, the Church, conscious of her political power, continued to exert pressure on the Jews "with the aim of
obtaining their capitulation."[4]

The Reformation did not appreciably improve the lot
of the Jews. Luther, after a brief moment of hope for their
conversion to his cause, which led him in 1523 to write his
Dass Jesus Christus ein geborener Jude sei, became so hostile toward the Jews that he advocated in his old age measures against them which rivalled any used during the Middle
Ages: burning their synagogues, closing their schools, driving them from their homes.[5] One might say that, until the
Enlightenment, the Church either used punitive measures to
punish the Jews for remaining Jews, or tried to coerce them
by various means to abandon their faith, thus forcing them
to cease to be Jews.

This brief history of Judenmission as it emerged in
the 19th century underlines both what is new and what remains the same. Nineteenth-century Judenmission--which has
its roots in the 18th century--emphatically rejected all force
and persecution; hostility, which had frequently been outright
hatred, was replaced by sympathy and goodwill. At the same
time, although the method changed, the goal remained the
same: conversion of the Jew through baptism, and his absorption into the Church.

Religious and Political Climate

Three major German thinkers--Schleiermacher, Harnack and Hegel--each contributed in their own way to a view
of the Old Testament which stripped it of most, if not all,
religious meaning as the Word of God. For Schleiermacher,
the writings of the Old Testament were legalistic and narrow-
ly nationalistic, expressing only the limited mentality of the
Jewish people. They had none of the breadth and universality of Christianity. Even the prophetic writings, even the
finest psalms, were seen to contain elements alien to Christianity, so that the Christian could not really use these writings for his own. The Old Testament thus becomes an obstacle to the Christian doctrine of God, and is best treated
as an appendix to the New, rather than as leading up to it.[6]

Harnack's views were no more positive than Schleiermacher's. In his book on Marcion he considered the

Church's retention of the Old Testament in the second century as correct; in the 16th, a mistake; and in the 19th, as "the consequence of paralysis in religious life and the Church. " [7]

The views of Hegel and his disciples (the chief among them being F. Christian Baur) were as influential in downgrading the Old Testament and Judaism as those of Schleiermacher and Harnack, though from a different perspective. For Hegel, ancient Greece was the norm. Compared to the Greek spirit and philosophy, Judaism is a barbaric religion, its God the "Demon of hate, " and Israel's history a repulsive tragedy. Even though the Old Testament points to the ideas which eventually become concentrated in Jesus, Christianity no sooner appears on the scene than it is divided into "Judaism" and "Paulinism." [8]

While the low esteem in which the Old Testament was held during the 19th century automatically cast its reflection and shadow on Judaism, the growth of German nationalism contributed its share to anti-Semitism. Kraus suggests that the new consciousness of the special role of the Germanic race now filled the void left by the religious belief in Israel's election. [9] The Jews, more than other minorities, were considered as a threat to unblemished national unity; hence they must be removed in one way or another, for every people that is conscious of its identity and dignity has the right to prevent contamination. [10] That this nationalism was not without religious overtones is evident from the fact that one of its most vocal proponents was the religious poet Ernst Moritz Arndt. He considered the Jews as having no place in the new Germany, because they were an essentially alien people, whose growth should be prevented. [11]

The threat might have appeared less great if the Jews had still been enclosed in their ghettos. But their emancipation at the end of the eighteenth century enabled them--at least in theory--to participate in the normal cultural, political and economic life of the country, thus arousing new fears, particularly among the more conservative elements of the population. "The old concepts of the Jews as Christ-killers are now adapted to the new conditions, so that the Jews appear as destroying the Christian-Germanic way of life" [Ernst-Ludwig Ehrlich, "Emanzipation und christlicher Staat." Christen und Juden, p. 169].

What was to be done to ward off this supposed

danger of a Jewish take-over? Some Germans saw the solution in the "elimination" of Judaism through baptism. Let
everything be done to win the Jews over to Christianity.[12]
The argument is familiar already from Luther's early writing, That Jesus Christ Was Born a Jew. It was to be used
again shortly, by exponents of Judenmission, but in a very
different spirit. In the present context it is tantamount in
purpose, though not method, to Hitler's "Final Solution."

　　　Writing in 1861, Philippson compared the attitude toward the Jews of the Protestant Church in Germany with
that of the Catholic Church. He maintained that while Prot-
estantism did not let loose the fire and sword of the Inquisi-
tion against the Jews, nor threaten them with compulsory
baptism, it replaced these overtly brutal methods with the
"gentler" and more subtle approach of proselytizing. "How
many caresses, assurances of brotherly love, of admiration of Jewish martyrdom were lavished upon the Jews, ...
but ... the small obligation asked for in return is baptism."
Whereas the Catholic Church turned its missionary efforts
outward, to foreign continents, the Protestant Church
"turned in the main to proselytizing among the Jews."[13]

　　　There is sufficient historical evidence to justify Philippson's description of the Church's ambiguous efforts to convert Jews. If this were the whole picture, Judenmission
would be purely and simply identical with unabashed proselytizing, for motives which have little to do with genuine love
of the Gospel on the part of Christians. This is not the
case, however--at least not in those of its representatives
to whom we shall now turn.

A New Approach

　　　Both Goppelt ["Israel and the Church...," pp. 352-
72] and Kraus [Versuche, pp. 176-79] find in 19th-century
Judenmission an approach to Judaism on the part of some
Christian theologians which was motivated by genuine appreciation of and love for Israel, and helped to bring about a new
attitude. From what has been said in the preceding pages,
it is clear that these elements do not stem from Neoprotes-
tantism, with its devaluation of the Old Testament. What,
then, is their origin?

　　　It is to be found in the heilsgeschichtliche Lutheran
theology of the 19th century, and in the impetus given by

Pietism to approach Judaism in terms of a "mission of
love." Its leading representatives are the Protestant theologians Christian Konrad von Hofmann, Franz Delitzsch, and
Christian Ernst Luthardt. According to von Hofmann, Israel's heilsgeschichtliche role has not ended, but is still, according to Romans 11:25 ff. , awaiting fulfillment. "The
aim of Jewish missions, therefore, is not to extinguish Israel by means of a general conversion, but to prepare it for
the great day of salvation which is awaiting it" [Goppelt, p.
353].

Nineteenth-century Judenmission will first be examined chiefly through the person and work of Franz Delitzsch
(1813-1890), a devout Christian and leading Old Testament
scholar, whose influence is still felt in Germany today through
the Institutum Judaicum Delitzschianum. Delitzsch's attitude
toward Judaism was characterized by two principal traits,
both of which are present in 19th-century Judenmission generally: a deep scholarly interest in Judaism, and the desire
to bring Jews to faith in Christ, which resulted in concrete
missionary efforts. That his own deepening faith acted as a
spur to his missionary zeal is apparent in a letter to Salomo
Buber which Delitzsch wrote five years before his death:

> At one period of my life I lived and moved in Jewish
> poetry; at another, in Jewish medieval philosophy; at
> yet another in [Jewish] literature, grammar and lexi-
> cography. Now, as I grow older, I am concerned
> primarily with practical matters and the religious
> questions that pertain to the Church and Synagogue.[14]

It is indicative of Delitzsch's learning that he, a fervent
Christian, was considered (by Jews) one of the founders of
the new 19th-century Wissenschaft des Judentums, precursor
of what has since come to be called "Judaica."[15]

In another letter, written to Jews in 1883, Delitzsch
spoke of the reason for his intensified studies of Judaism,
and of his desire to become "a Jew to the Jews":

> Men of Juda ... I have learned your language and lit-
> erature for no other purpose than to preach to you
> the Gospel of the crucified Christ. I recognize no
> higher purpose for my studies, next to serving the
> Church, than to persuade you, unceasingly, and with
> powerful arguments, to accept him whom you reject-
> ed, Jesus Christ [quoted in Barkenings, "Die Stimme
> der Anderen," p. 211].

It is difficult to imagine that a man writing thus today would
be looked upon kindly and with trust by Jews, and not be rejected as an unabashed proselytizer. If such was not the
fate of Franz Delitzsch, it was due to his integrity, which
won him the esteem of Jews.

Delitzsch produced a number of missionary writings.[16]
He attached greatest importance, however, to his translation of the New Testament into Hebrew, a work which engaged him for the last twenty years of his life. This translation won him admiration and respect among many Jews,
both learned and unlearned.[17] A Christian Biblical scholar
and Hebraicist, Rudolf Kittel, in his funeral oration for Delitzsch hailed the translation as "... a magnificent witness
of his warm love for the Jews, and one of the most brilliant
achievements of the history of German scholarship.... As
Luther gave the Bible to the Germans, so Franz Delitzsch
gave the New Testament to the Jews" [Allgemeine Evangelisch-Lutherische Kirchenzeitung, 1913, col. 220 f., quoted
in Barkenings, p. 211].

Delitzsch's considerable organizational talent resulted
in a number of concrete efforts to further Judenmission,
which not only outlived him, but survived into post-Hitler
Germany. In 1863 he founded the quarterly, Saat auf Hoffnung, which he edited for 18 years.[18] In 1871 he organized
various Lutheran groups engaged in Judenmission into the
"Evangelisch-lutherische Zentralverein für die Mission unter
Israel." The work which has had the greatest and most lasting impact, however, was the founding, in 1886, of the Institutum Judaicum in Leipzig, generally known as the Delitzschianum, and still today one of the major Institutes of Jewish
Studies in Germany.[19]

On the occasion of the 25th anniversary of the reopen-
ing of the Delitzschianum, its director, K. H. Rengstorf,
stated that it can "without a doubt be considered the legitimate continuation of Delitzsch's Institute" [Rengstorf, Institutum Judaicum, p. 29]. This brings us to the original purpose of the Delitzschianum, which was one of several institutes of Judaica founded in the 19th century.[20] The phenomenon was an outgrowth of a wider movement, sparked by
Christian students throughout Germany who were motivated by
interest in Judaism and by missionary zeal, the latter frequently the spur to the former. The institutes fostered a
more accurate knowledge of Judaism among Christians and
facilitated Jewish-Christian contacts. While they produced

relatively few professional missionaries to the Jews, they
instilled in a number of theologians a lifelong love of Judaism which, in some instances, passed the test of the Nazi
persecution. Rengstorf cites [pp. 17-18] Dean Heinrich Grüber of Berlin as the most outstanding representative of the men
who were deeply marked by this 19th-century movement. [21]

The Delitzschianum offered missionary training to
men who were already theologians. There were, however,
few applicants for this internship, and the project had soon
to be abandoned. Yet the high scholarly level was maintained under Delitzsch's successors: Gustav Dalman, Otto
von Harling--whose assistant Rengstorf became in 1926--
Hans Kosmala, and Rengstorf himself. Delitzsch's twofold
purpose was also carried on: to increase knowledge of Judaism among Christians, and to bring Jews to Christ.

Reference should here be made to the Institutum Judaicum founded in Berlin, in 1883, by H. L. Strack (1848-
1922). It differed from the Delitzschianum and the other institutes referred to above in one important respect. It was
devoted entirely to the scholarly exploration of Judaism--
particularly that of the intertestamental period--and wholly
devoid of any missionary purpose. Strack's scientific contribution to the field of Judaica is well known, above all
through his Kommentar zum Neuen Testament aus Talmud
und Midrasch, a work which he coauthored with P. Biller-
beck, and which "made the encounter with the Judaism of
New Testament times unavoidable" [Kraus, Versuche, p.
178]. Writing in a publication of the Berlin Institute in 1927,
H. Gressman underlined the Institute's determination to
steer clear of any missionary endeavors and maintain scholarly objectivity, particularly at a time when a new wave of
anti-Semitism was sweeping Germany. [22] In order to maintain this objectivity Jewish scholars were invited as guest
lecturers, so that theological debate between Jewish and
Christian theologians was made possible. It is Kraus' opinion that the Berlin Institute has inspired a large number of
theologians over the years.

While the Judaica institutes won friends among some
Jews, others looked upon them with suspicion. Rengstorf
[Institutum Judaicum, p. 17] considers this mistrust under-
standable and well-founded, given the heavy losses to Judaism in the 19th-century through "Taufjuden"--Jews who saw
baptism as the "entrance ticket" to Western civilization. [23]
This explanation, correct as far as it goes, seems to be but

half the truth at best. For Jewish mistrust of Christian
missionary activity goes back far beyond the 19th-century,
and is rooted in the age-old history of Christendom's enforced conversion of Jews.

Delitzsch was well equipped, through both his scholarly and his missionary interests in Judaism, to play an important role in combating the rising anti-Semitism of the
time, of which he was an implacable foe. This is particularly apparent in his controversy with the Catholic August
Rohling, who sought to discredit Judaism in his book, Der
Talmudjude.24 In his own words [quoted in Barkenings,
"Die Stimme," p. 213], Delitzsch defended the Jews against
"Totally fantastic accusations which arouse the monster of
popular rage against them." In 1890 he wrote:

> The attitude of the Church to the Jews was almost
> willfully aimed to strengthen them in their antipathy
> to Christianity. The Church still owes the Jews the
> actual proof of Christianity. Is it astonishing that
> the Jewish people is such an insensitive and barren
> field for the seed of the gospel? The Church itself
> has drenched it in blood and then heaped it with
> stones [Allgemeine Evangelisch-Lutherische Kirchen-
> zeitung, 1890, col. 552 f., quoted in Leuner, "From
> Mission to Dialog," pp. 386-87].

On another occasion he wrote that if even "a small particle
of this un-Christian race-hatred were to tinge our missionary work, ... it would constitute its self-condemnation"
[Saat auf Hoffnung, Vol. 18, p. 203, quoted in Kraus, Versuche, p. 177].

One might speak of "mixed motives" here, of which
Delitzsch made no secret. He declared on one occasion that
he was motivated in combating anti-Semitism not only by hu-
manitarian but also missionary considerations, hoping thus
to defend the Jews against their detractors and keep open the
door for Judenmission as well. Yet the atmosphere is very
different here from that described at the beginning of the
chapter, where baptism of Jews was seen as a way of end-
ing the "Jewish Question." It should also be kept in mind
that Delitzsch lived in an age in which Christianity had not
yet come to question and reassess missionary work in general, and Judenmission in particular.

Delitzsch was first and foremost a theologian, an

exponent of the heilsgeschichtliche Lutheran theology of the
19th century. In his view of the Old Testament he has nothing in common with Schleiermacher, as is illustrated by the
following passage:

> In the Old Testament the Lord is coming, is approach-
> ing, engaged in the self-proclamation of his manifes-
> tation. Let us transport ourselves back into these
> Old Testament times and follow in the steps of the
> One who is coming, pursue the traces of the Ap-
> proaching One, seek the shadow he casts on his Old
> Testament path through history, and above all try to
> understand the direction of the prophecies that an-
> nounce him [Franz Delitzsch, Messianische Weissag-
> ungen, 1890, p. 2 f., quoted in Kraus, Versuche,
> pp. 176-77].

Delitzsch believed that the Jew should undertake this journey
with the Christian, and recognize in Jesus the "great, holy,
divine man, whose manifestation divides the history of the
world in two" [p. 4].

Delitzsch's theology on Judaism was strongly influenced by an eschatological perspective. He saw Israel's salvation in terms of a remnant, rather than the pecple or nation as a whole. Israel had been chosen for the sake of
mankind, but the mass of the people did not live up to their
vocation. He thought they claimed as their prerogative what
was in reality free grace, and he opposed "national particu-
larism" to God's design for its universal role. [25]

Yet God continued to love his people: for the sake
of the promises made to the Patriarchs, but also "because
he saw in the mass a core [Kern]" that would welcome his
love and prove themselves instruments for his design. [26]
What, then, of the promises made to Israel? The mass has
forfeited their election, their role has passed on to those
among the Jews who believed in Christ, along with those
among the gentiles who accepted him. Israel was chosen
with a view to this remnant; one day the rest of the people
would also heed God's call.

Delitzsch rejected as having no foundation in Paul any
concept of national prerogative or restoration. Israel will be
judged and purified, but not destroyed. The day will come
when it will be saved. Theology has no way of depicting the
manner in which this will come about. [27] For Delitzsch,

Israel's history came to an end with Christ. For Israel had
been chosen in order that salvation, in the person of Christ,
might come forth from it. Apart from Christ and Christianity "the history of this people is an aimless history, written
in sand" [Sind die Juden, p. 27, quoted in Barkenings, p.
215]. Israel's history is of paradigmatic value, but limited
to Biblical times.[28]

    If we ask, What of the Israel that still exists today,
Delitzsch would answer that it deserves our compassion and
love, and that the Church has, to her shame, by and large
refused this. She has treated Israel with contempt, even
hate, thus becoming the "bludgeon of the divine curse"
[quoted in Barkenings, pp. 218-19]. No wonder, Delitzsch
exclaims, the Jews have closed themselves to the Gospel.
It was Pietism, not Orthodoxy, that opened the Church's
eyes to her true mission toward Israel. (As history was to
show before long, however, her eyes were not opened suf-
ficiently to stem the coming disaster.)

    Delitzsch has been called by his own century the
"soul of the entire Lutheran Judenmission," "its heart and
driving force" [Allgemeine Evangelisch-Lutherische Kirchenzeitung, 1890, col. 552, quoted in Barkenings, p. 218].
It may be said of 19th-century Judenmission in general that
there was serious theological concern with Israel's role and
vocation in the history of salvation. For Delitzsch, von
Hofmann and Luthardt, God's enduring faithfulness implied
Israel's enduring election, an election seen in terms of a
remnant, rather than the people as a whole. They look forward to the day when Israel will "crown its task in the
world by turning to its Messiah, thus glorifying the triumph
of God's grace" [Barkenings, p. 203]. God's election had
conferred upon Israel a unique status. In what way has this
status been modified or even cancelled out by Israel's temporary rejection of Christ, by the entrance upon the stage of
a new people of God? To what extent has Israel's vocation
passed over to the Church? Such were the questions that
preoccupied 19th-century Judenmission. These questions are
not basically different from those that were asked by the
early Church and which are still being asked today. The difference lies in the method of posing the questions.

A Change in Method, Not Goal

    Judenmission was not always free from political

involvement. It was supported at times by the proponents of
the "Christian State" as a means of getting rid of the Jewish problem, and became embroiled more than once in anti-
Semitic controversy. [29] Yet by and large it saw its task in
religious terms: preaching the gospel of Jesus Christ. It
fought anti-Semitism not only as a serious threat to its work,
but as basically un-Christian. Thus G. Dalman wrote, "One
can be a nominal Church--or confessional--Christian, and
join in anti-Semitic activities. But no Christian who lives
and moves in the sacred scriptures of the Old and New Testament can do so. There he learns to think differently
about Jews--not more gently or kindly, but more deeply and
seriously" [quoted in Barkenings, p. 207].

We agree with Barkenings' statement that 19th-cen-
tury Judenmission was a "constant challenge to the Church
to make Christianity credible through its own lived faith, its
critical effort to find its own place vis-à-vis Israel" [pp.
207-08]. The warnings of its spokesmen, that the Church
had failed in her task of love toward the Jews, went largely
unheeded, and have been tragically borne out by this century.
Judenmission failed, ultimately, in its efforts to arouse love
and interest for Israel among the population at large, to do
away with dangerous stereotypes, and to stem the rising
tide of anti-Semitism. It should not be forgotten, however,
that during the Nazi rise to power it was frequently men and
women engaged in Judenmission, as well as missionary organizations, who risked their lives to save Jews.

> There are countless instances that bear witness to the
> brotherly love of these Christians for their Jewish
> brothers. At the same time, we also know that this
> love and willingness to serve at times knew severe
> limits; Christians who wanted to give Jews God's sal-
> vation in Christ frequently refused to integrate them
> into their own Christian community [W. Dantine,
> "Kirche als Israel Gottes...," in Jüdisches Volk--
> gelobtes Land (Munich: Kaiser, 1970), p. 334].

The leading proponents of Judenmission were aware
of the limitations of their work, and hoped only to sow seeds
for the future. (This is indicated by the very title of Delitzsch's quarterly, Saat auf Hoffnung.) Delitzsch wrote in
1881: "We are a weak contingent. Slowly and painfully,
hoping against hope, in many disappointments, yet keeping
the hand to the plough, we furrow a fearfully stony field"
[Saat auf Hoffnung, Vol. 18, p. 199, quoted in Barkenings,

p. 209]. Barkenings suggests, "It is quite possible that today, after all that has happened to the Jews among us, the
humble renouncing of missionary effort at least in Germany
may better correspond to the intentions of those who fought
anti-Semitism from the ranks of Judenmission than the resumption and continuation of the work according to the old
manner" [p. 209].

The text contains clear reference to the Nazi period
and Holocaust. It is historical events, then, which lead
Barkenings to question Judenmission today, "at least in Germany." This could be called the "pragmatic" approach. It
is based not so much on a revision of theological arguments,
as on grounds of practicality, advisability, effectiveness,
timing, desire to redress ancient wrongs, etc. Elements of
this approach may be found among some of the post-1945
theologians whose views have yet to be examined. This
pragmatism appears valid, for the absence of historical in-
fluences on religious thinking leaves the latter hanging in a
vacuum, robbing it of all relevance or claim to have something to say to the men of today. One may ask, however,
whether it goes far enough. Barkenings' qualifying phrase
--no longer, perhaps, "a Judenmission ... according to the
old manner" (emphasis added)--is revealing, even if one can
only hazard a guess as to its precise meaning. It raises
several questions for us:

Can the Christian theologian today be satisfied with
abandoning old techniques and approaches, waiting for a
more propitious time--when the past will have been forgotten and old wounds healed--to resurrect these old approaches,
albeit in a revised form? Are there theologians writing in
Germany today upon whom the impact of the horror perpe-
trated upon Jews in their own lifetime and by their own,
frequently "Christian," countrymen, is such that we can
speak of a radical theological overhauling of their views of
the Church's relationship to Israel, hence also of Judenmission?

Chapter II

THE JEWISH CHRISTIANS

The problem of Jewish Christianity is as old as the
Church itself. In its earliest normative form Christianity
was a purely Jewish phenomenon. The first Christians
shared with their fellow Jews a common scripture, life and
worship. Although Christianity was considered a Jewish
sect, there were many sects within Judaism at this time,
each claiming to be Jewish and recognized as such by others.[1] There was controversy, at times sharp and bitter,
yet Judaism found room within its community for Christians
and non-Christians. Whatever the differences that separated
them, both Jews and Jewish Christians were Jews. Each
claimed to be the "true Jew," without, at this early stage,
denying the other's claim. The disputes that took place occurred within the same community. All were Jews, and the
community was one. "The Christian community, which had
its beginning in Palestine after Jesus' death, lived, socio-
logically speaking, at first like the Pharisees and the Es-
senes, as a religious group within the folk community of Israel, although it already understood itself to be the church"
[Goppelt, "Israel and the Church...," p. 353].

The first Christians worked from within the Jewish
community to bring their fellow Jews to faith in Christ.
They claimed continuity between this faith and Jewish tradition; the Jewish scriptures were their scriptures, and they
observed the Law of Moses.

The entrance of the gentiles into the Church and the
ensuing mission to the gentiles posed a wholly new problem
for the early Christian community, and required of the Jewish Christians far-reaching and radical adaptation to a new
situation. The key point at issue was whether the gentiles
could become Christians without first becoming Jews, through
circumcision and the observance of the Law. We know from

Acts 15 how the dispute was settled, in theory: the gentiles
were admitted to full membership in the Christian community, which henceforth consisted of Jewish and gentile Christians. There was to be no distinction, and both were to en-
joy full, equal rights. Jews who became Christians could
continue to be Jews.

> The Jewish Christians of the first centuries lived in
> solidarity with their people under the Law, which they
> understood as 'Law of freedom' (James 1:25; 2:12),
> not as 'Way of salvation,' or means to become just
> before God, but as expression of his will which they
> wanted to fulfill. Paul himself wished to 'be a Jew
> to the Jews' (1 Cor. 9:20). That Paul affirmed the
> life of Jewish Christians under the Law is seen most
> clearly from 1 Cor. 7:17-19 [Heinz Kremers, "Römer
> 9-11 in Predigt und Unterricht," Im Dienst für Schule,
> Kirche und Staat. Gedenkschrift für Arthur Bach
> (Heidelberg, 1970), p. 155].

The efforts of the Council of Jerusalem, to allow
room within one and the same faith community for both Jews
and gentiles were, as we know, doomed to failure. Before
long Jewish Christians lost both authority and status within
the Christian community. Gentile Christianity increasingly
turned away from Judaism and, after the catastrophe of the
Roman war, contributed to an already existing pagan anti-
Judaism. The prophets' criticism of Israel was now interpreted as anti-Jewish, and applied to the Jews by Christians who no longer felt any sense of solidarity with them.
What had been self-criticism became anti-Jewish polemic.

The same process was at work in the interpretation
of Jesus' words as recorded in the gospels: "They were not
any longer operating within the framework of Jewish self-
criticism. They hardened into accusations against 'the
Jews,' the synagogue across the street, and against the
people who claimed the same scriptures, but denied its fulfillment in Jesus Christ.[2] Thus, Jewish Christians came to
be regarded as heretics by Christians and as apostates by
Jews. Already beginning with the second century, the
Church became predominantly a Church from among the gentiles, and her original and uniquely Jewish character was
largely lost. By the fourth century hardly a trace is found
of Jewish Christians; they had ceased to exist as a distinct
entity.   (cont. on p. 56)

I. <u>In its broadest and most general meaning</u>, the term may legitimately be used to refer to that "Jewish amalgam which persists as a vital element in Christianity."[a] However hellenized the Church became in the course of time, certain Jewish elements, whether recognized as such or not, remained an integral part of her life and were never totally lost. In this sense, then, it can be said that every Christian is a "Jewish Christian." Some authors use the term "Judaeo-Christian" (or "Judeo-Christian") in English in place of "Jewish Christian," both in its general meaning and with regard to the early Church. We have opted for "Jewish Christian" for several reasons:

- "Judaeo-Christian" is a modern coinage, whereas "Jewish Christian" is based on the New Testament.

- "Judaeo-Christian" is today somewhat controversial. While those who favor its use interpret it as stressing the link and common heritage of Christianity and Judaism,[b] there are others, both Jews and Christians, who fear that it stresses the common ground while neglecting the very real differences.[c]

- German has only one term, the literal equivalent of "Jewish Christian" (<u>Judenchrist</u>--and <u>Judenchristentum</u>).[d]

II. <u>The early Church</u>. Here again, the term "Jewish Christian" in its broadest meaning designates all Christians of Jewish descent, e.g., the entire Jerusalem community which constituted the mother-Church of Christianity. Schoeps points out, however, that

... as the designation of a group, this name is ambiguous and open to misunderstanding. There were Jewish Christians, such as Paul and the Gospel writers, who prepared the way for the Gentile Christian Church. Then there were Jewish Christians who, being proud of their origin, formed separate groups within the churches and sometimes, perhaps, established congregations alongside the gentile Christian Churches.... Finally, there were Jewish Christians--also known as Judaizers--who gradually separated themselves from the majority and had a history of their own.[e]

Of the two last-named, the former remained within the Church, while the latter soon came into conflict with the mainstream and eventually became a heretical sect.[f] This sect was most commonly known as "Ebionites," sometimes also as "Nazarenes." According to Schoeps [<u>Jewish Christianity</u>, pp. 10-11], these names were originally titles of honor, but gradually acquired a pejorative meaning.

III. <u>Modern usage.</u> The term "Jewish Christian" continues to be used today for Christians of Jewish descent. In addition, "Hebrew Christian" began to be used in English in the 19th century. Both terms refer to Jews who have become Christians by baptism, and both are used by Christians only. "For Jewish scholars the term 'Jewish Christian' is a title of honor which they limit to the Jewish Christians of the first centuries. The Jewish Christians who were later forced by the Churches to give up their Jewishness they call 'baptized Jews,' which means to them apostates, traitors who have gone over to the enemy, quizzlings, etc."[g]

While "Hebrew Christian" has become a quasi-technical term in the English-speaking world, we shall use "Jewish Christian" to translate the German "Judenchrist," except when dealing with the Hebrew Christian Alliance.

The International Hebrew Christian Alliance

The growth in number of Jewish Christians during the
nineteenth century led to the founding, in England in 1866,
of the Hebrew Christian Alliance, which developed into the
International Hebrew Christian Alliance (IHCA) in 1925.[3]
The choice of name of the IHCA is explained by Ellison as
follows:

> We do not know who first coined the term 'Hebrew
> Christian'--it is older than the Alliance--but its use
> showed spiritual genius; it stressed the Alliance was
> to be a union of persons who felt themselves peculiar-
> ly one by reason of a common national origin, not be-
> cause of any peculiarity in their common faith. In
> most Continental languages such a term had been ei-
> ther unknown or unused, and the equivalent, 'Jewish
> Christian,' which came to be used instead raised
> among many theologians a strong but entirely unjusti-
> fiable suspicion that some form of Judaizing lay be-
> hind the Movement [The Church and the Jewish
> People, p. 150].

Ellison states the aims of the IHCA [150-51]:
   1.   To foster a spirit of fellowship and cooperation
among Hebrew Christians throughout the world.
   2.   To present a united witness on behalf of Christ
to the Jewish people and to the world.
   3.   To interpret the spirit of the Jewish people to
Christians, and the spirit of Christianity to the Jews.
   4.   To assist in Christian missionary efforts toward
the Jews.
   5.   To protect and defend Hebrew Christians where
necessary against anti-Semitism.

Jewish Christian Communities

Another phenomenon that originated in the 19th century resulted from a desire, among some Jewish Christians,
for Jewish Christian communities. It had two principal
causes. In part, it was a reaction against the situation in
which the Jew who became a Christian found himself.
Forced to leave behind his Jewish heritage and people, he
could not exist in the Church in any visible way as a Jewish
Christian; he had to cease being a Jew. A second spur was

provided not only by outright anti-Semitism, but by the less
than total acceptance and even hostility he often found upon
entering the Church, which added to his sense of homelessness and uprootedness. A number of prominent Jewish converts are associated with this movement, such as Jechiel
Lichtenstein, Joseph Rabinowitsch, Christian Theodor Lucky,
and Abram Poljak.

Among some of these groups, there was a trend toward autonomy and separation from the Christian Church.
In a series of meetings between 1931 and 1937, the IHCA
discussed the possibility of establishing a Hebrew Christian
Church, but ultimately took a decisive stand against it--an
attitude it still maintains today. At the same time, the
need for Jewish Christian communities was recognized as
normal and healthy, and as in no way impairing the unity of
the Church.

The Nazi persecution, particularly the attitude of the
"German Christians"--i.e., those (the majority) who cooper-
ated with the Nazi regime--gave a new impetus to the trend
toward autonomous Jewish Christian communities after the
war. Rejected and expelled by their fellow Christians,
many Jewish Christians had discovered a new sense of solidarity with Jews, whose fate they had been forced to share.
Some of them now sought voluntarily what had previously
been forced upon them: their own, independent communities. In an address in September 1948, Rengstorf considered this trend so strong that he warned against the danger
of a new schism: "A new division threatens Christianity
in our generation, a rift which has no precedent in the
Church's history: the division between those of her members from among the gentiles and those from among the
Jews" ["Die eine Kirche aus Juden und Heiden," Viva Vox
Evangelii, (Munich, 1951), p. 232]. In another article
from about the same period, Rengstorf takes up the theme
at greater length, and uses the term "Jewish Christian se-
cession" ["Judenchristentum heute," Saat auf Hoffnung 73
(1950), pp. 145-63; originally an address, May 1948].

Within the overall picture, however, Jewish Christians who seek an independent existence are a marginal
phenomenon. The attitude of the majority is represented by
a report drawn up at a meeting of the International Missionary Council's Committee on the Christian Approach to the
Jews at Basel in 1947. Some excerpts follow:

The people of Israel by virtue of their election by
God have been and remain a mystery incapable of being fitted into the normal categories of national existence. It is impossible to explain their existence
merely in terms of a religious community, and hence
it is in no mere idealistic sense that we unanimously
affirm that the Jew who by faith becomes a member
of the Church of Christ in a very real sense remains
a Jew, and may with full justification be called a Hebrew Christian.

We affirm our conviction that it is normally every
Christian's duty to 'abide in that calling wherein he
was called,' and hence it should normally be expected
that the Hebrew Christian will maintain his identity
both in his relations with the Church and with his
brethren according to the flesh. It should be considered legitimate and natural if this should lead to cus-
toms and theological language differing from that of
his gentile brethren. It is, however, certain that any
such differences are primarily the result of human
sin and frailty; they do not imply that the Hebrew
Christian has any privileged position in the Church,
and they will assuredly vanish in the perfection of the
eternal state.

We affirm that the manner in which the Hebrew Christian can best express and preserve his identity before
his own people is one to which he must be led by the
Holy Spirit. So long as the Hebrew Christian does
not misrepresent thereby the teaching of Christ nor
compromise with Judaism, the gentile Christian should
be prepared to show him all sympathy and understanding....

Convinced as we are that although national differences
do not necessarily disappear in Christ, national
churches represent a departure from the mind of
Christ for His Church. However such a concession to
human frailty may have been necessary, we would
profoundly deplore the setting up of a Hebrew Christian Church, the more so as there seems to be no
imperative reason for such an action. We confess the
lack of love and understanding for the Hebrew Christian in many local churches is such that the setting
up of local Hebrew Christian churches is unavoidable,
but we would urge that no such step be ever taken
unnecessarily....

> We recognize with grief that the Hebrew Christian all
> too often does not feel at home in the Church of
> Christ, and we call on the Church at large to real-
> ize that the main reasons are lack of love which
> cannot find room for the stranger, and the latent
> root of anti-Semitism which often poisons the
> Church's life where it is least realized.... [Ellison,
> "The Church and the Hebrew Christian," pp. 159-
> 60].

A Controversial Issue

In the 1960's the concept of Jewish Christian as in
any way distinct within the Church aroused fresh controversy.
The immediate occasion was a statement issued by the
"Consultation on the Church and the Jewish People," which
met under the auspices of the Lutheran World Federation's
Department of World Missions at Løgumkloster, Denmark,
in the spring of 1964. It referred to the use of the term
"Jewish Christian" and reads as follows: "Those who in
faith through baptism have put on Christ Jesus are all
Christians, without distinction, whether they have their origin in the people of the old covenant or among the gentiles.
Terms such as 'Hebrew Christian' and the like, introduce
unbiblical divisions into the church" [Lutheran World, XI,
No. 3 (July 1964), p. 266]. It is clear from the entire
context that the statement is motivated by the desire to foster unity and avoid the scandalous kind of division and discrimination which to this day remain a shameful blot on the
Church from the Nazi period.

Nevertheless, the position taken at Løgumkloster
aroused strong protest on the part of the IHCA, which set
forth its opposition in a statement issued in The Hebrew
Christian [November 1965; reprinted in Lutheran World, XIII,
No. 1 (1966), pp. 66-67]. A longer article by Heinz David
Leuner, European Secretary of the IHCA, took up the issue
in greater detail the following year, 1966, and is helpful in
this context ["Ist die Bezeichnung 'Judenchrist' theologisch
richtig?" Pastoraltheologie 55, No. 9 (Sept. 1966), pp.
372-79]. Leuner points out in the first place that the term
"Jewish Christian" has been used ever since the 19th century by a number of outstanding theologians, prominent
among them Delitzsch, and later Otto von Harling. In the
Nazi period Hans Ehrenberg, himself a Jewish Christian,
made use of it in his "72 Guidelines," one of the major

documents of the Confessing Church.[4] Karl Barth, in 1942,
wrote that "... only a perverted and distorted mentality
could oblige a Jewish Christian to feel ashamed of his Jewish origins, or a gentile Christian to reproach him for it.
To be a Jewish Christian is a high and ineradicable honor"
[Church Dogmatics II/2, p. 228]. Among contemporary
German-speaking theologians, Helmut Gollwitzer, Hermann
Diem, Walther Zimmerli and Theodor Vriezen all use the
term.[5]

        Furthermore according to Leuner the term has been
the subject of various studies since 1947, all of which have
stressed its legitimacy and value. The designation makes
clear that the Jew who becomes a member of the Church
does not, thereby, lose his bond with his own people, his
"brothers according to the flesh," from a Christian point of
view [Leuner, "Bezeichnung," p. 373]. Paul's statement in
Galatians 3:28, that "there is neither Jew nor Greek," etc.,
must not be misconstrued to mean that all distinctions have
now ceased to exist,[6] or that previous loyalties are to be
denied. Moreover, in a Church which has become predominantly a gentile Church over the centuries, the presence of
Jewish Christians reminds the Church of her Old Testament
heritage.

        Leuner argues that, if the gentile shares the bless-
ings of Israel only by being grafted on to the natural olive
tree, why should the Jewish Christian "step out of his calling, only to re-enter it after his conversion"? [Leuner,
pp. 373-74]. To force him to leave behind his Judaism is
a strange reversal of the situation against which Paul fought
in the early Church, namely, the demand that gentiles first
become Jews in order to become Christians. "It is nearer
the truth to say that a gentile must unite himself with the
history of the Jews--that is to say, with the historical un-
folding of the covenant--and play his engrafted role in fulfillment of it."[7]

        What is the special vocation of the Jewish Christian
in the Church? First, Leuner believes he is a sign that,
unlike any other nation, Israel is chosen as a people.
Above all, however, he is a "pledge of the eschatological
hope" that all of Israel will one day recognize Jesus as Messiah. Until that day the Jewish Christian is a sign of God's
enduring fidelity to his people, a safeguard that prevents
faith in Christ from becoming a mere philosophical system,
and a witness to the unity of Jew and gentile in the Church.

Only if he retains his distinctiveness as Jew can he bear
witness to this unity [Leuner, pp. 375-76].

While stressing the Jewish Christian's special vocation, Leuner emphatically denies--as does the whole IHCA--
that he occupies any special or privileged place within the
Christian community; still less, that there is any justification
for an autonomous Jewish Christian community. "There is
no No-Man's land between the Church and Israel" [p. 377].
The Jewish Christian must embrace both Christianity and Judaism, because Jesus belongs to both.

This does not mean, however, that Jew and gentile
are in an identical situation with regard to the Church.

> The New Testament belongs to the Old Testament, not
> to the ancient Indian Veda.... The denial of the legit-
> imacy of the term Jewish Christian results from the
> erroneous concept that Israel is, like other religions,
> a theological idea. This is precisely not the case!
> In contrast to all other religions, Israel is a histori-
> cal fact, placed by God in this world and maintained
> in existence by him [Leuner, pp. 377-78].

It is interesting to compare this view of Judaism with
that expressed by Rengstorf, in the article, "Judenchristentum heute," on page 57). For Rengstorf, it is self-evident
that Jesus himself, in his words and life, expected his followers to break with their people. Recognizing that religion
and people belong together in Judaism, Jesus knew that separation from the synagogue meant separation from his people
as well [the article, p. 158]. According to Rengstorf, Jesus'
own fate and the history of the early Church proved him
true, "despite the good will of the early Jewish Christians.
Neither their adherence to the Sabbath, nor the observance of
the ritual law, kept them from being treated as apostates and
heretics" [p. 159]. In Rengstorf's opinion, Paul provides the
theological basis for this: "When anyone is united to Christ,
there is a new world; the old order has gone, and a new order has already begun" (2 Cor. 5:17). Since, then, religion
and nation cannot be separated in Judaism, the Jewish Christian, while remaining "a son of Abraham according to the
flesh ... ceases, by attaining faith in Christ, to be a member of his people, which continues to resist Jesus of Nazareth
and even glories in its obstinacy" [p. 159].

It is obvious that we have here two radically different

conceptions of the nature of Judaism, and of the manner in
which the Jewish Christian's situation in the Church is conceived.

The controversy to which the Statement by the "Consultation" at Løgumkloster had given rise was not settled by
the objections of the IHCA. The Lutheran World Federation,
while taking cognizance of the problem, decided to initiate
further study "of the term 'Jewish Christian' which shall include consideration of its origin, its meaning and its implications for Christians in the State of Israel as well as elsewhere" [Lutheran World, XIII, No. 1 (1966), p. 66].

Jewish Christianity Today: Some Questions

It seems that for the first time since the days of early
Christianity, one can speak today of a Jewish Christianity
within the Church. Whatever one's interpretation of it, attitude toward it, or the diversity within it, it exists and is
active. Jewish Christians see themselves in continuity with
the Jewish Christians of the first century. Obviously, such
a continuity cannot be derived from the temporal order,
since the early Jewish Christian phenomenon did not long survive. Rather, it claims the ancient right for Jewish Chris-
tians--whether as individuals or groups--to maintain and express their cultural and ethnic origins. This is possible only if what for centuries has been uniformity in the Church
gives way to a greater diversity and pluralism. Jewish
Christians are in part reacting to having been "absorbed" by
a largely gentile Church, forced to cut every link that bound
them to their people and history.

This situation can be explained historically. The
early gentile Church feared the synagogue as a rival and enemy, a "phobia which persisted down the centuries," even
when Jews were powerless and oppressed. As a result,
"... the Church has for the most part been precluded from
even considering the possibility of the continuance of the Hebrew Christian as a separate and discernible element within
the Church.... So far from lamenting his complete assimi-
lation, it has greeted it as something entirely desirable [El-
lison, "Church and Hebrew Christian," p. 145].

Two other factors have contributed to the contemporary

Jewish Christian phenomenon. The first was the Judenmission which began in the 19th century, and resulted in growing numbers of Jews entering the Church. This missionary origin may in part account for the strong missionary aspect which frequently characterizes Jewish Christianity today. 8

The second is the fact that converts from Judaism often felt--and still feel--unwelcome in the Church, encountering there, even as Christians, the anti-Semitism they had known as Jews. This situation reached its zenith among the "German Christians" of the Nazi era--a memory still very much alive. Following is one particularly glaring example of the attitude of these "Christians" (an attitude which maintains that the Jew who becomes a Christian is not and never can be on a full par with other Christians; not even baptism can wipe out "racial" difference): Late in 1933, the highly respected Austrian ethnologist Wilhelm Schmidt, speaking in Vienna, maintained that

> the Jewish people had received the highest national
> calling ever bestowed upon any people: to fashion
> the human nature which the Saviour of the world was
> to assume, and make ready his coming into the world.
> The people as a whole fulfilled the first part of this
> task, but not the second; only a small minority was
> faithful. Therefore the Jewish people has failed in
> its national vocation. Such failure would inevitably
> distort the nature of any people; because the calling
> of the Jewish people was so high, the distortion is
> deeper and more far-reaching: corruptio optimi
> pessima...... This nearly 2000-year-old uprooted-
> ness and distortion of its character had, moreover,
> a real though secondary effect on the physical race.
> If a Jew becomes a member of the Catholic Church
> sincerely, out of full conviction, he has removed the
> strongest barrier that separates him from us, and
> the deepest roots of his being different from us.
> But the racial effects of this difference, which have
> accumulated in the course of 2000 years, cannot be
> eliminated at one stroke, not even through baptism.
> Only much time and interior effort can achieve this.
> Therefore, although the baptized Jew is one of us,
> his belonging differs from that of our German com-
> patriots. [W. Schmidt, "Zur Judenfrage," in
> Schönere Zukunft IX (1934), p. 408 f.; quoted in
> Greive, Theologie und Ideologie, pp. 219-20; empha-
> sis added].

The question of "once a Jew, always a Jew," was approached in a very different spirit by Karl Ludwig Schmidt, who saw it as a painful and urgent theological problem for the Church. Writing in Switzerland in 1943, at the height of the Nazi terror, Schmidt struggled with the question of whether a baptized Jew ceases to be a Jew:

> Besides practicing Jews, there are Jewish Christians, i.e., Christians of Jewish descent. While there is reason to rejoice that the Church of Jesus Christ from the first considered Jewish Christians as its own, there is equal reason to lament the attitude of the recent anti-Semitism, which, for so-called racial reasons, treats Jewish Christians on principle, as a whole and practically speaking, exactly like Jews.... Even though we automatically and totally reject anti-Semitism, this poses a very difficult question: Is the Jewish Christian no longer a Jew? In this connection let us for the present point out that the Jewish Christian Paul always knew himself related to Judaism, even as a Christian, and continued to feel himself a Jew... [Die Judenfrage im Lichte der Kapitel 9-11 des Römerbriefs. Theologische Studien No. 13 (Zürich: Zollikon, 1943, 2d ed. 1946), pp. 3-4].

To return to Jewish Christianity today. It does not seem possible to us to give one uniform description of it. As has been pointed out, the majority of Jewish Christians see their aspiration to retain the bond with their tradition and people as in no way conflicting with the unity of the Church, a unity which, in fact, they wish to deepen. (See Leuner, "Bezeichnung.") There are some groups, as already mentioned, that seek a greater, or even total, autonomy. [9] Finally, there are individual converts to Christianity who feel no desire to be part of a special group, but quietly try to live their Jewish heritage within the Church.

After what has been said so far concerning the de facto existence of Jewish Christians today, it should not be forgotten that there are those who, both among Christians of Jewish origin and other Christians, question the desirability of the concept of "Jewish Christian." These views have been discussed in connection with the Løgumkloster meeting. It would seem that the issue here is, ultimately, the nature of Judaism and Christianity.

At present two factors can be seen to be at work that may foster a Jewish Christianity. The first is that the "Judaization" of the Church, which for centuries was considered a danger, is today beginning to be desired as an asset. A growing number of Christian theologians (for example, Spaemann and Kraus) deplore what they consider the excessive hellenization of the Church, and the loss of much of her Jewish heritage. Restoring the Jewish element to the Church is seen as one way of redressing the imbalance, and some Jewish Christians themselves see this as part of their vocation. Unlike earlier times, when Jewish converts often became leading anti-Semites, men and women such as Paul Démann, John Oesterreicher, Charlotte Klein, and many others equally well known are today making a unique contribution in helping their fellow Christians gain a deeper understanding of Judaism. This shift in attitude toward a greater appreciation of what was once--and might have continued to be--the Jewish character of Christianity, lends new importance to the Jewish Christian question.

A second element is the existence of the State of Israel. While some proponents of Jewish Christianity, as well as other Christians, see it as a new opportunity for missionary efforts--an attitude which many outspokenly deplore--the concern of the present work is with another dimension of the existence of Israel. The already existing--though invariably small--Christian communities in Israel today find themselves in a situation that has not heretofore pertained: a small minority scattered among a vital, constantly evolving Jewish population, in its own country. There can be no doubt that this will profoundly affect the Christian communities there, although it is too soon to predict in what manner. Perhaps, in time, it will lead to a totally new kind of Jewish Christianity--the result, not of missionary efforts (whether on the part of Jewish or gentile Christians), but of a Christianity influenced by a living Judaism.

This leads us to raise a question which we are in no position to answer, yet which seems important. Is it conceivable, in the not too distant future, that a Jew could become a Christian without cutting himself off from his heritage and people, or being cut off by them? Our concern stems not from a desire to convert Jews, but rather from the existential situation: regardless of missionary effort, there always will be men and women who will come to faith in Christ; just as there always will be Christians who become Jews. The Jewish Christian, in other words, is, and

will continue to be, a fact in the Church. As Wolfgang Wirth
writes,

> In our days we once more have in our churches men
> and women who belong to Israel by birth and have be-
> come disciples of Jesus, not in order to become in-
> visible, nor to cast off Israel's burden, but in order
> to witness Christ, in whom they have recognized Is-
> rael's Messiah. Unfortunately these Jewish Chris-
> tians, who see their function in terms of a bridge,
> spanning both parts, are not yet generally recognized
> by Christians as a sign [of God's covenant].... It is
> part of our ecumenical task to welcome every Chris-
> tian who comes from Judaism for the sake of Israel,
> and to encourage him not to deny his origins and tra-
> ditions, which have come to him through his people
> ["Der ökumenische Aspekt der Begegnung mit den Ju-
> den," Judentum und christlicher Glaube, ed. C. Thoma
> (Klosterneuburg, 1965), p. 153].

How can his desire to retain his bond with his "brothers according to the flesh," and to be a link or "bridge" between
the two communities, ever be realized unless Jews for their
part are willing to maintain the bond?[10]

We can envision this possibility only if Christians--in-
cluding Jewish Christians--abandon the missionary enterprise
and convince Jews that they have done so. Given our heavily
burdened history, this will not be achieved easily. To this
day, the majority of Jews still expect most Christians who
approach them to be intent on conversion;[11] as we have seen
in this chapter, this fear is not without foundation. Although
the Catholic Church as such does not engage in missionary
work among Jews, the Lutheran Church continues to do so,
as do many fundamentalist sects, even and especially in Israel. It is inconceivable that, so long as the suspicion of
proselytizing persists, Jews would feel anything but hostility
toward their own who become Christian.

The creation of genuine Jewish Christian communities
could also contribute to changing the Jewish Christians' situation with regard to their own people. Such communities existed in the very beginnings of the Church, although they were
entirely gone by the fourth century. Today in the State of Israel
some groups have already sprung up that are evolving a new
Jewish Christian liturgy in the Hebrew language. The Israeli government is not hostile to these groups, and some

Israeli scholars are sympathetic to them and in close contact. If this trend continues, we may witness, for the first
time since the second century, a Jewish Christianity that is
genuinely Jewish and genuinely Christian, where the Jew can
feel at home without abandoning his traditions. Here again,
a prerequisite would be the complete renunciation of all missionary intent.

One further point may be raised in this context. The
virtual impossibility for Jewish Christians to remain members of their people has led some theologians to question
whether Jews who have come to believe in Christ should be
baptized.[12] K. H. Rengstorf, for one, condemns such a suggestion in no uncertain terms.[13] The question is worth considering, given the fact that the Jew who is baptized is considered a traitor by his own people (although this was not always so, as noted earlier). It is important that steps be
taken to make possible once more, within the Church, the rebirth of an authentic Jewish Christianity. To do so is, in
the words of C. E. Florival, "to pose the very delicate question of the relation between the Christian Church and living
Judaism."[14]

Conclusion

The renewed impetus of Judenmission which began in
the 19th century was motivated by a missionary zeal that differed from times past in that it rejected force; at its best,
it approached the Jew in a spirit of brotherly love. The
rapid growth of interest in Jewish studies, as typified by various "Instituta Judaica," while in large measure motivated by
the missionary objective,[15] nonetheless led to a greater appreciation of Judaism. (It should be pointed out that the best
work so far has been done with regard to Biblical Judaism;
the discovery of post-Biblical Judaism is still in its very beginnings.) Already in the 19th century men like Delitzsch
were questioning not only the traditional Christian methods of
conversion, but also traditional Christian teaching concerning
Israel's rejection.

The growth in the number of Jewish Christians and the
emergence, in the 19th century, of Jewish Christian communities and organizations, attest to a moderate measure of
"success" of Judenmission. Jewish Christianity today is no
uniform phenomenon. The sufferings, and the discrimination
from their fellow Christians, experienced by Jewish Christians led many to seek complete absorption into the Church,

and to relinquish all elements of their own tradition. Others, on the contrary, reacted by wishing to retain their Jewish identity within the Church. As demonstrated by the 1964 controversy resulting from the Løgumkloster Conference, the issue is not closed. The reaction to the two tendencies among non-Jewish Christians has also been mixed; some decry an identifiable Jewish Christianity as marring the unity of the Church; others welcome it as a means of strengthening the Jewish element in Christianity. This question also remains.

The main concern and goal of Judenmission may be described as follows: Israel's salvation in Christ, through baptism into the Church (the true people of God), carried out here and now by the Church's missionary efforts, which have been enjoined upon it by the Lord. The outgrowth of 18th-century Pietism, Judenmission has been furthered among major Church bodies principally by the Lutheran Church. In recent years there has been a tendency to consider the efforts of individuals and groups as inadequate, and to stress the missionary task as being the responsibility of the Church as organization. (See Chapter III.) If this trend persists, it will heighten the importance given to Judenmission by those Churches that endorse it.

At the same time, a growing number of theologians today are coming to question the very concept of Judenmission. This development is examined in Parts Two and Three of this book.

---

[a]Ben Zion Bokser, Judaism and the Christian Predicament (New York: Knopf, 1967), p. 364.

[b]E.g., The Institute of Judaeo-Christian Studies at Seton Hall University, directed by Msgr. John M. Oesterreicher.

[c]See Cohen, The Myth of the Judeo-Christian Tradition, 1970.

[d]In French the opposite pertains: there is the single term "Judéo-chrétien." This is translated rather arbitrarily into English by either term, as is evidenced by the fact that Jean Daniélou's book, La théologie du Judéo-Christianisme, appeared in English as The Theology of Jewish Christianity, while his article in Sacramentum Mundi is entitled "Judaeo-Christianity."

[e]Hans-Joachim Schoeps, Jewish Christianity; Factional Disputes in the Early Church, trans. by Douglas R. A. Hare (Philadelphia: Fortress Press, 1969), p. 9. Original German edition: Das Judenchristentum, 1964.

[f]Both groups are described by Justin Martyr in his Dialogue with Trypho, c. 46.

[g]Kremers, "Römer 9-11," p. 155. The accuracy of this statement by a Christian theologian is corroborated by the following text from a Jewish author: The United States Catholic, (February 1966, pp. 21-29) "refers to an apostate from Judaism as a 'Jewish-Christian' ... There is no more legitimacy in describing a Jew who left his faith to become a Christian as a 'Jewish-Christian' than there would be in describing a Christian who left his faith to become a Jew as a 'Christian-Jew.'" Ben Zion Bokser, Judaism and the Christian Predicament, p. 364; emphasis added.

Part Two

One People of God--Divided

Chapter III

THE 1961 BERLIN KIRCHENTAG

The inability of the Churches to face the Jewish Question in the years immediately following World War II has already been noted (see "The Period Covered," in the Introduction). Although individuals and groups were not inactive
during this time, the silence of the official Church was not
broken until 1948, when the "Reichsbruderrat der Evangelischen Kirche in Deutschland" met at Darmstadt in April,
and issued a statement on Judaism [Der Ungekündigte Bund,
pp. 251-54]. During the next 12 years various Church meetings took place, sponsored by one or the other organization
of the Lutheran Church in Germany.[1] A climax was reached
in 1961, with the tenth meeting of the "Deutsche Evangelische
Kirchentag" in Berlin. This meeting may be considered an
epoch-making event in the post-war history of Judaism and
Christianity for a number of reasons:*

    - It was the first time that the "Deutsche Evangel-
ische Kirchentag" (DEK) officially included the topic of Judaism on its agenda. The decision to do so grew out of the
previous DEK in Munich, at which an evening devoted to the
State of Israel had drawn an unexpectedly large number of
participants. Thus the theme of Judaism and the Church became part of the official agenda of the German Lutheran
Church.

---

*The Kirchentag as an institution has been called the Diet
of the German Churches. It goes back to the mid-19th century, and is largely the work of J. H. Wichern, who saw its
ecumenical significance in being "Not a union but a confed-
eration of ... the Lutheran and the Reformed confessions
... and the United type."[2]

- For the first time, a special task group was constituted by the DEK to deal with the question of Judaism and
Christianity: the "Arbeitsgruppe für Juden und Christen."
The work of the steering committee ("Arbeitsgruppenleitung,"
or "AGL") was rendered difficult not only by the complexity
of the theological questions, but because 1961 was the year
of the Eichmann trial, so that the meeting was held in an already charged atmosphere.

- The AGL decided to include a Jewish theologian,
Rabbi Robert Raphael Geis, among the official speakers. In
the words of Dietrich Goldschmidt and Hans-Joachim Kraus,
this meant that, for the first time since Christianity's break
with Judaism, a Jewish speaker was able to address a large,
official gathering of Christians on an equal footing and in an
atmosphere of freedom and respect [Ungekündigte Bund, p.
10].

- An unexpectedly large number of people--in the
thousands--attended the workshop, testifying to the interest
in Judaism at that moment in Germany's history [p. 10].

- The papers and discussions of AG VI ("Arbeitsgruppe VI," as it came to be called) aroused a vehement
controversy in the ecclesiastical press in the ensuing months,
centering largely around the issue of Judenmission, even
though this was not the official or explicit theme of the meeting.

    The proceedings of the DEK, published in Stuttgart in
1961, were later expanded into a volume that contained, in
addition, follow-up work done by the AG VI, which had meanwhile become the "Arbeitsgemeinschaft für Christen und Juden beim Deutschen Evangelischen Kirchentag." Various
articles showing the controversy in the press, papers given
at meetings at Arnoldshain and Frankfurt, and other valuable
historical documentation were also added. [3]

    Despite the widespread interest in the work of the
AG VI and the breakthrough which it signified, its work did
not meet with universal acclaim. In some quarters--particu-
larly in the official publications of the Lutheran Church--
vehement opposition was voiced to some of the views presented. [4] Goldschmidt and Kraus liken these criticisms to
wanting to wash one's feet without getting them wet. [5] They
contrast them with the change in mentality that was apparent
among many participants during the DEK: the realization

that a radically new attitude by Christians toward Jews was called for, and that the traditional Christian superiority complex would no longer do. An honest reappraisal of the history of the Church and its failures must be undertaken. The Church's relation to Judaism is ultimately a theological matter which touches the Church in its very core, since it, too, is a covenant community [Ungekündigte Bund, pp. 13-14]. A new understanding of Judaism and its relation to the Church will, therefore, have repercussions for the whole of Christian theology and affect every aspect of the life of the Church: its relation to the world and its understanding of itself and of its mission.

The Controversy over Judenmission

In contrast to the secular press, which reported the deliberations of the AG VI matter-of-factly and objectively, the reaction in several ecclesiastical and theological journals was far from dispassionate.[6] The most negative view is perhaps summed up by G. Hummel: "Anyone who took home what the AG had presented ... could do nothing else, logically, than deny all faith-relevance of Jesus and the New Testament for Christians, and describe the whole history of Christian proclamation down to this very day as being on the wrong track" [Christ und Welt, July 28, 1961, quoted in Ungekündigte Bund, p. 161].

The various criticisms of the press amount to accusations that Christianity has capitulated to Judaism, and abandoned Jesus as the Christ for the whole world. The sharpness of the controversy is indicated by the use of phrases such as "selling Church history down the drain," "distortions," "dangerous Judaizing," and "relapse into Judaism."[7] In one way or another the fear is expressed that the views voiced by the speakers at the Kirchentag imply an abandoning of the Church's mission to the Jews, and a betrayal of Christ's command to preach the gospel.

The AGL set forth the results of the workshop in a statement accompanied by explanatory remarks. It is the fourth and last paragraph of this document that proved to be the main focus of the critics' attack. It reads as follows:

In face of the false assertion, widely held in the Church for centuries, that God has rejected the Jewish people, we ponder anew the apostle's words:

'God has not rejected his people whom he foreknew'
(Rom. 11:2). A new encounter with the people chosen
by God will confirm, or re-awaken, the awareness
that Jews and Christians both live through the faithfulness of God, that they praise him, and serve him
everywhere among men in the light of biblical hope
[Ungekündigte Bund, p. 125].

The paragraph which elaboratores upon this point reiterates
that Christians and Jews owe their continued existence to the
fidelity of the one God in whom both believe, and who has
freely chosen them. Both have received a task and call to
bear witness to him. Hope has been promised to both.

This statement, along with the opening sentence of the
entire document--"Jews and Christians are linked in an unbreakable bond" [unlösbar verbunden]--make the document unacceptable to Kurt Wendlandt.[8] To say that an unbreakable
bond unites Jew and Christian, and that God has not rejected
the Jewish people, is to give Judaism an equal validity with
Christianity as a way to God. But how can there be a way
to him outside of Jesus Christ? What meaning does Christianity's mission to the Jews have, if both religions are valid?

Paul Reinhardt takes exception to the same phrase,[9]
because it passes over in silence what separates Jew and
Christian: faith, or lack of faith, in Jesus as Messiah.
The most vehement attack, however, comes from J. G.
Mehl, who qualifies the phrase as "the latest fad," "bound-
less exaggeration," and denies that any supporting evidence
for it can be found in the New Testament ["Kirche und Synagoge," p. 9]. For although the Jews were the first to hear
the gospel, through their rejection of Jesus Christ they forfeited all claim to be the chosen people. Jesus' Jewish origin is of "merely historical" significance. Since his coming,
the God whom the Jews worship is no longer the same as
the God of Christians [p. 8].

Mehl denies not only an "unbreakable bond," but any
spiritual bond whatever between Jew and Christian. Far from
being spiritual brothers, as the AG VI would have it, the
Jews have now become the "Synagogue of Satan" (Rev. 2:9
and 3:9). It follows that any working together based on spiritual and religious kinship is out of the question and mere
sentimental enthusiasm [p. 11]. "There is Judenmission,"
writes Mehl, "there is a movement, 'the Gospel for Israel,'

but there can be, today, no Christian-Jewish cooperation in the religious sphere which has a legitimate basis in scripture" [p. 11].

For Mehl, the only proper relationship of Christianity to Judaism is a purely missionary one [p. 17]. The people of God, chosen from all eternity, takes on different forms in the course of history. Once it had been the Israel according to the flesh; since Pentecost it is the Church, "outside of which there is no salvation" [p. 16]. Insofar-- and only insofar--as the Jewish people enters the Church, can it again become part of the chosen people [p. 17].

The obligation to Judenmission is stressed by others than Mehl, and the lack of emphasis given it by the AG VI is deplored and considered dangerous. Thus Martin Wittenberg, in his reply to Mehl [pp. 18-25], disagrees with the latter that Israel is rejected and that, since the coming of Christ, it no longer worships the same God as do Christians [pp. 23-24], yet he considers the failure to stress Judenmission as a blemish on the entire work of the Kirchentag.[10]

Kurt Wendlandt asks whether the Church has been mistaken all these centuries in its consciousness of being the "true Israel according to the Spirit," and in considering as its "noblest duty" the proclamation of Jesus Christ to the Jewish people [Lutherische Monatshefte, I, No. 2 (1962), p. 83]. He reasons that if the Jews are indeed, as H. J. Kraus and others of the AG VI maintain, "God's chosen, beloved people," it follows that the Church is not the people of God, and "the Lord Jesus Christ died and rose in vain" [p. 83]. This is a surrender of the New Testament's universalist claim to salvation, and Christians might as well start thinking about converting to Judaism [p. 82]. There is only one people of God for Wendlandt, according to scripture: either the Jews are still chosen, or they are rejected.

The obligation to Judenmission is seen as identical with bearing witness to Jesus Christ. This leads Paul Reinhardt to the startling conclusion that it is improper, at a Protestant Kirchentag, for anyone officially to address the Christian community who does not himself confess Christ (hence, for him, the inevitable lacunae in R. R. Geis' paper). The Church must proclaim Jesus of Nazareth to the Jews as their Messiah [p. 80], and resist the facile temptation to skirt the Christ question in a "culpable silence" which results from wanting to reduce confrontation with the Synagogue to mere Philosemitism [p. 81].

It would seem that Hansgeorg Schroth hits the nail on the head when he writes, with reference to these views: "It is not the New Testament statements that are wrong. What is wrong, however, absolutely wrong, is their use by Christians against the Jews; the impertinent, arrogant manner in which Christians deduce from them a divine prerogative and consider themselves as sole 'possessors' of Christ" [Ungekündigte Bund, pp. 180-81].

There is common agreement among the critics that the AG VI has distorted and misread scripture, especially Romans 9-11. In Reinhardt's opinion, only such a misreading can lead to the one-sided view that Israel is still chosen: Romans 11:2, that God has not rejected his people, must not be taken in isolation, but as part of the whole of Romans 9-11. Paul speaks, after all, of the "branches that have been broken off," which obviously means that they are now dead--even if at some future time God can bring them back to life.[11] This is a direct reference to remarks made by Günther Harder at the Kirchentag.[12] Do his remarks warrant the vehement criticism they aroused? Does he advocate a "betrayal of the Gospel"?*

Harder bases his arguments largely on Romans 11.[14] He points out that Paul makes a distinction between the "rejection" and the "hardening" of Israel, denying the former (Rom. 11:2), but affirming Israel's obduracy in not accepting Christ (Rom. 11:7). Yet Israel remains loved by God for the sake of the Fathers, and because God's gifts, once bestowed, are not withdrawn (Rom. 11:29). It is God's will, then, that Synagogue and Church exist side by side, at least until "the fulness of the gentiles has entered" (Rom. 11:25) --to which text Harder adds the words, "the Church." This does not mean, however, recognizing the Synagogue as an "independent way to God apart from Jesus Christ" [Ungekündigte Bund, p. 138]. Christianity recognizes the

---

*Harder was one of the founders and most active members of the AG, and his paper became the main focus for critics, leading to further elaboration on his part and further criticism on theirs. Harder is also the founder and director of the "Institut Kirche und Judentum" at the "Kirchliche Hochschule" of Berlin.[13]

Synagogue insofar as it consists of the Israel chosen by God.
It denies its recognition, however, "as Synagogue, that is,
as the gathering, outside the name of Jesus Christ, in which
the chosen Israel finds its religious form" [p. 138].

Harder reiterates this view the following year, in
responding directly to Reinhardt's criticisms.[15] Christians
may not speak of Israel as a salvation community ["Heil-
saussagen über Israel zu machen"], nor consider Judaism
as a way to God, or as a "being-with-God."[16] Yet Harder
takes issue with the 19th-century theologian Theodor Klie-
foth who concluded that Israel, in rejecting Jesus Christ,
"steps back into the ranks of other nations." Israel's existence and history since Christ, as well as Romans 11, are
evidence of its special place.

Harder sees Christianity's relationship to Judaism in
terms of tension. There is communion, because Christians
are the wild olive branches, in living relationship with the
root. Both believe in the Living God and their election--
Israel without Christ, Christians only through him. There
is tension, because Israel refuses to understand itself in the
light of Christ. This means that the Church, while stressing its bond with Israel, remains bound to give witness to
Israel of Christ. It will not fail in this witness, the fears
of some members of the AG VI notwithstanding. For how
can the Christian speak of God, of Israel, of election, without speaking of Christ? "There is no other name given to
men under heaven in which they can be saved" (Acts 4:12).
These words remain valid. At the same time, witness to
Jesus Christ necessarily includes witness to Israel, since
Jesus was Son of David and a Jew.

Harder, then, insists that the Church owes Israel the
proclamation of Christ; but it must be given humbly, not ar-
rogantly, not as though the Church possessed him.
No wonder that the centuries-old triumphalism of Christianity arouses painful memories among Jews. All that Christians can do is to point humbly to God's wealth in Christ,
a wealth destined for Christian and Jew alike.

It should be apparent from what has been said so far
that Harder rejects neither Christ-witness nor Judenmission.
The latter, he believes, must change its traditional character. Not only should it be free of all arrogance and superiority, but it must also take a different approach from that
of its origins in modern times--in Pietism. The Pietists

were concerned with individual conversion, and consequently
put all men--pagans, Jews, unbelieving Christians--on the
same level, applying the concept of mission to all alike and
in a similar fashion. Jews rightly objected to being considered on a par with pagans, Harder points out [Ungekündigte
Bund, p. 140]. (One need not add that they object even more
strongly to being objects of Christian mission at all.)

In Harder's view, the 19th century gave rise to another ambiguity: several Christian missionary societies were
established as organs of the State, to work for conversion of
the Jews so that, through baptism, they might be absorbed
into society and thus cease to exist as Jews. This kind of
Judenmission, Harder insists, is a thing of the past. As the
World Council of Churches stated at Amsterdam in 1948, witness of Christ toward Israel is a concern of the Christian
community as a whole, not only of certain organizations [pp.
140-41].

It seems to us that Harder's reasons for advocating
a new form of mission to the Jews are ultimately pragmatic,
conditioned by historical events. This is evident from his
phrase that "the present situation, especially in Germany today" [p. 141], requires dialogue, not mission as the appropriate encounter with Judaism.

At the same time, his approach to dialogue shows that
he respects what the Jew may have to say to us and teach
us. True dialogue for him presupposes two factors. The
first is a willingness to listen to the other, because we know
that what he has to say is worth hearing. Christians can
learn from the Jews' passionate desire to do God's will,
from their experience of God's intimate relation to his people
in history, their praise of God, their ardent hope for a better world. Secondly, dialogue requires unconditional and patient love: unconditional, because it does not insist that the
other first change--that Jews become Christians--before en-
gaging in dialogue; patient, because it waits for God to act.

Some months later, in a paper given at Arnoldshain
in January 1962, Harder elaborated on his earlier remarks.[17]
The apostolic witness to Christ as recorded in Acts, to which
Christian proclamation must adhere at all times, demands of
Israel a changed outlook--recognition of Jesus as Messiah [p.
146]. "It does not exclude Israel from salvation," but sees
in those Jews who recognize Jesus the true Israelites.
Through faith in Christ the Jew achieves his true destiny [p. 146].

The exclusive character of the Christ-witness does not permit the Christian to see Judaism as a "fully valid way to God." He will not deny Judaism's special place and election, "but cannot concede it eschatological salvation."[18] Only in Christ can men find salvation. This explains Christianity's twofold attitude toward the Synagogue: a "Yes" as the gathering of God's people, a "No" insofar as this gathering takes place outside Christ [p. 146].

In Christ God will give us all things (Rom. 8:32). For Harder, this "all" includes the Old Testament, the consciousness of being chosen, and the promises--which have been bestowed upon us in Christ even though we were a "no-people" (Rom. 9), with no claim on our part to these riches either through natural descent or merit. Harder believes that our witness to Christ must, therefore, include three points [pp. 157-58]:

1. The Old Testament remains the book of the Jews,[19] we do not wish to take it away from them. It is true that, as Paul writes in 2 Corinthians 3, a veil lies over Moses (i.e., the Law and whole of the Old Testament), for the scriptures yield their full meaning only in the Spirit. Yet God still speaks to Israel through his word, making known to them his will, his jealousy, fidelity, glory and grace. Therefore the Jews remain a special people among the nations of the earth.

2. Israel's election remains valid. Our consciousness of being chosen is not acquired at the price of Israel's election. Romans 9-11 clearly states that Israel is not rejected. Jesus Christ is the fulfillment of Israel's way, and we are chosen only through him. The Jews are still beloved by God for the Fathers' sake, even though they oppose God's plan in Christ. When Paul speaks of continued election he has in mind the whole of Israel, not only individual Jewish converts. Against Reinhardt ("Zur gegenwärtigen Diskussion," p. 100), Harder maintains that all of Israel is affected by the remnant mentioned in Romans 9, so that the uniqueness of the Jewish people is not a thing of the past, but is embodied in Jewish existence down to our own day [Lutherische Monatshefte, I, No. 2 (1962), p. 325].

3. God's promises to Israel still apply to the Jewish people, for their ultimate fulfillment will include Israel. The goal of history is the one chosen people of God, a

new mankind made up of Jews and gentiles under the
lordship of Christ. There can be no final and complete
salvation for the Christian which does not also include
the Jew.

Until that time comes (Harder continues), the Christian community must bear witness to Christ in love,
proclaiming the message entrusted to it in its entirety:
God's grace and judgment, his promises and threats.
We shall be kept from false security 'insofar as we remain in grace' (Rom. 11:22). This awareness will enable us at one and the same time to carry on the dialogue in love, and not to betray our mission [Ungekünd-
igte Bund, p. 159].

While Harder presents his arguments in that spirit of
charity and humility which he asks of the whole Christian
community, his views can hardly be qualified as theologically audacious or unambiguous. He maintains the continuing
election of the whole of Israel, but does not concede that Judaism is a way of salvation. Judenmission should give way
to dialogue, at least for the present, yet the Christian community waits for the day when Jews will acknowledge the
lordship of Christ. Thus conversion of the Jew--if not now,
later, if not through Judenmission then through dialogue--
still remains an essential part of Christian witness.[20]

The fact that such relatively moderate views provoked
vehement and harsh criticisms and accusations among members of the Lutheran Church is an indication, it would seem,
that the subject of Judenmission touches a raw nerve in
Christian theology. Approaching it from the opposite end,
one might say that the more general discussions by the
Kirchentag of such themes as election, covenant, and
"people of God," gave rise to a heated controversy about the
Church's mission to the Jews.[21] This shows the subject of
Judenmission to be not a peripheral one, but very much at
the center of Christian theology vis-à-vis Judaism today.

In the Kirchentag controversy can be found the basic
issues posed in the Introduction to this book: Christians as
the only true People of God in the full sense of the term,
Christ as the sole and universal way of salvation, and the
nature of Christian mission. The mere fact and vehemence
of the controversy are signs that there is no longer one
single, simple answer to these questions, to which anyone
claiming to be a Christian must subscribe. The very

ambiguities and contradictions in some of the theological arguments brought forward--e. g. , Israel is still chosen, yet
must not be considered a salvation community--is evidence
of a search for a new approach to the perennial questions
facing the Church with regard to Israel.[22]

Chapter IV

JUDENMISSION AND THE ECUMENICAL QUESTION

In the previous chapter, the 1961 Kirchentag was considered solely from the point of view of Judenmission. This should not cause us to lose sight of its wider importance in the history of post-Hitler Germany. It led to a greater confrontation with the Nazi past of the Church than had hitherto taken place, brought the question of Judaism and the Church to the forefront of popular consciousness and, particularly through the work of the "Arbeitsgemeinschaft für Juden und Christen," marked a new era of theological concern with this question. The volume which resulted from the Kirchentag suggests in its very title, Der Ungekündigte Bund--the "unbroken" or "still-valid" Covenant--the willingness of Christian theologians to re-examine Judaism's relationship to Christianity.

The companion volume, which appeared in 1966[1] is, as the subtitle indicates, also the work of the "Arbeitsgemeinschaft." As in the earlier volume, the proceedings of the KED in Dortmund and Cologne take up less than half the total number of pages. The remainder brings together theological material that elaborates upon the main themes of the two meetings, and a 50-page annotated bibliography [prepared by Dr. Ursula Bohn--see Ch. 3, note 13]. A further point of similarity with the earlier volume is the significance of the title: "The Divided People of God": one single people that has suffered a split, cleavage, or, to use a theological term that now gradually comes to the fore, a schism. This concept will be examined in some detail--since it represents a certain new departure in the considerations of Judaism and the Church, of Judenmission and, more basically, of ecumenical theology in general--but first the use of "ecumenical" should be clarified.

80

"Ecumenism"--A New Meaning

The term "ecumenical" has a long history, dating
back to New Testament times.   It has occurred in a variety
of meanings over the centuries.   Although it is generally understood today to refer to the unity and concerns of all the
Christian Churches, this meaning is of relatively recent origin, making its first appearance in the 19th century. [2]

William Temple, Archbishop of York and later of
Canterbury, who was one of the leading figures in ecumenism in the first part of the 20th century, described the ecumenical movement as "a great new fact of our century."[3]
Yet, in the overall panorama of Church history, some his-
torians of ecumenism maintain that the whole history of the
"Christian Church from the first century to the twentieth
might be written in terms of its struggle to realize ecumenical unity."[4]   Stephen Charles Neill writes that, although divisions had been present in the Church "almost from the beginning..., division has never been finally acquiesced in as
the normal condition of that Church.   The vision of perfect
unity, sometimes faint and elusive, has always been before
the eyes of Christians, and in every age some have been
ready to pursue that vision."[5]   Centuries were to pass, however, before the Churches as churches became seriously concerned.   In the sense, then, that the ecumenical movement
has become a concern of the Churches as such, and has
gained a considerable measure of popular support among
Christians at large, it is a phenomenon of the 20th century,
engaged in the effort to promote unity among the various
Christian Churches.

Another interpretation of ecumenism, however, began
to make its appearance in the late forties.   Scarcely noticed
at first, it has come to be applied by a growing number of
theologians today not only to Christians of all persuasions--
Roman Catholic as well as Orthodox--but to Jews as well.
Indeed, according to Robert McAfee Brown, the word ecumenical today is used in so broad a meaning that it suggests
"a spirit of cooperation and goodwill among all men whatever
their theological or religious persuasion."[6]   We touch here
upon a new phenomenon: the suggestion that the Jews belong
within the ecumenical context--a context that had hitheto been
considered exclusively intra-Christian.   What led to this approach?   What are its implications?

In 1948 a Belgian Benedictine, N. Oehmen, used the
phrase "schism in the divine economy" with reference to the
break between Israel and the Church. The concept gradually gained ground. Thus Stephen Neill speaks of the "state
of permanent schism" in which the Church exists since its
separation from Israel; and calls this the "original schism"
within the people of God, "far more serious than any division within the Church...."[7]

The study on Israel and the Church published by the
Reformed Church of Holland in 1959 strongly advocates placing Israel within the ecumenical context:

> We may ... see our relation to Israel in an ecumen-
> ical perspective, by considering the division between
> the Church and Israel as the first schism within the
> one body of God's community. Israel was the cradle
> of ecumenism. This concept is so closely linked to
> the Jewish people that an ecumenical movement severs
> itself from its own source if it does not concern it-
> self with this people. For without Israel, the Church
> cannot experience her ecumenical character in ful-
> ness [Ger. ed.: Israel und die Kirche (Zürich: EVZ
> Verlag, 1961), p. 43 (emphasis added)].

A Catholic theologian, Bernard Lambert, sees the
Church's ecumenical mission as twofold. It is directed first
of all toward continuing the reconciliation of the Cross--
healing the division in mankind between Jew and gentile.
Secondly, its aim is to reestablish union among Christians.
Since the schism between Israel and the Church underlies
all Christian schisms, "Judaism could be the key to the im-
passe in which Christians have become caught," and play a
decisive role in Christian reunion [quoted in Gespaltene
Gottesvolk, p. 290].

In a somewhat similar vein, K. E. Skydsgaard asks
whether our ecumenical effort has not become "strangely
lifeless and inoffensive because it is not radically inspired
by Israel and the Bible?" ["Israel, the Church and the Unity
of the People of God," Lutheran World, X no. 4 (Oct. 1963),
p. 350]. We must not "overlook the fact that the division
between Judaism and Christianity was from the beginning a
division within the Jewish people itself' [p. 345]. The
Christian Church began with a break, a schism. When the
Church came into being, the people of God was split [p.
349]. "In short: here we have the 'ecumenical problem'

in its most central difficulty" [p. 350].

The schism doctrine* will be examined in greater detail in the pages that follow. These remarks are merely intended to indicate the shift in the ecumenical scene from an
intra-Christian concern to one which not only seeks to include Judaism, but considers it as the starting point and
sine qua non of the ecumenical movement. [8]

Let us now turn to the writings of three theologians
whose views of Judaism center around the concept of schism,
and who have influenced the German scene: N. Oehmen,
Paul Démann, and Heinrich Spaemann.

The Eschatological Perspective

The first to extend ecumenism beyond the Christian
pale was the Benedictine N. Oehmen, of the Abbey of Chevetogne in Belgium, in an article entitled "The Schism in
the Divine Economy."[9] (Renate Maria Heydenreich, in drawing attention to this article and the concept of "proto-
schism" [i. e., Urschisma], speaks of the "enormous fruit-
fulness" which this concept can bring to ecumenical theology
[Gespaltene Gottesvolk, p. 223]). Oehmen identifies the end
of time with the end of the "exile of the House of Jacob
amid the 'desert of the nations'," when the basic schism
which has caused all other schisms will be ended. This
schism has divided Israel into two parts, one believing, the
other unbelieving. The division is temporary only, it will
one day be healed through the conversion of the Jews. It is
clear from scripture that this will not be the work of human
effort, and that God alone can bring it about (Ez. 36).
Hence missionary efforts are useless. The healing of the
schism is not a phenomenon within the historical process,
but will be achieved only at the end of history [Irénikon, p.
29].

A text from Zechariah 4:6ff. provides Oehmen with
images that speak of this wholeness at the end of time, images which he expands into a parable. The cornerstone of
the new Temple was laid by all the prophets and holy men
of the Old Testament, right up to the apostles. The keystone, however, is still missing, so that the building is still

---

*We owe the terms "schism doctrine" and "schism theologi-
ans" to Alan Davies, Antisemitism, p. 156.

incomplete. One day God himself will find the keystone
"among the believing Israel of the last times," the "children
of the prophets (Acts 3:25)." Meanwhile, this stone lies
buried beneath the rubble of the old Temple, which signifies
unbelief [p. 31]. Before the advent of Christ the debris
will be cleared away, for every mountain and hill shall be
brought low, and there will come forth the "believing remnant of Israel with a shout of joy: 'Grace, grace be upon
Israel!' " Then at last the Church will be whole, with that
inner unity of the Spirit which is indestructible, and which,
hitherto invisible and interior, will at last become external
as well [p. 31].

     A theme can be found here that will occur again with
theologians of this type: that the Church is imperfect, incomplete, without Israel. Only when Israel believes--Oeh-
men refers to the "conversion of the Jews"--will the keystone complete and perfect the building. Until then, something is yet lacking.

The Church, Israel, and the Nations

     One of the theologians most influential in placing Isra-
el within the ecumenical context was Paul Démann. [10] In
1953 he published an article entitled, "Israel and the Unity
of the Church," [11] in which he sharply distinguished between
Israel and "Missionsvölker" ("missionizable peoples"). For
it is of the nature of the Christian missonary task, in Démann's view, to implant and give flesh to the Gospel in an
environment and soil which have, until now, been alien to it.
Since Israel is the root and mother-soil out of which Christianity has grown, the concept of mission does not apply
[Gespaltene Gottesvolk, p. 256].

     There is a further difference between Israel and the
nations. While the Church faces many new problems in missionary lands, no past history stands in its way and blocks
the Gospel message. In this regard, too, Israel's situation
is different: for the history of the relationship between Judaism and Christianity is heavily burdened.

     On both these counts, then, Démann considers Isra-
el's situation closer to that of a branch of divided Christendom than of "Missionsvölker": a common tradition and origin
have been disrupted at one time, and this break has resulted
in rivalries, hostilities, injustices and bitterness that have

left a deep mark [p. 257]. And yet, those who have been
torn apart need each other; division means imperfection and
incompleteness. In the case of both Israel and the Christian
Churches, the goal is the restoration of unity. "The origin,
development and nature of the fundamental schism that separates Israel and the Church show clearly that all considerations with regard to the restoration of the unity of Christendom can be applied in a marvellous way, and at times much
more clearly, to the reintegration of Israel into the
Church."[12]

Démann developed these ideas at greater length in an
essay published in 1961 ["Kirche und Israel in oekumenischer
Sicht. Katholische Besinnung auf Israel seit 1945," in
Christen und Juden, pp. 270-83]. Despite the difference
constituted by the lack of a common faith in Christ that binds
the various Christian Churches across their divisions, Israel clearly belongs within the ecumenical, rather than missionary perspective. For there is much that is similar: in
both cases, a once existing unity has been broken, with consequent hardening and polarization. Yet there is the desire
today on the part of many to resume the dialogue, and to
create conditions which will make this possible: removing
obstacles and distortions, atoning for the past, achieving mutual respect, a return to scripture, the deepening and puri-
fication of one's own faith and relationship to God, etc. [p.
281].

In describing the missionary endeavor, Démann goes
beyond his earlier remarks. It will take one of two forms:
either the effort to make Christ present in a country and culture that do not know him, or, attempting to bring as many
"unbelievers" as possible to baptism; that is, striving for
individual conversion [p. 273].

Neither form fits Israel's situation. The primitive
Church's proclamation to the Jews may be called "missionary" in the broad sense of the term, but the concept had a
very different meaning then from the one it acquired subsequently. For this early proclamation occurred from within
the same salvation community, the same people, tradition
and culture. No adaptation of the message was needed--al-
though this quickly became imperative as the Church turned
toward the gentiles.

This original missionary activity from within Démann
considers also today as the only legitimate attitude of the

Church toward Israel. It must be rooted in the Church's
effort to come to a deeper understanding of its Biblical heritage and origins. Any other missionary attitude would oblit-
erate the difference between Israel and other religions, which
have remained, historically, "outside Revelation and salvation history" [p. 274]. Due in part to sociological factors
and the growth of missionary activity in the 19th century,
this difference tended to become obscured. [13]

Démann's stress on the difference between Israel and
the nations with regard to the Church is one of his main
concerns, and puts him squarely among the Schism theologians. [14] Israel is neither a stranger to us, nor different
from us. Rather, we are discovering today that it is a
part--separated, but not definitively--"of the one and only
people of God" ["Israel und die Kirche," p. 278]. Although
this people was split in two at the decisive moment of history, we know on the basis of the New Testament and of the
Old, "read in the light of Paul" [p. 279], that God does not
repent of his gifts (Rom. 11:29), and that Israel, though separated for the time being, is not rejected, but still loved
(Rom. 11:28). [15] Israel remains a witness to Sinai and the
Covenant, hence "bound to the destiny of the people of God."
From this it follows that it neither is nor ever can be an
object of mission, like other nations. For it does not exist
"outside" the Church. [16]

The Church is linked to Israel through the past, its
origin in "the depth of her [the Church's] own existence as
people of God." This means that it can proclaim Jesus
Christ to Israel only in the form of a constant, on-going dialogue and debate ("Auseinandersetzung") that takes place within the people of God itself: between those who have come to
believe in Christ, and those "who remain far from him" [p.
279].

Démann believes that we have come to a critical turning point in Christian-(Catholic)-Jewish relations today, and
that a change in mentality is asked of us: a shift from a
missionary to an ecumenical outlook. He sees this change
as being achieved more easily by Catholics than Protestants,
because missionary work toward the Jews has been less organized and more sporadic among Catholics. [17] Protestants,
on the other hand, have the advantage of a long-standing interest in Israel, and more experience in ecumenical work
["Kirche und Israel," pp. 282-83].

Such a change in mentality, urgently needed though it
is, cannot, in his view, as yet be taken for granted. For
the traditional missionary attitude is widespread and has
deep roots. It manifests itself frequently in greater zeal toward Jews[18] than toward other Christians or non-Christians,
revealing an echo of the bitterness which a triumphant medieval Christianity experienced in the face of unremitting
Jewish resistance. Démann sees in this attitude the convergence of several complex elements:

- "an obscure consciousness" that Israel's election
  has never been revoked;

- a sincere (if at times unenlightened) apostolic zeal;

- the desire to justify one's own faith;

- a certain anti-Jewish, or antisemitic attitude [p.
  275].

Another factor adds to the ambiguity: missionary efforts toward the Jews today leave Christians--both Catholics
and Protestants--somewhat ill at ease and arouse in them
a feeling of embarrassment, at least "among the best of
them" [p. 276]. If we ask after the meaning and source of
this malaise, the Nazi persecution and Holocaust appear as
the most immediate and direct cause. These in turn opened
the eyes of Christians to the centuries of Jewish suffering
that had preceded them and faced them with a painful question. After all that the survivors of this decimated people
have undergone for their faith, should Christians still try to
separate Jews from their people?[19] In other words: "After all that has happened, do we have the right to 'convert'
the Jews? Must we not first try to convert ourselves and
the Christian world, particularly in its attitude toward Jews?"
[p. 277].

At the same time, theological factors have also been
at work since 1945: the rediscovery of our own faith and
continuity with Israel, of Israel's primary function in salvation history, which makes of it the Christian's "elder brother," whom one respects and hesitates to instruct, despite
the conviction of having received, in grace, a revelation
that surpasses his [p. 277].

Do these feelings, Démann pertinently asks, have a
sound theological basis, or are they in the last analysis only an exaggerated sensitivity, growing out of the understand-
able desire not to wound Jewish sensibility yet further?

[p. 278]. It is his opinion that the malaise goes far deeper than a mere "tactic," and is rooted in a still vague, but deeply felt rediscovery of the real dimensions of the problem of the Church and Israel, and the desire to explore its Biblical, historical, ecclesiastical and ecumenical aspects [p. 278]; in other words, of Israel as an ecumenical problem which affects the entire Church.

It would seem that Démann's views here go beyond the "pragmatic" approach encountered so far, and touch some basic theological issues which are expressed rarely if at all. Given Israel's role, vocation and history, does the Christian have the right (the word is Démann's) to convert the Jew? His description of the growing malaise among Christians with regard to the Jewish people appears less facile and contradictory than the "answers" that the Jews as a whole are hardened though not rejected, still people of God, but not fully so until their conversion to Christ.

Démann still believes that the Church as church must proclaim Christ to Israel, but he sees this as an intra-Church, an ecclesiological problem, much like the early proclamation of the first Jewish Christians toward their fellow Jews [p. 273] (see Chapter VI, part 1). He rejects individual conversions as inadequate, though the German text ["dessen Lösung nicht allein durch individuelle Konversionen erreicht werden kann" (emphasis added)] suggests that he does not exclude such conversions. They would end the separation between Israel and the Church, but not solve the problem in a positive sense. His earlier formulation of the problem of individual conversion may shed light on Démann's meaning here:

> The end to the disunity of the people of God cannot come about only through occasional individual conversions. For we could easily imagine that their multiplication would lead to Israel's being "sucked up" ("Aufsaugen") and to its gradual disappearance; how, in this case, could we achieve a reincorporation and salvation for the whole of Israel? [Gespaltene Gottesvolk, p. 258].

A one-sided missionary and individualistic approach would, furthermore, "obscure the meaning of Paul's magnificent text in Romans 11, as well as of the nineteen-centuries-long unique history of suffering of the Jewish people."[20]

Despite the ambiguity in phrases such as "reintegration" of the Jewish people into the Church, their having no existence "outside" the Church, etc., taken as a whole, one can agree with R. M. Heydenreich that, in Démann's approach, the "missionary dimension is not intended to be understood as 'Judenmission' " [p. 224]. We find the strongest evidence of this in another--a Jewish--quarter. Given the sensitivity of Jews to attempts at conversion on the part of Christians, this reaction from André Neher may have great significance:

> No matter at what level, Jewish-Christian relationship has, for the Christian, a sacramental significance. The Jew is a potential convert. This is what perpetuates the difficulty of my approach to Christianity.... Among all the various possibilities of viewing the subject of the conversion of the Jew, one recently suggested by P. Démann is noteworthy. Based on an exegesis of Romans, it suggests putting off this conversion to the ultimate moment of time, the moment of God, who himself will bring about the collective return of the Jewish people as such. In such a perspective, the individual conversion of Jews no longer has a sacramental meaning, and Jewish-Christian encounter, at the individual level, can take place in a climate of serenity [L'Existence juive, pp. 242-43].

Israel's Return--The Perfecting of the Church

Heinrich Spaemann is another theologian for whom the separation of Israel and the Church is the basic schism that mars the unity of the people of God. His concern with the ultimate reunion of the divided parts raises questions with regard to the Church's mission to Israel that are somewhat different from Démann's, though on some points the views of both men overlap.[21]

At the center of Spaemann's vision is the Church, which in God's plan is meant to be a Church from among the Jews and gentiles. Without Israel the Church is incomplete, imperfect and impoverished, hence it inevitably longs for the day when it will be reunited with Israel. This perfecting of the Church will also be the perfecting of Israel, for both need each other and belong together. Jesus' high priestly prayer is too often applied only to Christian unity [Christen und das Volk der Juden, pp. 13-14].

The Church considers itself the true Israel [p. 25].
But Jesus called the Jew Nathanael a "true Israelite" (John
1:47) even before he became his disciple, and we may not
refuse this title to the Jewish people, at least to those who
take the Covenant seriously and live in expectation of the
coming of God's kingdom, even if they cannot yet recognize
in Jesus the Messiah [p. 26]. Their inability to do so may
well be due to the failure of Christians to live up to their '
faith. "Just as Israel's failure to believe in the Messiah
was largely responsible for a Church from [only] among the
gentiles, so Christianity's failure to imitate Christ in deed
and truth is largely responsible for the continued existence
of the Synagogue." For how can Jews believe in his coming, when Christians hinder that transformation of the world
which the Messiah is to usher in, according to scripture?[22]

Ephesians 2:11-22, which speaks of Christ breaking
down the wall of separation, makes it clear that our salvation is a sharing in the salvation of Israel. (We are "Mit-
erlöste Israels.") Christ died for his people and for all
men, thus drawing us into the Covenant [p. 38]. This text,
Spaemann suggests, which speaks of him as our peace, making Jew and gentile into one new man in himself, can serve
as a guideline for our attitude toward Israel: we must make
this peace a reality for the Jews, proclaiming it and passing it on, thus making visible for them Jesus' fidelity to his
people. Until we do so, the reunion of the whole of Israel,
the old and new people of God, cannot take place, and the
longing for the Parousia remains unfulfilled. That we, the
gentile Christians who have received this peace from Christ,
are to pass it on to those for whom it was destined in the
first place, is a reversal of the original order and involves
the humiliation of the Jewish people, who now take second
place. In carrying out our task we must remember that we
have been called to share in the inheritance of our "elder
brother" through no merit of our own [pp. 38-39].

Spaemann believes that it is essential to the reunion
of the people of God that Israel come to faith in Jesus as
the Christ. Until they recognize him, the Jews' eyes are
held, as it were. This is expressed in a passage which is
intended as a challenge to Christians to love Jews and treat
them as brothers, but which also reveals--inadvertantly per-
haps--the way in which the author sees post-Biblical Judaism and its future destiny.

Before the day of faith can dawn for Israel, before the

veil which still today conceals the Messiah from them
can be removed from their hearts, our eyes must
first learn to see, and to recognize and love in this
people, the elder brother. How else can Israel recognize God our Father, the Father of our Lord Jesus
Christ, as its God? Only the recognition of one's
brother is recognition of God--for Israel as for us.[23]

We find the phrase, "a veil covers the hearts of Israel," less striking than the implication that Israel does not
yet recognize "God our Father ... as its God." Spaemann
does not say that Israel does not recognize God our Father
as the Father of our Lord Jesus Christ, but: Israel does
not recognize our God as theirs. Could it not be said that
Israel's God is "God our Father"? The Jew might observe
that he does not need to recognize God our Father as his
God, since he is "already with the Father."[24]

Spaemann points out that, as the history of the Church
shows, every schism within the people of God carries with it
the danger of one-sidedness and impoverishment. What is
true of the divisions within Christianity is still more true of
the schism that antedates all these--that between Israel and
the Church. The consequences, for the Church, of having
become a "Church from among the gentiles and not [also]
from among the Jews"[25] are impoverishment, and the loss of
certain charisms: Israel's gift for transposing the command-
ments into concrete deeds--a dynamic understanding of his-
tory--a profound experience (hence real living out) of the
Covenant relationship--faith in God's promises and the consequent elan of setting out into the desert and unknown future
--Israel's messianic impatience ["Kirche und Israel," pp.
76-77]. The Church needs the stream of Jewish life, which
has dried up ever since the schism. For Israel was in a
unique way the living bearer and embodiment of revelation,
and brought this heritage to the primitive Church. Without
the Jewish community this concreteness became a piece of
doctrine [p. 74].

Israel in its turn has incurred a loss by having become a people of God from [only] among the Jews and not
[also] from among the gentiles. Spaemann's conclusions are
more tentative here, phrased in the form of questions rather
than statements: could the loss of gentile Christianity not
expose Israel to the danger of wanting to be only a nation
like all others, or of remaining in the ghetto, or of assimi-
lation or dissolution in a world that rejects Revelation?[26]

The question is raised at this point whether it is possible
for the Christian theologian--or for any "outsider"--to know
what is good (or bad) for the Jew. Would Jews agree that
they need Christianity? Moreover, the dangers to which
Spaemann considers Judaism exposed without a gentile Christianity range from the narrowness of ghetto existence at one
end to that of complete dissolution at the other. What is
left to the Jew? Becoming a Christian? Does this not also
imply a dissolution of sorts, the disappearance of Judaism
as Judaism?

Spaemann sees failure as well as loss on both sides.
"Israel has failed to believe in love made incarnate. We
... have failed to witness to this love."27 [It would seem
that the two resulting demands are unequal: in one case, the
Jews' conversion to Christ; in the other, the Christians' living up to what they profess in faith. Spaemann never uses
the term "conversion," yet what else can the phrase, "Israel has failed to believe" in Jesus Christ imply?] Only in
finding each other will both prodigal sons have fully returned
to the Father, making possible an exchange of their respective gifts. This coming together "will renew the face of the
Church, restoring her features as they were in the days of
her birth and first love, a Church from among both Jews
and gentiles" [p. 79].

Spaemann interprets history in theological terms.
Following the mainstream of Christian tradition, he attributes
the age-old suffering of the Jewish people to their failure to
recognize the Messiah, toward whose coming their entire existence had been geared. This failure had terrible consequences for them: they destroyed their own foundation, are
dispersed all over the world, and "made to partake in
Christ's suffering without experiencing the comfort and power
of his resurrection."28 The identification of Jewish suffering with that of Christ represents a considerable advance
over the view so frequently found, that the Jews suffer because they are cursed by God. Yet their suffering is still
seen as something they brought upon themselves through their
"faithlessness"--the word is the present author's.

The establishment of the State of Israel is also viewed
in a theological perspective, as resurrection from the dead
["Kirche," p. 8], and proof of God's love and fidelity toward
his people. At the same time, Spaemann sees the new State
as a step toward reunion, which for him means the Jews'
conversion to Christ. Now that they are once again gathered

together as a people, we may hope that they will become a
people "of the Risen Lord, and will at last reach the land
toward which they have been journeying since Abraham...,
recognizing the Lord on the shores of Lake Genesareth, as
did the disciples after their long night" [p. 21]. Through
all the vicissitudes of world history God continues to lead
his people toward salvation [p. 21-22].

Spaemann's deep love for Israel is unmistakable, as
are his appreciation for the uniquely Jewish dimensions of
faith, recognition of Christianity's failures, desire for reconciliation and longing for reunion. Despite these positive
elements in his approach to Judaism, however, it seems
evident that he looks upon it as a temporary and imperfect stage, to be surpassed on the day when the Jews will
recognize Jesus as Lord. He visualizes the reunion of the
people of God through the conversion of one part.

The reflections of Jacob Agus, an American Jewish
theologian, on the schism between Israel and the Church
provide some interesting points of similarity, as well as
contrast to much of what has been said above. The passage
here quoted was written in response to Jean Daniélou,
whose works are well known in Germany:

A word about the author's [Daniélou's] reflections on
the 'Schism of Israel.' What he sees as the separation of Israel from the historic stream, we see as
the growth of the Christian branch from the Jewish
tree, even as several centuries later, the Moslem
branch grew out of the same tree. All three
branches, Rabbinic Judaism, Christianity, Islam, have
grown from the same trunk. (Judah) Halevi assures
us that, in the fulness of time, the ripe fruits of all
the three branches will contain the same seeds. But,
we are not living at the end of history. What then
shall the relations of Judaism and Christianity be?[29]

While Agus shares the Christian theologians' concern with
the relationship of Christianity to Judaism, their respective
roles, and hopes for eschatological unity, his approach to
the question might be described--depending on one's perspec-
tive--as either vaguer or broader in scope; at any rate as
more tentative and less dogmatic.

All in all, the picture is not clear, nor free from
ambiguities. Thus, Dom Emmanuel Lanne deplores Israel's

separation from the Church and the resulting imbalance, yet
employs terms that come close to traditional stereotypes.
Judaism presents the "monstrous paradox" that an entire
people rejected the faith which was its raison d'être, thereby becoming a non-people [quoted in Gespaltene Gottesvolk,
p. 250].

The main change effected by the Schism theologians
is that of placing the Church's separation from Israel within
the ecumenical context, seeing in it the schism of all
schisms ("Urschisma"), graver than all subsequent breaks,
hence its healing as the most urgent task of ecumenism.
Israel is a people sui generis in the history of salvation,
linked to Christianity in a manner that places it on an altogether different plane from that of the rest of the nations.

If, in the minds of its proponents, the schism concept provides new grounds for hope toward solving the ecumenical problem, it also raises some problems of its own.
Davies asks: "In what sense can a movement born out of a
desire for Christian reunion properly occupy itself with either
Judaism, as a non-Christian religion, or the Jewish people
as a historic entity?" [Antisemitism, p. 155]. He observes
that the new definition of ecumenism "is at almost total vari-
ance with its older definition. The confusion which has followed, especially at Evanston, is scarcely surprising. Can
this new definition be accepted as a viable theological foundation for the ecumenical movement and its programs?" [p.
156].

That the question is well taken is graphically illustrated by the confusion that surrounded the Vatican II Declaration on the Jews. What had been conceived by Cardinal
Bea's Secretariat as an independent "Decree on the Jews"
during the preparatory work for the Council, was subsequently suggested as part of the Decree on Ecumenism, only to
end up as the next-to-last paragraph of the Declaration on
World Religions. [30] The shifting fate of the Declaration, and
the still widespread feeling that it does not quite fit where it
eventually came to rest, are symptomatic. The Viennese
theologian Clemens Thoma--a Catholic, writing three years
after the Canadian Anglican scholar Alan Davies--echoes the
latter's concern as he looks back to Vatican II:

> Considering the Council texts, one could put the puz-
> zle this way: Whenever Christians wish to enter in-
> to conversations with Jews, they are uncertain

whether to prepare for a dialogue with another partner or for a presentation of their Christian stance;
whether to look on Judaism as mysteriously one with
the Church or not. This leads to the anxious question: Can a Christian ecumenical view ever do justice to Judaism in its long historical development--
an autonomous development that took place independ-
ently of Christianity--as well as in its present concrete existence with its manifold concerns? ["Points
of Departure," in Brothers in Hope, The Bridge.
Judaeo-Christian Studies, Vol. V (New York: Herder
and Herder, 1970), p. 159].

The theologians whose views have been examined in
this section are all struggling with the question Israel-
Church, in an effort to find a new theological basis for this
ancient problem. They posit an original unity between Judaism and Christianity which is seen to subsist down through
the centuries, maintaining one single people of God, despite
the break that occurred with the coming of Christ. We have
elsewhere [see note 12] expressed some doubt as to this
"original unity" and its restoration, but both concepts are an
intrinsic part of "Schism theology." The healing of the
schism, or restoration of unity, is the goal of history. Until it is achieved the Church is not fully herself, for she
needs those aspects of Israel's life which it alone, as the
original recipient and bearer of divine revelation, can bring
to the world. As such, Israel is the Church's partner in
dialogue--an equal partner--and may never be made into an
object of mission. Judenmission is a denial and distortion
of Israel's continuing vocation as people of God, and of the
fact that the Church may claim this title only thanks to and
by sharing in Israel's election. Moreover, it arrogates to
man's own efforts what can ultimately only be the work of
God.

The "shape" which this unification will take is not
clear--a fact which is perhaps to the credit of the theologians in question. Terms and phrases such as "reintegration"
(Démann), "conversion" (Oehmen), perfecting of the Church
(Oehmen and Spaemann), "veil over their hearts," "failure
to believe in Christ" (Spaemann), suggest that the reunion
presupposes Israel's conversion to Christ. At the same
time, Démann warns against the absorption ["Aufsaugen"]
of Judaism by Christianity, which suggests that Judaism is
in some way meant to retain its own unique form. Skydsgaard's statement, that the eschatological reunion will be

the triumph, not of Judaism and Christianity over each other,
but of God over his people's torn condition, [31] also leaves the
door open for further exploration.

"Judenmission" and "Heidenmission"

A related aspect of Judenmission should be examined,
one that has been touched upon a number of times in passing:
the question whether mission to Israel is to be considered on
the same level as mission toward other non-Christians or
gentiles. * We have seen the question raised in the context
of ecumenism, and by critics of the 1961 Kirchentag. Underlying it is, once again, the fundamental question of Judaism's relation to Christianity. Is this relationship special,
unique, or is it on a par with that of any other religion?

Let us begin with the most negative, extreme and
simplistic attitude, expressed by two of the sharpest critics
of the 1961 Kirchentag, Wendlandt and Mehl. (See Chapter
III.) Neither man sees Judaism as different from other religions in its relationship to Christianity. For Mehl, Judaism since the coming of Christ has lost all privileges it
once had over pagans, and stands under the same judgment
as they. "The old people of the history of salvation has become salvationless ["heil-los"], and is no better than the
pagans."[32] Quoting John 8:24, "If you do not believe that I
am He, you shall die in your sins," Mehl adds his own
gloss: "regardless of whether you are Jews or fetish wor-
shippers!" ["Kirche und Synagoge," p. 11]. Since the defin-
itive rejection of the Gospel by the "Church of the Synagogue,"
every synagogue is, according to the New Testament, a
"Synagogue of Satan" (Rev. 2:9, 3:9), at least as much as
every idol-worshipping temple of pagans [p. 11].

For Wendlandt also, Jews are no better off than pagans, despite their belief in one God. We have already referred to his quotation from Luther, but it bears repeating
in the present context:

> Whatever is outside Christendom, whether it be pa-
> gans, Turks, Jews or false Christians and hypocrites,
> even if they believe in and worship only one God, they

---

*The German word "Heiden" is translated as "gentiles"
rather than "pagans," since the latter has a pejorative, not
to say contemptuous, ring about it.

do not know what he intends for them ... hence they
remain in eternal wrath and damnation. For they do
not have the Lord Christ, nor are they graced and
enlightened with gifts through the Holy Spirit [Luther-
ische Monatshefte, Feb. (1962), p. 82].

In this perspective the question ceases to be a problem, for the answer is unequivocal. Starting from the premise that the Covenant once made with Israel is no longer valid, the Jews have forfeited any and every claim as people of
God; their one-time privileges in no way give them any special prerogative or position since the coming of Christ.

This extreme view represents the opinion of only a
minority, however, though it is a vocal one. During a discussion held at the 1961 Kirchentag, Theodor Vriezen, in
answer to the question whether Jews are the same as pagans, replied unequivocally that they remain Jews, members
of the chosen people. Through the Jew Jesus and the Old
Testament, they are more intimately related to Christians
than any other people [Ungekündigte Bund, pp. 64-65].
Paragraph four of the statement by the AG VI of the Kirchentag stressed, as we have seen, the "unbreakable link" between Jews and Christians [p. 124].

More than ten years earlier the question had been
raised in a discussion at Basel between a Jewish youth group
and Karl Barth.[33] While it was only one of 11 questions
addressed by the group to Karl Barth, it was dealt with at
some length. The Jews asked Barth how Christians could
morally justify the right to missionize the Jews, a people
which represents a pure religion, whereas Christianity, in
the eyes of Jews, appears as a compromise between Judaism and paganism.

In his reply, Barth rejected the concept of Judenmission as invalid, when understood in the same sense as mission toward gentiles. He deplored the use of the term itself, because it completely fails to reflect the true relationship between Israel and the Christian community. The two belong together for Barth. In and through Christ both are
members of the same people: Israel is going toward Christ,
while the Christian Church takes its origin in him and
comes from him. Israel fails to perceive this unity between
the two, but in the Christian perspective, to be a Christian
is to be a true Jew. For the whole of the Old Testament
is oriented toward one moment, its fulfillment in Jesus

Christ. Any missionizing of Jews on the part of Christians is--or should be--out of the question, for the Jew must on his own attain to the realization that Old and New Testament belong together [Freiburger Rundbrief, p. 20].

J. H. Grolle, speaking at the 1963 Kirchentag held in Dortmund, also rejects the term Judenmission on principle. For although the New Testament bears clear evidence to the fact that the early Christians proclaimed Jesus Christ to their fellow-Jews, Grolle points out that the approach, and particularly the vocabulary, used by the apostles when dealing with Jews is radically different from that employed toward the gentiles.

> Whenever, in Acts, Paul meets with Jews, he argues
> from the Old Testament. We have here an inner-
> Jewish situation ... they argue about a text and dis-
> cuss it, just as the rabbis in Talmudic times ...
> seeking to convince one another. This is conversa-
> tion; not monologue, but dialogue.... Because the
> encounter in the New Testament, between Christ-wit-
> nesses and other Jews, is always carried on in this
> form of dialogue, the term 'mission' is inappropri-
> ate [Gespaltene Gottesvolk, pp. 52-53].

A lengthier discussion of the concepts of Judenmission and Heidenmission is undertaken by Walter Holsten, in an article of the same title.[34] Holsten raises several questions at the outset: are both terms useable today, have they become too ambiguous, and do they have anything in common? The answer to the last question depends, in his opinion, on one's view of mission. If it is taken in the traditional sense as referring to the "total activity of the Christian Church among non-Christians," then Jews and gentiles are in the same category. Such a view presupposes, in the words of Schlunk, "Christianity's superiority over all non-Christian religions and moralities" [quoted in Holstein "Judenmission und Heidenmission," p. 113]. It assumes that the covenant with Israel is no longer valid, and that a radical discontinuity has severed the old people of God from the new.

Holsten points out, however, that we find in the New Testament both continuity and discontinuity, common ground and difference. A new people has indeed been called from among the gentiles, a people in which there is no distinction between Jew and Greek (Gal. 3:28). Yet the former

distinctions still remain, and Paul continues to address the
gentiles under that name (e.g., Rom. 11:13, Eph. 3:1, 2:12).
At the same time, both peoples are bound together in the
fidelity of the same God. They belong together as the "beginning and end of one single history, whose center is
Christ," and in this belonging-together stand over against
the gentiles [p. 116].

Thus, if a radical discontinuity and a broken covenant are posited, Jews and gentiles are in the same category; the former are at best the highest point of religious
development outside Christianity. If, on the other hand, we
stress continuity, then the gentiles stand in a unique relationship to Israel. They are gathered from their various
religions into the one people of God, Abraham becomes their
father, and they are grafted onto the true olive tree,
"against their nature" [p. 118]. In the latter perspective,
Holsten questions whether we may speak of Judenmission as
in any way parallel to Heidenmission. Like Barth and
Grolle, he considers the term misleading and unfortunate,
because it obscures the special relationship existing between
Christianity and Israel.

Some years earlier E. L. Ehrlich, a Jewish theologian writing in Switzerland, had taken strong exception to the
Christian missionary approach to the Jews, maintaining that
it made all genuine dialogue impossible.[35] Holsten, in the
article with which we are here dealing, refers to Ehrlich's
article and claims that, in actual fact, Ehrlich rejects only
a certain form of Judenmission, rather than mission as
such. For, he says, Ehrlich points out that both Judaism
and Christianity have been given a mission by God. For Judaism, it is formulated in Isaiah 43:10, "You are my witnesses." For Christianity, it is stated in Acts 1:8, "You
will be my witnesses." Ehrlich adds that this task both
"separates and unites" Jews and Christians. From this Holsten concludes that Ehrlich's severe criticism of Judenmission points the way for true mission: it must be carried
out in humility and dialogue ["Judenmission," p. 122].

At this point a further question arises for Holsten:
are not the very elements that render Judenmission unacceptable today also applicable to the concept of mission in
general? Humility and dialogue, after all, are called for
not only with regard to the Jews, but to all men. The
Christian stands under the obligation of addressing the same
question to Jew and gentile alike: do you believe in Jesus

as Savior of the world? [p. 124]. Yet there is a difference
for Holsten, in at least two respects. First, Christianity
already exists in a dialogical mode with regard to Judaism,
whereas other gentiles must yet be drawn into this dialogical
relationship. Secondly, the guilt which Christianity has incurred toward the Jews is far greater than that toward any
other people. On both counts, then, Heidenmission is less
ambiguous than Judenmission [p. 124].

Holsten concludes that "concern for Israel must ultimately be what has been called 'service for Israel'"
["Dienst an Israel"], a service which may take many forms,
but without which neither mission, nor witness, nor dialogue
are credible. Witness to Israel, in turn, is not possible
without such service [p. 126].

Holsten does not, however, reject Judenmission, despite the misgivings expressed. This becomes clear from
an article written the following year[36] where he considers
the same question in the ecumenical context. If one accepts
the view that Israel is an ecumenical problem, indeed, at the
very heart of the ecumenical problem, then the concept of
Judenmission seems to be inadmissible: "Anyone who de-
clares that the Jewish question is an ecumenical problem
seems forced to reject Judenmission, which in this perspective seems no more possible or legitimate than mission toward various Christian groups" ["Ökumenische Probleme III,"
p. 513]. But are the two really irreconcilable?

Holsten answers yes, if one no longer grants the validity of Israel's Covenant. This is not necessarily implied,
however, for Delitzsch and all of 19th-century Lutheran Judenmission in general posited the still-valid covenant with
Israel. In that perspective, the Christian mission toward Israel consists in "reminding the Jews of the history of God's
great deeds, and in proclaiming to them the anticipated end
of that history in Jesus of Nazareth..." [p. 515]. Israel is
at one and the same time part of ecumenism, and outside of
it. Outside of it, for the time being, since it does not recognize Jesus Christ [p. 516], but part of it in hope, because
of God's fidelity, which intends a healing of the schism.
This "not-yet" produces a tension, and constitutes the basis
for Christian mission toward the Jews, in order that "all of
Israel may be saved" (Rom. 11:26) [p. 517].

While Judenmission differs radically from Heidenmission for Holsten, he considers the concept legitimate insofar

as the Christian is always bound to missionary proclamation, even toward members of his own community. Despite
the ambiguity which today is inherent in the term and the
undeniable fact of Israel's unique relationship to Christianity,
"mission" itself need not be understood thus ambiguously,
and remains a basic Christian task for Holsten. While no
man may be made into an object of Christian mission, every
man--including the Jew--must be placed into a situation of
freely deciding for or against Christ.[37]

Holsten's views have been dealt with at some length
because of his detailed treatment of the question. It appears that when all is said and done, and despite the various distinctions he makes, Judenmission remains for him
part of the Christian's task, as it does for the other authors
considered in this section.

A somewhat different slant is given to this subject by
K. H. Rengstorf. He suggests that debate on whether a distinction should be made between mission to Jews and gentiles is already a thing of the past, and that there is a growing realization today, at least among Lutherans, that the task
of Christian mission is "to call and lead the whole of mankind under the lordship of God" ["The Place of the Jew...,"
Lutheran World XI, No. 3 (July 1964), p. 289]. For Rengstorf, Christian mission is an essential task of the Church at
all times, and mission to the Jews is at its center. This is
clearly expressed in the following text: "Christianity ...
must never surrender what is contained in the word 'mission,' also and especially not with regard to the Jews; otherwise it would surrender itself. For Christianity stands or
falls with Paul's words, that the gospel is 'the power of God
which saves all those who believe in it, the Jews first of
all...'" [Rengstorf, "Begegnung statt Bekehrung: welchen
Sinn kann das jüdisch-christliche Gespräche für Christen
haben?" Juden--Christen--Deutsche, p. 268]. The text is
all the more remarkable in that it appears as part of an essay entitled "Encounter Instead of Conversion." It renders
well the official attitude of the Lutheran Church.

Gerhard Jaspers, for his part, suggests that mission
to the gentiles will succeed only insofar as Christians first
convert Jews.[38]

Can one, then, speak of a radical questioning of Judenmission in the ecumenical context after all? By way of
answer let us turn to a Dutch theologian, Kornelis Heiko

Miskotte, who has exerted a profound influence on German
theologians. (H. Gollwitzer [in an unpublished interview,
Berlin, Spring 1970] attributes to Miskotte a greater impact
upon his own generation than anyone else.) In an essay written as long ago as 1934, but published in German for the
first time in 1970, Miskotte writes:

> The subjective possibility of revelation lies, in the
> case of the Jew, in his 'birth,' in the case of the
> Christian, in his 'rebirth.' Christianus fit, non nas-
> citur. But at this point Judaism poses the question:
> 'What right do Christianity, and the Church, have to carry
> on missionary work among the Jews?' What do we
> mean when we talk of the Jew's 'conversion' to Chris-
> tianity? From the Jewish point of view, this is ident-
> ical with separation of a member of the Jewish people
> all over the world, separation from the original com-
> munity and entrance into a later sect. For, no mat-
> ter how widespread Christianity may be quantitatively,
> ... qualitatively it is nothing else than a part of Is-
> rael... [title essay in the collection, Das Judentum
> als Frage an die Kirche, (Wuppertal: Theologischer
> Verlag Rolf Brockhaus, 1970), p. 12; emphasis in
> original].

Miskotte cites Herman Cohen's answer to a Protestant clergy-
man, when asked whether he did not miss the sense of divine intimacy in his life of faith. "What!?", exclaimed Cohen;
"The Lord is my shepherd, I want for nothing!" Miskotte
goes on to comment: "Indeed, if by mission we understand
bringing others to a pure concept of God, or teaching them
a higher morality, or the exemplary living of a more profound religion, then the concept is utterly meaningless as applied to the believing Jew" ["Judentum als Frage...," p. 13].

     For Miskotte, it is not a question of Israel's not per-
ceiving an already existing unity (Barth), or of Christianity's
mission to remind Israel of God's great deeds in its history
(Holsten). Apparently, the difference in Miskotte's attitude
lies in his having some awareness of, and taking seriously,
the Jew's own consciousness of his relationship to God. For
the majority of Christian theologians whose writings have
been so far dealt with, Israel is still an object to be looked
at from the Christian perspective, and to the understanding
of which Christianity alone holds the key.

     At this point in the present study several theological

trends can be discerned. One can say that a twofold shift has taken place which affects the way in which the Church sees her mission toward Israel. The first, in the realm of ecclesiology, perceives Israel no longer "out there," as one alien people among other peoples of the world (although more problematic for the Church than the others). Instead, Israel is now seen to occupy a unique, privileged place which, in the view of some theologians, makes the traditional missionary approach out of place. If Judaism is Christianity's mother-soil, if there is but one people of God, how can the Church "missionize" the Jews? If we speak of mission at all, we can do so only in the sense of "missionary activity from within" (Démann): of the Church's efforts to understand more deeply that tradition to which she owes her origins and a large measure of her heritage.

The second shift in the missionary perspective can be characterized as moving from the present, the here and now, to the end-time, or eschatological perspective. The conversion of Israel as a people will not occur within history, but only at its end. It will be the work of God, not of man. Hence again, missionary work is out of place. There will indeed always be conversion of individuals, but Christians should not make deliberate efforts to bring this about.

It should be noted that the abandoning of missionary work does not mean abandonment of the concept of conversion to Christianity. Most of the theologians studied in Part Two look forward to the day when Israel will be converted, recognize Christ as its Savior, and become fully integrated into the one people of God, the Church composed of Jews and gentiles.

This view is clearly stated by the French theologian K. Hruby:

> This election [of Israel] ... is also an election with respect to Christ. It is in Christ that Israel truly becomes the prophetic people and instrument of salvation for mankind; Christ is the goal, the fulfillment of Israel's election. Since Christ's death on the cross, it is the whole Body of Christ, all those who believe in Him, who become the chosen people. Still, this does not end the special election of Israel which will continue as a distinct body, until--at the end of time--it will be reintegrated with the Body of Christ

from which it is now separated (cf. Rom. 11:26) [Hruby, "Reflections on Dialogue," <u>Brothers in Hope</u>, p. 119f.].

Part Three

Beyond Mission?

Chapter V

MISSION OR DIALOGUE?

The title of this chapter is not of the author's making. The phrase, "Mission or Dialogue?," is frequently used by theologians today to designate one of the most controversial aspects of the debate surrounding Christianity's relationship to Israel. It may be rephrased as follows: should mission be replaced by dialogue? The answers given range from a clear-cut affirmative to an equally clear-cut denial, across a variety of qualifications and nuances. An examination of the different positions in this context may allow the evolution in the missionary approach to be perceived under a new aspect. Let us begin by clarifying the meaning of the term "dialogue."

The word is used so frequently today as to be in danger of losing its meaning. Yet it is difficult to find an adequate substitute for it. Genuine dialogue implies a dialectical relationship which is characterized by mutual respect, partnership and equality, freedom, willingness to listen to and hear others, see them as they are, challenge them and be challenged in turn with whatever risk this may entail. *

The attitude and mentality required for dialogue were described by Hans-Joachim Kraus in an address delivered at the 1963 Kirchentag in Dortmund. It represents a challenge, by a leading German Christian theologian to a large Christian audience, to open themselves to a new possibility and manner of encountering a Jew.

_____
*Although in German "Gespräch" and "Dialog" are frequently used interchangeably, "dialogue" in English goes beyond mere conversation.

How can I love the other if I do not know him, if I
know nothing about him? Coming to know him means
abandoning my own secure position, giving up my emphatically asserted point of view, listening with openness to what he has to say to me.

Will tonight's gathering have contributed a little toward eradicating deep prejudices of Christianity, and
uprooting overgrown weeds? This alone concerns us,
who for years have been striving for a new Christian-
Jewish encounter and understanding. We are not
handing out some cheap sort of tolerance. Tolerance,
and still more uninformed Philosemitism, are meaningless, empty words. The love of Christ that drives
the Christian on ... is long-suffering; it has the cour-
age to listen to the other at length and patiently to
seek him out, come to know and see him as he really is. Such love is outgoing, it goes to meet the oth-
er--the friend, the brother. It is not jealous. It
renounces that all-too-hasty Christianity which, nar-
row and breathless, rigid and inhuman, knows only
the intimidating Either/Or: either conversion, or
damnation. He who truly seeks the other does not
throw himself upon him, but goes forth to meet him,
in the desire to understand and hold converse with
him.

Our guilt against the Jews is enormous. The zeal of
a self-assured, proud, and superior Church has led
to countless confusions and distortions. The Christian has behaved like an arrogant film star, who can
play his role in his sleep, and, given the right cue,
is able at once to recite his great confession of
faith as monologue ["Bekenntnismonolog"]--'in charity,'
of course (as prescribed by the stage directions of
piety). And yet, at the heart of the basic text in
which Paul writes of the Church's relationship to Israel, stands the warning to the Church: 'Be not
proud, but beware!' Love does not seek its own.
It forgets itself. It does not constantly circle around
its own possession of faith, it is free for the other
... [Kraus, commentary on I Cor. 13:4 and 5a, Gespaltene Gottesvolk, pp. 44-45].

Such a dialogue represents a radically new departure
in Christianity's relationship to Judaism. In the words of
H. J. Schoeps, "For nineteen centuries Jews and Christians
went through history side by side. They frequently glanced

at each other, but no dialogue took place, nor could it have taken place" [Jüdische Geisteswelt--Zeugnisse aus zwei Jahrtausenden, Geist des Abendlandes, ed. V. H. Noack, 1953, p. 333; quoted by Kraus, Versuche des Verstehens, p. 173]. For the medieval Church was all-powerful. "The triumphant Church spoke, condemned, excommunicated, cast out--in the name of her dogma and the power of possessing the sacraments. It took the "keys to the kingdom" into its hand and closed the gates... took hold of the keys again and opened, organized missions and issued invitations..." [Kraus, Begegnung mit dem Judentum (Hamburg: Furche, 1963), p. 69].

In such a climate, no wonder that whatever theological discussions did take place between Jews and Christians hardly qualify as dialogue. While discussions between individuals during the 11th and 12th centuries were, on occasion, characterized by mutual respect, the 13th century saw the beginning of public disputes organized by the Church between representatives of Christianity and Judaism. The cards were a priori stacked against the Jews, who confronted the Church in all its power and might. It was the Church who threw down the gauntlet and issued the challenge.[1]

The two largest and best-known of these disputations took place in Spain: in 1263 at Barcelona, between the Dominican Pablo Christiani, a former Jew, and the Talmudic scholar Nachmanides Moses ben Nachman; and in Tortosa, from 1413-1414, between Vincent Ferrer and a number of Jewish Scholars.[2] If one remembers that Christianity was then at the height of its power, while Judaism was becoming more and more oppressed, it is small wonder that the outcome of these disputations was never in doubt. The Jews invariably found themselves on the defensive and in danger of reprisals, regardless of the skill of their arguments. Thus, as a result of the Barcelona disputation, the Dominicans instigated a lawsuit against Nachmanides, who was eventually forced, at the age of 70, to leave Spain, and who died in Jerusalem.

A New Climate

For the first time since post-apostolic times, a climate prevails in the Church which makes dialogue possible. Many factors, both theological and historical, have contributed to this new situation. On the one hand, developments within the Church are leading to a revised attitude toward

Israel. The Biblical renewal, the emphasis on the Church
as community and people of God, the ecumenical movement
--all these provide a framework and basis for a new vision
of Israel. Centuries of alienation and hostility, during which
Christians were aware almost exclusively of the differences
and contrasts between Judaism and Christianity, are giving
way today to a discovery not only of a common heritage,
but also of a common hope: the hope for the kingdom of
God, which for the Jew still lies wholly in the future, while
the Christian awaits only its final consummation in the Parousia.

        Along with these theological developments, circum-
stances of a historical nature have played an important role
in the changed outlook on the part of the Church. The disappearance of the ghetto and the emancipation of the Jews
made possible contact between Christians and Jews where,
for centuries, walls had sealed off the two communities from
each other. At the same time, this contact led to new ten-
sions and forms of anti-Semitism, which eventually came to
a climax in the unparalleled explosion of hatred in the Nazi
era and the Holocaust. This in turn caused an awakening of
Christian conscience and soul-searching, regarding the part
which Christianity had played in these developments through
its distorted teachings on Judaism.

        At the same time, the loss of political power by the
Church and the growing diaspora of Christians, at least in
certain parts of the world, are today giving them a minority status not unlike that which for so long was the lot of
the Jews. This has led to a lessening--if not yet complete dis-
appearance--of Christian triumphalism, and the dawning realization that Christians may have something to learn from
the centuries-old Jewish experience of diaspora. A secular-
ity, which challenges the faith and traditions of both Judaism and Christianity, is also contributing to a sense of solidarity and shared destiny.

        Finally, the birth of the State of Israel is raising
questions for the Christian which force him to reflect about
the role and meaning of Judaism for the world, and the re-
sultant tasks for the Church.

        All these factors combined, many of them occurring
simultaneously, have resulted in a hitherto unprecedented
willingness to take Israel seriously.

> Only one thing is of any use now: a radical meta-
> noia, repentance and re-thinking; we must start on a
> new road, no longer leading away from the Jews, but
> towards them, towards a living dialogue, the aim of
> which is not the capitulation but simply the under-
> standing of the other side; towards mutual help, which
> is not part of a 'mission,' to an encounter in a true
> brotherly spirit [Küng, The Church, p. 138].

Since dialogue is a two-way street, some remarks
about Jewish attitudes are appropriate here. There are leading Jews today who openly call for dialogue. The first to
do so since World War II was Leo Baeck, on the occasion
of his first return to Germany in 1948.[3]

> Certainly, 'there is a time to keep silence, and a
> time to speak.' But now, it seems, is the season
> for speaking. On us today, it seems, is laid a sol-
> emn obligation that the Jewish and Christian faiths
> meet openly--faiths indeed, not only boards or
> writers or orators. It may turn out one day a sin of
> omission if they carelessly or timidly or presumptu-
> ously shrink from asking and answering the right ques-
> tions ["Some questions to the Christian Church from
> the Jewish point of view," in The Church and the
> Jewish People, p. 103].

Leo Baeck is not alone. In Germany, Robert Raphael
Geis works closely with Christian theologians, and many distinguished American Jewish scholars are willing to engage in
dialogue with Christians. One must be careful, however,
not to give an exaggerated picture of Jewish openness to or
interest in Christianity. By and large, the Orthodox community rejects any religious dialogue with Christians.[4] Speaking more generally, Christians should not expect the same
theological preoccupations with Christianity on the part of
Jews that Christians feel toward Judaism. Christianity as a
religious phenomenon concerns Jews in general very little.

If one may speak nonetheless today of a willingness,
among a limited but growing number of Jews, to enter into
dialogue with Christians, this is due to several factors:
the lessening of fear, the slow beginning of trust here and
there, an appreciation on the part of some Jewish scholars
of the New Testament and the person of Jesus--even of
Paul; the realization that Christianity has retained fundamental Jewish elements, chief among them the Hebrew

scriptures, and worship of the God of Abraham, Isaac and Jacob.

It is not only an awareness of the common ground, however, that will stimulate dialogue. As Arthur Cohen writes, "... to the extent that we begin in this time to communicate anew with Christians as believers who believe differently, but seek to learn from us in truth what it is that has sustained us during the centuries that have elapsed since the time the Church cut us off in our living members and refashioned us as a Christian myth, we may be beginning the joint work of coredemption...." [5] Thus we may speak today of a climate--widespread though by no means universal--in which dialogue can take place, a dialogue that is frequently fostered by religious leaders and theologians on both sides.

In Germany, the dialogue which had begun prior to the Nazi period climaxed in Buber's famous debate with K. L. Schmidt in 1933, and broke off the same year. It resumed again 15 years later, in the fall of 1948 at Darmstadt, at a meeting of the "Deutsche evangelische Ausschuss für Dienst an Israel" organized by K. H. Rengstorf, (and at which Baeck made his first appearance in Germany after the war).

Different Positions

The first position held, concerning the question, Mission or Dialogue?, is represented by a segment of the Lutheran Church which insists on organized missionary activity toward the Jews. [6] It advocates dialogue, but within carefully circumscribed limits. This view is reflected in the booklet, Das Zeugnis der Kirche für die Juden [ed. Reinhard Dobbert (Berlin: Lutherisches Verlagshaus, 1968], which we shall take as an example of this attitude.

The necessity for dialogue is here admitted, but its function is a very limited one. Dialogue can contribute to a deeper understanding of one's own Christian tradition, but may under no circumstances take the place of mission [H. Becker, "Gibt es ein Zeugnis der Kirche für die Juden?," Das Zeugnis, p. 30]. To pose the question in terms of either/or is to misunderstand the nature of Christian mission, which has always, so Becker claims, included dialogue [p. 14]. Mission, according to him, was always conceived, "at

least in theory," primarily as dialogue, in which the partner was not to be "talked out of" his position, but convinced. [7]

For Becker, the Christian may engage in dialogue only under certain conditions. Paramount among these is his
motivation. If his concern is merely to bring the Jew to
live the Sinai Covenant in greater fidelity, he has already
abandoned his own faith-position and dialogue "will deterior-
ate into an intra-Jewish dispute" [p. 30]. He must seek
more than new knowledge and insight: he must intend to convince and convert. "There is hardly a more binding duty for
the Christian Church than mission. It is the essence of all
religion--the assumption, that it is given to every man to
recognize the truth; that every man must be taken seriously.
The Christian Church will at long last have to take the Jew
seriously by seeking to convert him to Christianity" [W. S.
Schlamm, Wer ist ein Jude. Ein Selbstgespräch (Stuttgart:
Seewald Verlag 1964), p. 74; quoted by Becker, "Gibt es ein
Zenguis," p. 31]. The concept of "taking the other seriously" is used here in precisely the opposite sense from the
one it commonly has today. Instead of perceiving and letting
him exist in his own truth, "taking him seriously" means as-
similating him to ourselves.

Genuine openness to the other is not only rejected as
a condition for dialogue, but considered dangerous and unde-
sirable. Entering into dialogue implies a threat to his faith,
for the Christian, as for any other man [p. 29]. Hence he
should engage in it only if he is a priori certain of his position. This position will be given a more detailed analysis
shortly. For the time being, let it merely be suggested
that, although it appears to endorse dialogue, in actual fact
this position mistrusts it to the point of repudiation, and considers mission, with conversion as goal, as the only legitimate approach.

A second argument commonly found today which favors
a substituting dialogue for mission is based on the exigencies
of this particular moment in history (e.g. Harder, Rengstorf). In view of the guilt which Christianity has incurred
toward the Jewish people and the history of enforced conversions, the concept of mission inevitably erects barriers and
closes doors. It is for Jews what the red cloth is for the
bull, and invariably makes dialogue impossible. The word
"mission" itself has become so pejorative in the minds of
Jews--and even of some Christians-- as to constitute a

mental block.[8] Hence it must be abandoned. Christians
must renounce mission, and instead, direct their efforts to
creating a climate of trust in which dialogue can flourish.
This is also the view of the Dutch theologian J. H. Grolle.[9]

This presupposes on the part of Christians the admission of Christianity's failures and guilt. "Just as in
Christian worship confession of sin precedes confession of
faith, so also in our relation to Judaism the Confiteor must
precede the Credo" [H. D. Leuner, "From Mission to Dialog" Lutheran World X, No. 4 (Oct. 1963), p. 387]. The
credibility of the Christian message has been impaired by
the Church's attitude toward Israel.

Christians must recognize and admit their own shortcomings and limitations, and be willing to renounce a centuries-old triumphalism. Instead of singling out the failures
of the Jewish people, let them admit their own. In the
words of the Viennese theologian Clemens Thoma, "the
Church is not the mistress, but the sister of the Synagogue.
In speaking with her sister, she can legitimately appeal to
the New Testament only if she admits that she represents
Christ imperfectly" ["Points of Departure," in Brothers in
Hope, The Bridge, Vol. V, p. 167].

The recognition of past sins and the consequent renouncing of mission in favor of dialogue do not necessarily
imply the renouncing of mission as such. This is clearly
stated by K. H. Rengstorf ["Begegnung statt Bekehrung,"
in Juden, Christen, Deutsche, pp. 268-69]. Although
Christians must come to see that it is they themselves who
prevent Christianity from being credible, and the Church
has repeatedly failed in preaching Christ's message of love,
he says, Christianity may never renounce what is implied
in the word "mission," neither in the case of the Jews, nor
of other men [p. 268]. The question at issue, for Rengstorf, is not the fact of Christian proclamation, but the manner in which it is made.

Another position questions the Church's missionary
approach on the basis of a theological view that sees Israel
as people of God. It is formulated in the Study on Israel
and the Church undertaken by the Dutch Reformed Church
[Israel und die Kirche (Zurich: EVZ Verlag, 1961)]. Given
Israel's privileged position and enduring status as people of
God, mission to Israel is out of place and must be replaced
by dialogue. Christians must take Israel seriously. This

does not imply a minimizing of the uniqueness of Christ's
Revelation in his Church, nor indifference. The Church
will approach Israel in the consciousness of her missionary
character, but aware of its privileged place among the nations [p. 42]. A clear distinction must be made between Israel and other nations. Hans Küng writes that

> the Church can never seriously take up the task of
> 'missionizing' the Jews. The Gospel cannot be pre-
> sented to the Jews as something alien and external to
> them. The Jews were never previously guilty of a
> false faith; before the Church existed they believed in
> the one true God and before the Church existed, not
> simply through the Church, the Gospel was preached
> to them [Küng, The Church, p. 142].

This position is carried further in the same document, as well as by J. H. Grolle ["Judenmission oder Gespräch?", in Der Zeuge, 3. Folge, p. 7]. The Church's
right to missionize Israel is here questioned because of Israel's character as missionary people--the missionary people
par excellence. Before all other nations, Israel has received the task to bear witness among mankind to the living
God, and to be a light among men to the ends of the earth.
"This is the missionary peak of its election" [Israel und die
Kirche, p. 42]. Israel is the real missionary people.
"And one does not carry on mission among missionaries"
[Grolle, "Judenmission oder Gespräch," p. 7]. (The opinion that Israel is missionary by its very nature is shared by
some Jews, while disputed by others.)

The traditional situation is here reversed. Mission
--yes--but as the birthright and privilege of Israel, rather
than of the Church. Insofar as the latter is missionary, it
owes this to its Jewish origins and a sharing in Israel's
privileges [Grolle, p. 7].

The advocates of dialogue decisively reject the accusation that to substitute dialogue in place of mission is a betrayal of Christian witness. Christians cannot but give witness to Christ, also in dialogue [Grolle, "Judenmission...,"
p. 8]. Their willingness to let the other challenge and question them will in itself transform dialogue into witness. In
answering questions put to them by Jews, such as, why do
Christians consider the Old Testament our Bible, why do
they claim to be "Israel," they will inevitably be led to
speak of Christ, not in a naive effort to win Jews over to

Christianity, but rather in justifying their own faith as it is
challenged by Judaism [Harder, Ungekündigte Bund, pp. 154-
55]. Dialogue, so its advocates say, inevitably means for
Christians confession of Jesus Christ as Savior of all men.
Without this confession it would degenerate into mere talk
[Leuner, "From Mission to Dialogue," p. 394]. There can
be no question of a "religious levelling" ("eine religiöse
Gleichmacherei"), nor of renouncing the specifically Christian mission. This view is expressed by Harder also in ten
theses presented under the title, "Mission and Dialogue"
[Gespaltene Gottesvolk, p. 283].

John Oesterreicher, while emphatically rejecting any
proselytizing intent of Vatican II, writes that

> ... It is quite correct to say that it is the mark of
> the Church to be missionary. In other words, only
> at the price of ceasing to be, could she forget that
> she is sent into the world to serve men and offer
> them the healing power of Christ. The Church must
> bear witness to Him. Even without preaching, she
> bears this testimony by her very presence, and so
> does the individual Christian. This witness wells
> forth from the very heart of the Christian existence,
> and no Christian can change it without unmaking him-
> self [Rediscovery of Judaism, 1971, p. 39].

There are Jews who agree with this position, because
they too consider Christianity missionary by nature. For
Leo Baeck, "the fact that the pious Christian awaits the day
in which Judaism will find its way to Christianity" is not a
barrier; "genuine hope never separates, it leads to understanding" ["Das Judentum auf alten und neuen Wegen," Judaica, Vol. 6 (1950), p. 147].

The assertion that dialogue under certain circumstances does not constitute a betrayal of the Christian message or a glossing over of differences is expressed also by
Arthur Cohen:

> This is a time ... when men must speak out of their
> differences and over the chasm that separates them.
> It is not that Christians should suspend their faith
> that they may learn to speak well and learnedly with
> Jews or that Jews should inhibit their eccentric singu-
> larity that they may learn to identify the better with
> Christians. It is that Christians must learn to speak

through Jesus Christ to that in the world which is un-
transformed and unredeemed and Jews must learn to
speak out of Torah with a sagacity and mercy which
brings the world closer to its proper perfection.
There is a new communication--not of artificial traditions and hypothesized concords, but a communication of friendship in the holy spirit which is an order
of love that is born out of faith in the urgency of the
quest, rather than in the certitude of discovery [Myth
of the Judeo-Christian Tradition, pp. xx-xxi].

The last position to be examined is that taken by certain authors such as Heinz Kremers and Hans-Joachim
Kraus, who believe that only a total renouncing of Judenmission can open the way to true dialogue. Kremers sees such
a renouncing of mission as resulting not simply from historical considerations and the awareness of the Church's guilt,
but from the full recognition that Israel is still Israel [Das
Verhältnis der Kirche zu Israel (Düsseldorf: Presseverband
der Evangelischen Kirche im Rheinland, 1965), p. 25]. Judenmission is a denial of God's covenant with Israel. "The
Church must renounce all Judenmission.... By Judenmission we understand all attempts by the Church to draw Jews
away from their people, which is still today more than a
people, that is to say, the Covenant-community Israel, in order to make them members of the Church of the gentiles"
[p. 25].

Dialogue must indeed replace mission, and great care
be taken that it not become a new and covert form of Judenmission. "The Jews must be subject as well as object in
this dialogue, that is, genuine partners" [p. 27]. On the
basis of the Old Testament, which Christians and Jews have
in common, both should interpret for each other their respective traditions: the Christian the New Testament, the
Jews the Talmud. Through such open, honest discussion
among equals there will come about mutual understanding and
greater knowledge, and each will be challenged to a new
depth of understanding and living his own faith [p. 26ff.].
What this may mean for the Christian is hinted at by Martin
Stöhr, who asks whether Israel's way of constantly questioning, of doing without dogmatic systematization, may not be
more worthy of God's revelation in history than the Christian
systematization of dogma. [10]

It is here that this position goes beyond any examined
so far. Genuine dialogue involves the willingness to confront

ultimate questions about one's own faith. This is emphasized also by Kraus, who sees such a questioning ("Sich-in-
Frage-stellenlassen") as the one essential condition for encounter and dialogue [Begegnung mit dem Judentum, p.
108], without which the other will not be understood in his existential reality. "Judaism today confronts Christianity with
question upon question. . . . Nothing is more important than
a greater willingness to listen on the part of Christians,
nothing more urgent than letting themselves be questioned by
the other" [p. 124].

An Interpretation

The term "dialogue" is used by all the authors examined above; but obviously it covers many different meanings.
According to one extreme (Becker, et al.), dialogue may
shake one's own faith, hence it is a threat and dangerous.
The Christian should engage in it only to the extent that he
is secure in his position, certain that his Church is the sole
true people of God and faith in Christ the key to understanding scripture. Thus, according to the followers of this interpretation, the ultimate and only legitimate goal of dialogue
is conversion.

The term is here emptied of its content. It is true
that its use in relation to the concept of mission is new.
The advocates of this position have abandoned the term "Judenmission," they speak instead of "service of Israel" and
"witness." In place of the old proselytism, and its frequently accompanying use of constraint, force and violence,
there is an effort toward openness, understanding and respect of the Jew. And yet, is there anything more here
than a change in vocabulary? Beneath the appearance of
words and good will, it seems that the basic positions remain unchanged; that this concept of dialogue is, in reality,
a new and subtle form of Judenmission. The Christian may
open himself to the Jew only in order to assimilate him.
In order to save his own faith from destruction, he must de-
stroy the other's faith.

Men like Kremers and Kraus, on the contrary, are
determined to free dialogue from such ambiguity. Opening
oneself to others and coming to know them, welcoming them,
will of its very nature lead Christians to relinquish their
security. It asks of them the willingness to let themselves
be challenged to the very depths of their certitudes and

convictions--to incur the risk of relativizing their own vision of the truth.

For these men, substituting the word "dialogue" for
the word "mission" is no mere change in vocabulary. It is
the expression of a radical change in religious outlook. Dialogue between Christian and Jew, far from being a matter of
good will--if it is only that, it betrays the other and oneself, is an evasion of the truth and hides the issues at stake
is a confrontation which involves a risk. It can take place
only if one is willing to renounce all desire of power over
others and manipulation of them, including the desire to convert them. It presupposes accepting the Jew for himself, as
one who is different--more, as one who in his own right is
the bearer of a truth which is not that of the Church, a truth
which the Church may even stand in need of. It is based on
the premise that the Jew has something to give the Church.

As we have already seen, the accusation is frequently
made against the advocates of dialogue that they betray the
Gospel. The representatives of the position here examined
also reject this accusation, but on somewhat different
grounds. They maintain that recognition of the specificity of
Israel and at the same time affirmation of the truth of the
gospel, is precisely what constitutes true dialogue. They believe that it is not a question of an either/or--either the
truth of Christianity and the negation of Israel, or the acceptance of Israel and the negation of the truth of Christianity;
that we must hold in tension both the differences and simi-
larities, and accept the fact that dialogue will send us back
to ourselves and the question of our own identity.

If one accepts these premises certain questions inevitably arise. What becomes of faith, of the Church, of truth?
How is it possible to affirm the uniqueness of salvation in
Christ, the Church's universal mission? Some seek a solution at the level of Christian moral perfection. They point
out that faith is never lived perfectly, that Christians have
through their sins and failures impaired the credibility of
Christianity (Rengstorf, Harder, Leuner), that the Christian's
witness to Christ is never adequate on this earth, and that
the pilgrim Church has not yet attained its goal. Gerhard
Jaspers writes that the Jewish question is a constant reminder to us of our un-redemption, of the shortcomings in our
Christianity; we ourselves are the real hindrance to Judenmission, because we scandalize Jews instead of "arousing
them to jealousy" ["Gibt es für die Kirche heute einen

Sendungsauftrag an Israel?" Fragen der Judenmission. Judaica, 17 (1961), pp. 129-40]. In this view, dialogue takes
place to the degree that Christians on the one hand, and
Jews on the other, do not yet fully live their vocations.
When that day comes, all differences will disappear.

This attitude would seem to bypass the main issue
and water down the full force of the problem. It projects
true communication into an ideal vision of the future, and
skirts the heart of the matter. For it is not, ultimately, a
matter of moral conduct, but rather, of the understanding of
truth: of accepting the other in his difference and uniqueness, also where his faith is concerned. Martin Stöhr has
well formulated the gravity of the question: "If we speak no
longer of mission to Israel, but of dialogue with Israel,
what will be the consequences? How will our ecclesiology
and soteriology be affected by the awareness that two confessions engage with each other in conversation (and polemics?)"
["Diskussionsbericht," in Antijudaismus im Neuen Testament,
p. 196].

Chapter VI will attempt to consider these major questions raised by Stöhr.

Chapter VI

THE CHURCH AND ISRAEL:
SOME THEOLOGICAL IMPLICATIONS

Those theologians, considered at the end of the previous chapter, who give a central importance to dialogue, have repudiated the word "mission." They speak of Judenmission only in order to point out its ambiguity and misleading theological implications. For men like Kraus and Kremers, dialogue can begin only at the point where mission ends. In approaching Israel the Church must renounce all intent of conversion. Not only missionary activity, but also the concepts of mission and conversion must be abandoned.

Such an approach leads to a new way of posing certain theological questions about the Christian faith. The kind of communication implied here does not take place by speaking about dialogue, but about the profound issues confronting one's own tradition, and sends us back to our own identity.

In considering certain theological implications that result from this kind of dialogue, one's concern should be to try to understand how the desire to open the door to genuine communication with Israel leads to a posing of questions that are new, and that will have repercussions upon Christian dogma and the identity of the Church. Two main areas will be considered: The Church as People of God; and Jesus Christ as Savior. In each case three elements will be briefly indicated:

the new way of looking at Israel which is emerging today;

its repercussions upon the way of viewing Christianity; and

the possibilities for a dialogue which accepts at one and the same time the givenness of certain basic

119

differences, and the call to communication through these
differences.

1. THE CHURCH, PEOPLE OF GOD

The traditional affirmation that the Church is the
people of God, the new and true Israel, people of the New
Covenant inaugurated in Jesus Christ, implied for classical
theology the refusal to recognize the claim of any other
group to be people of God. If a new people has been called
into existence by God, the old has outlived its function and
no longer has validity.

A radical discontinuity is implied in this view. Israel is rejected, and the Church, which has taken its place, is
the new Israel, who must refashion the forms it has taken
over from the old, giving them their true content. A new
mankind has come into existence, which is "Israel" more
perfectly than the old people of God ever was.[1]

This dialectic of exclusion, of either/or, is the basis
for Judenmission: there is only one people of God, the
Church, hence Israel is no longer people of God; the Jewish
people as such has lost its role; there are only individual
Jews, whom the Church must seek to convert with every
means at her disposal.

Israel--Also People of God

The ecumenical movement introduced a new dimension
into Christian theology. It now became necessary to hold in
tension simultaneously the unity of the people of God, and
the fact of a pluralism, whereby various groups claimed to
be that community of faith. Different Christian groups now
"also" claimed to be people of God. From this it was but
one further step that led certain Christian theologians (e.g.,
the Schism theologians) to assert that Israel is "also" people
of God: that particular human group which has received the
promises, preserves the faith of Abraham, and remains
chosen people. Israel today is still the people of the Covenant.

This broadening of the ecclesiological perspective,[2]
together with a new reading of Romans 9-11, has thus led
to the recognition of the specific character of Israel's

election, the originality of its faith, the fact that, as people,
it occupies a unique place among the nations and in relation
to the Church in particular, yet is not part of the Christian
oecumene.

The affirmation--accepted by a growing number of
theologians and frequently repeated--that Israel is still
people of God, does not, however, resolve the question as
to the manner in which dialogue between Israel and the
Church can take place. How is it possible to maintain the
unity of one chosen people, and at the same time the plurality of two groups, each claiming to be this people? It is at
this point that many efforts stop. The fact of one people of
God is affirmed, but the "how" of the relationship and communication between the Church and Israel is left unanswered.

The Church--Also Israel

The way toward a solution which is opened up today
by some theologians seems to be the following. Israel is
People of God; the Church is born of Israel; thanks to her
Jewish origins she too is people of God. Claiming a newness with regard to the old Israel, she at the same time
claims to be that very Israel from which she has received
her faith. A Jewish sect in her origins[3] she remains Israel, but open, now, to all nations. She is people of God only because she is "also" Jewish. She can claim that title
only by assuming, not by excluding, all that comes to her
from that people who was first called people of God, and
who still remains people of God.

Karl Barth, whose interest in Israel is longstanding
and who has exerted a great influence on contemporary theologians who deal with this question, wrote in 1950:

> The Jews are without any doubt at all the chosen
> People of God down to this day, in the same sense
> as they were from the beginning according to the Old
> and New Testaments. They have God's promise, and
> if we Christians from among the gentiles also have
> this promise, then we have it as those chosen along
> with them, as guests come into their house, as
> branches grafted on to their tree [Barth, "Die Juden-
> frage und ihre christliche Beantwortung," Judaica
> Vol. 6 (1952) p. 72; emphasis added].

Hans Küng writes in a similar vein: "The transference of
the name 'Israel' to the Church can ... never be exclusive
in character, but at best an extended application according
to Paul's parable of the olive tree (Rom. 11:17-24).   The
Jews are the rightful bearers of the title and the Gentiles
are only the grafts on to the old stem" [The Church, p.
115].

The influence of Paul's key chapters on Israel in
Romans 9-11 is explicit in both these passages, as it is in
the case of nearly all contemporary authors who acknowledge
the continuing election of Israel [see Chapter III, note 14].
Harder uses the same image of the olive tree to point to the
"insertion" of the Church into Israel: "In Romans 11 the
Apostle Paul uses the image of the grafting of a wild olive
branch into an olive tree.   This means that we have a living
link to Israel.   Only in this way are we also linked to God's
promises which apply to Israel.   If we deny this relatedness,
our Christian faith becomes a mere Weltanschauung" [Unge-
kündigte Bund, p. 139].

Krister Stendahl, in an address delivered to Jewish
and Christian scholars at a Harvard Colloquium in the fall of
1966, has gone further, to our knowledge, than any other
theologian in drawing certain conclusions from the Church's
origins as a Jewish sect:

It is clear to me that Christian theology needs a new
departure.   And it is equally clear that we cannot find
it on our own, but only by the help of our Jewish colleagues.   We must plead with them to help us....
We need to ask, in spite of it all, whether they are
willing to let us become again part of their family, a
peculiar part to be sure, but even so, relatives who
believe themselves to be a peculiar kind of Jews.
Something went wrong in the beginning.   I say 'went
wrong,' for I am not convinced that what happened in
the severing of the relations between Judaism and
Christianity was the good and positive will of God.   Is
it not possible for us to recognize that we parted ways
not according to but against the will of God?   ["Judaism and Christianity," p. 453].

Stendahl does not minimize the difficulties that stand
in the way of such a solution, on both the Jewish and Christian sides.   His proposal is at odds with many of his Christian fellow theologians, who tend to see the Church's

severing from Israel as having been not only inevitable, but necessary, divinely willed, and a blessing. [4]

"Intra-Jewish" Dialogue?

Leaving aside the somewhat controversial question of whether or not Christianity may be considered a Jewish sect, the new emphasis placed on the Jewish dimension as permanent and constitutive of the Church's life represents a radical shift in perspective, and transforms the nature of dialogue itself. No longer will it be the dialogue of two communities--the Church and Israel--extrinsic to each other, but a dialogue at the interior of Jewish tradition, an "intra-Jewish dialogue" (the phrase, Inner-jüdisch, is Helmut Gollwitzer's). The Church and Israel are partners in this dialogue, brothers who are separated--not, indeed, in a fraternal relationship, but in their being sons and daughters of one and the same, the God of Abraham, to whom the promise was given of a posterity "vast as the sand on the seashore."

This intra-Jewish dialogue, far from having the pejorative connotation given it by some thologians, is now seen as an ongoing debate between members of two groups who share a common origin, election, and faith in the God of Israel, and who live in the same Covenant of God's mercy and fidelity. The radical divergence of their ways over the past 1900 years does not--or need not--negate the "indissoluble link" that continues to unite them more closely than any other two religious groups. Out of the common effort to understand their respective and different traditions--the Talmud and the New Testament--on the basis of the scriptures they hold in common, there can come a deep and sympathetic mutual understanding, new insight into their own faith traditions, a sense of solidarity and, on the part of Christians, a profound gratitude for the privilege of sharing in Israel's heritage.

It is this last attitude which is most apparent in a sermon on Romans 11:33-36 preached by Hermann Diem as early as 1946. [5] Diem reminds his Christian congregation that "salvation has come from the Jews to us, the Church of Christ, who have come to believe in the God of Abraham, Isaac and Jacob; who have inherited God's promises to Israel even though we are from among the gentiles and therefore had no claim to them; to us, who have been taken up

into God's Covenant with Israel." We have become incor-
porated into his people. The God who led Israel out of
Egypt has become our God, and repeats in our lives the
same saving deeds he wrought for them.

It is obvious that this new sense of "Jewishness" presupposes a rediscovery by the Church of the Jewish elements
in its tradition, and will in turn reinforce them--or restore
them where they have been lost from sight. There is concern, stimulated by the Biblical renewal, among many Christian scholars today to try to restore the balance in what has
become, in the minds of some, an excessively Hellenized
Christianity. This has heightened the interest in Judaism.
Others hope for the "Judaization" of Christianity as one of
the fruits of closer contact between the Church and Israel.
(See, for example, Israel und die Kirche, pp. 38-40.)
Kraus speaks of the impoverishment Christianity has suffered through the loss of a Biblical anthropology, the concreteness of Jewish thought, the emphasis on historical reality, on the deed, and the Jewish understanding of Thora as
a way of life, a "walking in the ways of the Lord. "[6]

K. H. Miskotte describes another aspect of Israel's
existence, which acts as a constant challenge to Christianity.
For the Christian, redemption has occurred and lies in the
past; the Jew refuses to recognize this redemption, lives in
expectation of it, and works for its coming. Thus he is a
constant reminder to the Christian that the latter also still
awaits the fullness of the Kingdom. This fundamental aspect of Israel's existence, which acts as an irritant for the
Church, is described by Miskotte as follows:

All of Judaism's questions to Christianity are over-
shadowed by one single question.... Judaism awaits
the Messiah and the Kingdom. This attitude and life-
orientation is a challenge to us whether we too live
in a trans-personal expectation.... We must go yet
further: an entire people bases the meaning of its
apartness, and the unspeakable suffering connected
with it, upon the expectation of what is to come. Regardless of the personal attitude of individual members of this people, God places it as objective witness, as visible sign of the Parousia, the manifestation, the coming of Christ [Das Judentum als Frage
an die Kirche, pp. 15-16].

Miskotte sees Israel as constantly raising questions for the

Church. (See also Kraus, near end of Chapter V.) Through
his refusal to settle down, through his constant restlessness,
the Jew by his very existence can shake the Church from her
complacency.[7]

Thus there is a growing realization among Christian
theologians today that the Church needs Israel in order to be
fully herself, and for her own self-understanding:

> If we enter into debate with that which is Jewish, we
> understand better our origin, our unity, our task and
> our future as Christians. It is true that this is dif-
> ficult for us, for all that we encounter in the Juda-
> ism of old as well as today challenges, as nothing
> else does, our being Christian. Judaism must be-
> come for us a scandalon, a scandal--but a scandal
> which, if we take it upon ourselves, heals just as the
> Cross heals [W. Wirth, "Der ökumenische Aspekt
> der Begegnung mit den Juden," p. 145].

Israel is seen as necessary to the Church because it
constitutes part of her own being by virtue of her Jewish
origins, as well as an outside questioner and challenge. It
is able to perform both tasks, precisely because there is a
"common ground and difference" between Christianity and Israel.[8]

2. JESUS, SON OF ABRAHAM

We have taken this title, which is not a classical
Christological one, from Matthew's genealogy (Matt. 1:1).
We think it has several advantages. It is scriptural, yet not
worn thin through use; it points to Jesus' "Jewishness"
through his descent from Abraham, Father of the Jewish
people; it is not a Messianic title, such as "Son of David,"
which would be unacceptable to Jews; and it would be difficult for Christians to find any grounds on which to object to
it.

Faith in Christ is the foundation of the Church. It is
at one and the same time the Church's link with Israel,
through Jesus the Jew, and the sharpest point of division between the two, through Jesus the Christ. For the Christian,
the confession of Jesus Christ, Son of God and Savior of the
world, is the central affirmation of his faith, while for the
Jew such an affirmation is in the realm of blasphemy. All

other issues that divide the two communities come to a head
in the question concerning Jesus Christ. Acceptance of him
as Messiah, God-Man, sole mediator between God and man,
or failure to accept him as such, constitutes so radical a
line of separation that it can neither be concealed nor
crossed.

If that is so, we may ask whether dialogue about Jesus is possible at all. Why not resign ourselves to the admission that communication between Jew and Christian can
take place in many other areas--some of them admittedly
peripheral--but that, as far as Jesus Christ is concerned,
there can only be silence? Such an admission would place
Christology outside the realm of the Jewish-Christian dialogue, and impose upon the latter clearly defined limits:
"No trespassing beyond this point."

This is the attitude of many Jews and Christians--
even among those who believe in dialogue. They prefer to
avoid the subject of Jesus, rather than risk sharpening the
break or conjuring up ancient hatreds and stereotypes which
both sides have tried for decades to exorcise.

And yet, what is the point, ultimately, of a dialogue
in which the central difference is evaded? It would seem
that all those efforts analyzed previously--leaving behind
of triumphalist absolutism toward Israel, going beyond
good will, trying to attain to a genuine understanding
of the other's truth--are in danger of being nullified if the
central question, that surrounding the person and work of
Jesus, is excluded from the discussion. Despite the unavoidable difficulties, an attempt must be made to pursue
the theological quest of faith--the faith of Abraham--also,
and especially, with regard to the Jesus of first-century history and the Jesus of Christian faith.

The Jesus of History

For centuries, neither Christianity nor Judaism had
come to terms with the fact that Jesus was a Jew. Christians failed to understand why he should have come out of
Judaism, while Jews tended to ignore Jesus and his significance for world history. Today, however, a change is well
underway. Thanks to exegetical and historical studies,
Christians have "discovered" that Jesus of Nazareth was a
Jew. At the same time, some Jews are coming to accept
and revere him because he was a member of their people.

The fact that Jesus is a Jew, though obvious to the point of triteness, was, however, frequently paid little more than lip service on the part of Christians, who tended to see Jesus far more in opposition to the Jews than as one of them.* There was also the tendency to identify Jesus with those aspects of Judaism which hold a privileged position in Christianity, such as the prophetic tradition, rather than with the Judaism of his time, that of the rabbis and Pharisees, with which the gospels frequently show him in conflict.

Beginning with the late 19th century, Christian scholars came to recognize the importance, both for an understanding of the Church's origins as well as the person of Jesus, of a knowledge of first-century rabbinic Judaism, the environment of Jesus' life and work. Familiarity with the milieu that gave birth to Jesus came to be seen as essential to the Christian understanding of the New Testament. The various Judaica institutes established at that time, while many were in part aimed at Judenmission, also had as their goal a more thorough and scientific knowledge of Judaism. (The Institutum Judaicum founded by Strack in Berlin, however, was established solely for scholarly purposes without any missionary intent.) This trend has gained momentum in the present century, providing a wealth of studies of Jewish Christianity by Christian scholars, and giving to Judaica a respected place in many Christian university curricula.

In our day this knowledge of first-century Judaism has been vastly enriched by a new phenomenon: a growing interest in Jesus among Jewish scholars. The works of men such as Josef Klausner, David Flusser, Robert Aron, H. J. Schoeps, Schalom Ben Chorin and Jules Isaac, to mention only a few, have contributed immeasureably to our insight into the Jewish milieu of Jesus.[9] Even a glance at any one of these studies reveals to the Christian the originality and depth which a Jew can bring to an understanding of the New Testament background.[10]

That this interest in Jesus is not merely academic is evident from Buber's famous words: "From my youth on I saw in Jesus my great brother" [Two Types of Faith (New York: Harper Torchbooks 1961, p. 12]. Less well known

---

*The reference is not to the grotesque yet by no means unsuccessful attempts made by the Nazis to purge the figure of Jesus of all Jewish elements and to make him into a blond Aryan, but to the average Christian mentality over the centuries.

is an elucidation of this statement made by him some years
later: "The Jews ... are 'brothers' of Jesus.... Jews
know Jesus from within in a way which remains inaccessible
to those peoples who acknowledge his lordship."[11] In citing
this text, R. R. Geis comments that Jesus' life and work
can be understood in all their depth and scope only through
his Jewishness. "A Jew can, after 2000 years, understand
Jesus' word and deed, life and death, as a piece of himself" [Versuche, p. 129].

     Rather than accuse the Jews of "appropriating" Jesus
and taking him away from us, as Herbert Hug has done,[12]
Christians have good reason to marvel that he in whose
name countless Jews have been persecuted and murdered
over the centuries has in our day come to be loved and ad-
mired by some of them. We have already quoted the way
in which Buber conceived his relationship to Jesus. Let us
cite here one more testimony--a striking example of the
"intra-Jewish" dialogue--from a contemporary Jewish scholar,
Schalom Ben Chorin, given to a Christian audience in Germany:

          Even if Jesus of Nazareth is not everything for me
          that he is for many of you, he is still for me, for
          me as a Jew, a central figure without whom I cannot
          conceive my life--also and especially my Jewish life
          .... I make Buber's words [of the great brother]
          my own, but should like to add that, the longer I live,
          the closer have I come to the figure of Jesus along
          the road of my life. At every turn of this road I
          find him standing, and ever and again he addresses
          to me the question of Caesarea Philippi: 'Who am I?'
          And ever and again I have to confront him and an-
          swer. And I am certain that he will continue to ac-
          company me along the road and appear to me, even
          as, according to legend--he met Peter on the Via
          Appia, and according to Acts, Paul on the road to
          Damascus. Ever and again I encounter him, and
          ever and again we hold converse together out of the
          commonness of our Jewish origin and the Jewish hope
          for the Kingdom ["Jüdische Fragen um Christus,"
          Juden, Christen, Deutsche, p. 147f].

     It is possible, then, to speak of a breakthrough as
far as the Jewishness of Jesus is concerned, among both
Christians and Jews. Christians have come to recognize
that knowledge of Jesus' milieu gives them a deeper understanding of the founder of their faith and the origins of the

Church, while a growing number of Jews look upon Jesus
with admiration and pride as one of their own. On this
point, communication and understanding are not only a possibility, but already a reality. Jesus the Jew, Son of Abraham, today draws many Jews and Christians closer together.
For some Christians, at least, knowledge and love of Jesus
the Jew have become identical with knowledge and love of
his people:

> In reality, Israel and Christianity are intimately re-
> lated. If we encounter Jesus in the way he addresses
> us, and let him take hold of us, then we are taken
> hold of by the God of Israel, and hence must en-
> counter also the people itself. If we encounter Isra-
> el, we also encounter Jesus. The more we under-
> stand this, the clearer become both the meaning of
> Jesus and the meaning of Israel [Wirth, "Der öku-
> menische Aspekt," p. 160].

And yet, he of whom Paul writes that "he has made
gentiles and Jews one in the body of his flesh and blood,
breaking down the emnity which stood like a dividing wall
between them" (Eph. 2:14f.), remains even to this day the
great divide between them.

The Christ of Faith

The precise point that constitutes the heart of the
difficulty should be located: it is not Jesus of Nazareth,
Son of Abraham, a Jew among Jews. It is the Christian's
claim that in Jesus of Nazareth the Kingdom of God has
come among men--the confession of Jesus as the Christ--
that is the central issue. "That is the creed: I believe
that Jesus is the Messiah; and its chiastic correlate: the
Messiah is Jesus" [Stendahl, "Judaism and Christianity,"
Harvard Divinity Bulletin (Oct. 1963), p. 5].

It is true that Israel has known Messianic movements
and false Messiahs at different times in its long history,
and that the followers of Jesus were neither the first nor the
last Jews to acclaim their leader as the Messiah. Rabbi
Akiba's endorsement of Bar Kochba's Messianic claim did
not prevent Akiba from becoming one of the greatest and
most revered figures in Judaism. Most of these false Messiahs, however, were recognized as such before the end of
their lives and the Jews, disappointed in their hopes, resumed their Messianic expectation once more.[13]

In the case of Jesus, however, the situation was very different. Although we cannot speak of one uniform Messianic expectation either in the scriptures, or in first-century Judaism, it is clear from the Gospels that Jesus disappointed the current Messianic expectation of his time. The loss of political freedom and the smarting under the Roman yoke had given new impetus among large segments of the population to the expectation of a Messiah who would restore independence to Palestine. We know that Jesus' own followers were expecting him to be this kind of Messiah: "Lord, will you at this time restore Israel's sovereignty?" (Acts 1:6). Not once, but time and again, Jesus went against this current of Messianic expectation, refused to be acclaimed as political leader (e. g., John 6:15), and stressed the other-worldliness of his kingdom (John 18:36). In place of political power there was to be suffering and death, which seemed to the people at large, and even to his followers at the time, the destruction of all their hopes, and the negation of his Messianic claim. (See Luke 24:21.)

At the same time, the Gospels show Jesus speaking with an authority that could not but appear blasphemous to the religious leaders of the people. John's Gospel in particular depicts him as claiming oneness with the Father, and through its use of the "Ego eimi" formula (see Eduard Schweizer, Ego eimi, 1939), an authority that went beyond that of the Scribes and Pharisees. He offers to all, in his own person, that life which they thought to have through their descent from Abraham and the faithful observance of the Law. "I am the way, the truth, and the life" (John 14: 6). [14] One is tempted to say that it was inevitable that precisely the most religious and devout of his contemporaries would see in Jesus' person and claim a radical threat and challenge to their most sacred beliefs and traditions.

Yet this was the man whom his followers proclaimed Messiah, after his death. And from that time on Christians have staked their faith upon the belief that in Jesus of Nazareth God's promises to his people have been fulfilled. To quote Stendahl once more, "all that is said and came to be said of Jesus has its genetic center in the claim that he was the Messiah, that with him or through him the messianic age had drawn nigh. His teaching, his actions, his gracious and his harsh words all relate to this one claim" ["Judaism and Christianity," p. 4].

Thus, it was not Messianic faith as such that divided

the Church and Israel in the first century, nor is it the dividing line today; for this faith both held, and still does hold, in common. Each conceives of it, however, in radically different terms. The Christian believes that in Jesus Christ the Kingdom of God has appeared and redemption is accomplished, although only in germ. For him, Christ's coming marks the center of human history, a new starting point in time. A new power is at work in the world, though it will be manifest only at the end of time.

The Jew, on the other hand, does not "perceive any caesura in the course of history. We know of no mid-point in it, but only a goal, the goal of the way of God, who does not pause upon his way" [Martin Buber, quoted in Schoeps, Jewish-Christian Argument, p. 151]. He looks at the world and sees it unchanged: torn by fear, war, injustice and disease. These, to him, are unmistakable symptoms that redemption has not yet come, that the prophets' vision of peace and unity lies still in the future.

Buber has well described the difference in this respect between Christian and Jew: "Now to the Christian, the Jew is the incomprehensibly obdurate man, who declines to see what has happened; and to the Jew, the Christian is the incomprehensibly daring man, who affirms in an unredeemed world that its redemption has been accomplished. This is a gulf which no human power can bridge" ["Brennpunkte der jüdischen Seele," 1930].

And yet, despite this "gulf," the Christian also prays for the coming of the Kingdom. Even though, for him, the Kingdom has already come in Christ, he still awaits its full manifestation in the Parousia. It has come, and has not come; it is present and operative, yet hidden except to the eye of faith. Thus his life is lived in the tension of the between-time, of the "already" and the "not yet." And the Jew, who refuses to admit "enclaves of redemption" [Schalom Ben Chorin's phrase, "Jüdische Fragen...," p. 142] in the midst of an unredeemed world, can be a constant reminder to the Christian that he too still waits. In the words of Arthur Cohen:

> The Christian comes to depend upon the Jew who says salvation has not yet come, to interpret for him what happens when power collapses, how men shall behave when the relative and conditional institutions of society crumble, for the Jew is an expert in unfulfilled

time, whereas the Christian is an adept believer for
redeemed times only. The Christian comes to de-
pend upon the Jew for an explanation of unredeemed-
ness. [Myth of the Judeo-Christian Tradition, p. xx].

It is an oversimplification, therefore, to say that the
Christian lives wholly out of the past, and the Jew wholly
turned toward the future. Despite fundamental differences,
both share a common expectation. Nor should it be forgotten that the word and concept of redemption are not a Christian invention, but part of Christianity's Jewish heritage.
Israel's God is the saving God who led his people out of
Egypt and wrought mighty wonders for them. Otto Michel,
in comparing the Jewish and Christian faith in redemption,
writes:

> When the [Jewish] wise men say that one day all
> feasts will cease, they mean without a doubt that the
> abiding memory of God's unique deed will remain the
> central and lasting event. In the prayer of Jewish
> tradition the motive of redemption also plays a last-
> ing role. The salvation which is prayed for is noth-
> ing else than the return of salvation in history ["Jud-
> ischer und christlicher Erlösungsglaube," Juden,
> Christen, Deutsche, pp. 300-30].

Thus, the Jewish and the Christian Messianic faiths, while
differing in some essentials, also have much in common that
can be explored further, and which may lessen the gap between the two traditions.

Ben Chorin writes, "We may indeed pray together:
'Your kingdom come'; for the faith of Jesus which shines
forth from this marvellous prayer, the Our Father, unites
us--but the faith in Jesus separates us" ["Jüdische Fragen
...," p. 142].

The faith in Jesus the Christ, Son of God and Savior
of the world, constitutes the fundament of the Christian's
faith; for the Jew it verges on blasphemy. Can there be any
hope of communication here--not for the sake of convincing
each other, but in order to come to a deeper joint understanding?

One attempt to resolve the difficulty is made by Karl
Rahner. Rahner suggests that the man who "throws himself
into the arms of the unspeakable God" already implicitly

believes in Christ, whether he knows it or not ["Bekenntnis
zu Christus" in Juden, Christen, Deutsche, pp. 151-58].
If one postulates the anonymous Christian, as Rahner does,
then there is every reason to hope that "he exists also, and
especially, in Israel," and that behind Israel's No to Jesus
Christ there is already concealed its redeeming Yes to him.

One interpretation of the above is that this approach
robs Jews of their freedom and identity, and imposes upon
them the Christian vision of truth. This impression is re-
inforced by the manner in which Rahner asks certain questions in this same essay: Can you--the Jew--seriously expect the fullness of the Kingdom of God within history?
Could a purely human Messiah really be Messiah? Is it not
evident that those who truly believe in eternal life, which
ends history and is not of this world, have the best chance
to build a bearable life in this world, "since neither despair
nor hybris can, ultimately, be of help here?" [p. 154]. The
implication is that the Jew is prone to both, and that only
the Christian's faith leads to a truly constructive, hope-
filled existence here on earth.

The concern here is not with the question of whether
this argument will stand up in the face of history, and of the
Jew's so obvious contribution to human progress. It does
seem, however, that Rahner's approach offers no real possibility for dialogue, for understanding the other and respect-
ing them as who they are, precisely in their otherness.
What is quite acceptable as a personal confession of Christian faith relapses into the old absolutism, and closes doors,
if it is proposed as the one and only vision of truth. For-
tunately (from the present author's point of view) this is not
all. Other possibilities have been found which, though they
are few and tentative, seem to go to the core of Christian
dogma and Christology.

Trinitarian Doctrine

The dogma of the Trinity has always been rejected by
the Jews, to whom it seems to threaten the unity of God. It
was evolved by the Church in those centuries when Christological heresies were rampant, and when its alienation from
Judaism was complete. According to Kraus, the formulation
of this dogma spelled the final impossibility of resumption of
dialogue with Israel [Begegnung, p. 116]. Kraus suggests
that if exchange with Judaism had still been possible at that

time, Christianity might have evolved a trinitarian doctrine
more oriented along historical lines, such as are still found
in Ignatius or Ireneaus. "But the history-less, inner-trini-
tarian speculation ... could arise only in a Church who had
lost, along with her Jewish partner in dialogue, also the
historical dimension" [p. 116].

Kraus believes that Christian theology is today being
challenged to nothing less than a radical revision of Christology, beginning with the dogma of the Trinity. Instead of
reacting apologetically to criticisms, one should take seriously, for instance, J. Klausner's question, Why is there no
place within our trinitarian theology for I Cor. 15:28: "And
when all things are thus subject to him, then the Son himself will also be made subordinate to God who made all things
subject to him, and thus God will be all in all" [Jesus and
Paul, quoted in Kraus, Begegnung, p. 117].

To Kraus, this means the willingness on the part of
the Church to seek a new way of confessing the teaching
the Trinity. To go yet further: rather than merely a new
way, he asks, do we not need a "totally new orientation of
a historically oriented Christology, a much more concentrated and clear relatedness with the Old Testament?" [Be-
gegnung, p. 117].15

The Dutch Reformed Church, in its Study on the
Church and Israel [Israel und die Kirche (Zürich: EVZ Verlag, 1961)], has advocated just such a rethinking of trinitarian dogma. Its reason for so doing is the awareness that,
given Israel's central confession of faith of the unity of God
as expressed in the Shema (Deut. 6:4), the Church's trinitarian doctrine has tended to be misunderstood by Jews as
polytheism. In view of this, the Study suggests that "the
Church surely has good reason to ask herself to what extent,
through the formulations in which she little by little crystal-
lized this doctrine, she herself has contributed to this mis-
undestanding" [p. 16].

More Than One Christology?

Dogmatic formulations of Christology are not found in
the New Testament itself, but are the outgrowth of prolonged
theological speculation that was frequently aimed at combat-
ting heresies, in a Church which had become almost totally
hellenized.16 Kremers cautions against absolutizing them.

For contemporary New Testament scholarship makes it clear that there is no one New Testament Christology. Instead, the New Testament seeks to understand the miracle that "God was in Christ" through different modes of thought [see Kremers, Verhältnis der Kirche zu Israel, p. 28].

One example of the variety of these modes, which cannot always be readily harmonized with one another (e.g., Jesus' becoming the Son of God in the Resurrection, his anointing as Son of God in the baptism, his pre-existence, etc.) is found in the area of Messianism referred to earlier. In Acts 3:19-21, Peter speaks of the coming of the Messiah as being still in the future, and that this Messiah will be Jesus. We have here an expression of the first Christians' faith in the Parousia. While later generations of Christians struggled with the problem of the "second coming," the first Christians, according to Stendahl, sought an answer to the question: "In what sense and to what extent was the life and death of Jesus a coming of the Messiah? This is the problem to which the different gospels, and the traditions underlying them, give their answers, some tentative, some increasingly clear" [Stendahl, "Judaism and Christianity," p. 5]. They centered around the resurrection, and the coming of the spirit as promised by the prophet Joel. "One prayed in the Lord's Prayer: let your will become manifest on earth as it is now manifest in heaven.--Maranatha." Such language, which is "cut out of the same cloth as that of Judaism" [p. 5], reflects an experience and piety that grew on Jewish soil.

As dialogue between Israel and the Church resumes, it may help Christian theology to make room once more for the principle of dogmatic pluralism, which was so much in evidence in the early Church, and still prevailed at the Council of Florence, until "it became obscured during the Counter Reformation, and even more so in the past century, when the Church felt obliged to take stringent measures to stave off various forms of relativism" [Avery Dulles, "Dogma as an Ecumenical Problem," Theological Studies, vol. 29 no. 3 (Sept. 1968), p. 409].

Perhaps the most promising element in the discussions examined is the new willingness on the part of at least some theologians to reexamine even the most fundamental Christian dogmas and to relativize doctrinal formulations, knowing that they can never contain adequately, once and for all, divine revelation. [17]

It may be this new openness in the Church which
gives some Jews today a sense that they too may have something to receive from Christianity, so that Arthur Cohen can
write: "The Jew ... must look to Christianity to ransom
for him his faith in the Messiah, to renew for him his expectation of a nameless Christ" [Myth of the Judeo-Christian
Tradition, p.xx]. Thus, if there is today a new openness
among Christian theologians, it can be matched on the Jewish side. A text by H. J. Schoeps illustrates this:

> The Christian who, according to his faith, comes to
> the Father through Jesus Christ, that is, through the
> Church in which Christ lives on, stands before the
> same God whom we Jews confess, the God of Abra-
> ham, Isaac and Jacob, the God of our teacher Moses,
> the God whom Jesus of Nazareth also addressed as
> Father.
>
> This basic fact, which we can admit at all times,
> guarantees our inner relatedness to Christianity and
> opens up at all times the possibility of mutual ap-
> proach. Its limitation, of course, lies in the fact
> that we cannot recognize the Christ--that is, the Mes-
> sianic title of Jeschu ha Nozri, with regard to Isra-
> el....
>
> The Church of Jesus Christ has not preserved a por-
> trait of her Lord and Savior. If Jesus were to re-
> turn tomorrow, no Christian would know him by his
> appearance. But it could well be that he who comes
> at the end of days, he who is the expectation of the
> Synagogue as well as the Church, will bear the same
> features for both. [18]

It is in the nature of this study, however, that our
primary concern is with developments in Christian theology.
There are signs that a new and radical historical consciousness, and the understanding of dogmas as time-conditioned
formulations, are opening the way for a dogmatic pluralism
that has not existed in the Church for centuries. Catholic
and Protestant theologians can share this common ground,
according to Avery Dulles. He makes his own the following
remarks by the Lutheran Carl E. Braaten:

> Dogmas are things of history; they arise in history;
> they have a history; and they generate a history of in-
> terpretation in which earlier meanings are transcended
> through incorporation into new and quite dissimilar

formulations[;] ... the trinitarian and christological
dogmas ... are [not] exempt from the new interpre-
tations in an age of radical historical consciousness
["Reunion, Yes; Return, No," Una Sancta, 23 (1966),
pp. 32-322; quoted by Dulles, "Dogma...," p. 412].

This new attitude on the part of Christian theologians should
make possible and facilitate the kind of radical reexamina-
tion of trinitarian and Christological dogma considered to lie
at the heart of dialogue between Israel and the Church.

CONCLUDING REMARKS

The three main parts of the study having examined various approaches to Christian mission, some concluding remarks may now be hazarded, grouped under two main headings: a survey and evaluation of the various concepts of Judenmission; and some proposals for making possible continued dialogue between the Church and Israel.

1. SURVEY AND EVALUATION

Can one speak of an evolution in the missionary concept over the past twenty-five years? The answer is very likely both yes and no. Yes--because the traditional concept of Judenmission is being widely questioned in Germany today, in many cases rejected altogether. No--insofar as this traditional concept is still alive, indeed, is being strongly advocated by some. If we speak of evolution at all, then, it is not evolution in the chronological order. Rather, various approaches are found side by side; hence it may be more accurate to speak of a spectrum of missionary concepts. In this respect there is no doubt that where there had once been one dominant view, today there is great variety (this in itself may rightly be called an evolution).

Judenmission

The term is used here in its traditional sense: conversion of Jews through active missionary effort involving special missionary organizations and trained personnel. The goal is baptism and entrance into the Church, with the consequent disappearance of the Jew as Jew.

While St. Paul left the Jewish people the privilege of "being adopted as sons of God, the experience of seeing something of the glory of God, the receiving of the Covenants

139

made with God, the gift of the Law, true ways of worship,
God's own promises" (Rom. 9:4), Judenmission concentrates
on converting the Jews. Concrete missionary activity is
justified through a theology of mission which, in order the
better to show the specificity of faith in Jesus Christ, denies to those who claim the faith of Abraham all authentic
knowledge of God and his revelation. The faith of the Christian is light, the faith of the Jew darkness. While the
Church has full knowledge of the scriptures and the key to
their interpretation, Israel understands them only partially
and behind a veil, as it were.

This traditional Judenmission is based on a vision of
the Church as the sole organ of salvation for mankind. All
non-Christians are considered potential Christians, and the
Church must actively work for their conversion. Unless it
engages in missionary work, it is unfaithful to the mission
entrusted to it by Christ. Once converted, converts are as-
similated to the body of Christians and no longer have their
own specific mode of expressing their faith. Christianity
draws them into itself, in the name of love and truth, for the
sake of their salvation.

The attitude here described, which seems strangely
out of date in an ecumenical age, is by no means dead--not
even in Germany, not even in the post-Holocaust era, as is
witnessed by the Kirchentag controversy. It should be obvious that those who hold it (e.g., Reinhardt, Mehl, Dobbert,
Becker, et al.) see no religious validity whatever in post-
Biblical Judaism. Hence they draw the logical conclusion:
the sooner Jews disappear as Jews by becoming Christians,
the better. It is, in a sense, but a subtler version of Hitler's "Final Solution" (Those engaged in Judenmission would
vehemently--and no doubt sincerely--reject such a notion.)
The Viennese theologian W. Dantine observes that one can
hardly blame the Jews for suspecting Judenmission of being
nothing but a "pious, Christian-humane form of a 'Final Solution,' aimed at destroying post-Biblical Judaism through
Christianization" ["Kirche als Israel Gottes," Jüdisches Volk
--gelobtes Land, p. 335]. A Jewish reaction to Judenmission, coming from one of the great Jewish theologians of our
time, Abraham Heschel, sounds still more shocking: "I had
rather enter Auschwitz than be an object of conversion."[1]

A variant of the view just described considers Judenmission incumbent upon the Church, but not within the memory of Hitler (e.g., Barkenings). The guilt of Christianity

toward the Jews is admitted and is seen as an obstacle to
Christianity's credibility. The underlying attitude, however,
both with regard to the nature of Israel and of the Church,
remains unchanged. The new developments in the approach
to Judenmission appear to stem principally from two concerns: theological reflection about the people of God, and
the desire for dialogue.

Healing the Schism

A growing number of theologians today maintain Israel's election (Harder, Rengstorf, the Schism theologians, et
al.). Israel is still people of God. Indeed, there is only
one people of God, which exists in a state of division, or
schism, ever since the break between Christianity and Judaism in the first century. The validity of post-Biblical Judaism is recognized, the Jews are loved and respected.

Yet there is a limit. Judaism is an imperfect, temporary stage, for only explicit faith in Christ constitutes
full salvation. The Church is the true people of God in the
real sense of the term, even though Israel is "also" people
of God. Israel's "eyes are held" (Spaemann) until it recognizes Jesus as Messiah. In that day, Israel as a people
will be converted to Christ. This conversion will be the
work of God alone; hence Judenmission, in the sense of active missionary work, must be abandoned.

We find traces of a view which is very close to the
one here outlined, but differs from it in one important respect. It does not necessarily conceive of the Jews' conversion to Christianity; indeed, it questions the legitimacy
of the concept itself (Démann, Skydsgaard). While this view
also looks forward to the healing of the schism and the restoration of unity, the future shape of that unity is left open.

Those who see Israel as people of God frequently
have a keen appreciation for Judaism's contribution to the
world, and to the Church. They consider Christianity as
having been impoverished for centuries by the loss of Jewish Christianity. The balance must be restored; the Church
needs Israel.

One may agree with this insight, but should perhaps
be cautioned against "using" Judaism as an end for Christianity's perfection. The Jewish Christians may be taken

as an example. The opinion has already been expressed
that ways should be found to make a genuine home within
the Church for Jewish Christians, without cutting them off
from their own people. Christians would, however, fall into a new kind of proselytizing if they were to look upon Jews
primarily as a way of helping them (Christians) to become
more Jewish, and thus welcome them into the Church--or
even draw them into it--in order to make the Church more
complete. The Church can profit from Judaism "from the
outside" as well as "from within"--if Jews remain Jews,
and precisely as Jews are willing to engage in honest dialogue with Christians.

The recognition--however limited and circumscribed
--that Israel is still Israel, has led to another development:
the awareness that Israel's status is unique, among all the
peoples of the world as well as in relation to the Church.
Hence there can be no question of Judenmission. As the
primary and original recipient of revelation and people of
God, through whom God's promises to Abraham and the revelation of Sinai have come to the Church, Israel can in no
way be the object of Christian mission. On the contrary,
Israel is God's chosen instrument for bringing his name to
the nations, and the Church's mission is only a sharing in
that of Israel (Dutch Reformed Church).

Dialogue in Place of Mission

This phrase covers a wide variety of approaches, sum-
marized here under two headings.

(A) Witness to Christ Is Paramount. Many theologians today (Rengstorf, Harder, Holsten, et al.) advocate dialogue in place of mission. Whether for pragmatic reasons,
or because of Israel's special status as people of God, traditional Judenmission is no longer considered acceptable or
appropriate. Terms such as "witness" ("Zeugnis") and
"service" ("Dienst") now replace "mission." The Jew is not
an "object" of mission, but a partner in dialogue (though one
might question whether the concept allows for genuine equality). The Christian goes out to Jews in a spirit of service
and brotherly love, rather than superiority and proselytizing;
He must, however, give witness to Christ in all circumstances, including dialogue. Dialogue with the Jew will be
carried on in humility and respect, in the awareness of
Christianity's many failures and guilt.

Proponents of this approach hope that a dialogue carried on in such a manner will eventually open the Jew to
Christianity: thus, conversion is still the ultimate goal, although here, too, Judaism's continuing election is recognized. Yet it is at best only an imperfect stage, which will
one day give way to the full truth of Christianity.

(B) Dialogue Without Reservations. A small minority among those theologians who advocate dialogue with Jews
do so in a spirit of radical openness, willing to let the dialogue lead where it may (Kraus, Kremers, Miskotte). They
are aware that this requires the readiness to let go one's
own secure position and entails the possibility of losing the
ground under one's feet. Conversion? Perhaps, but who is
to say of whom, and to whom? Dialogue of this kind does
not imply a letting go of Christ, but of our ways of conceiv-
ing him, our dogmatic formulations, also in the area of
Christology. We must be ready to have our images of God
broken open time and again, allow ourselves to be questioned and challenged by the Jew even at the deepest level of
our faith ("Sich-in-Frage-stellen-lassen").

Such an attitude obviously involves risk. However,
unlike those for whom the risk of dialogue is an argument
against it (e.g., Becker and Dobbert), and who are willing
to engage in it only out of the security of their own religious
stance, the advocates of the position here described consider
such risk an essential condition for dialogue. Without it,
the Christian retains his customary attitude of superiority
and his claim to be the sole possessor of truth.

Some Distinctions and Questions

The first distinction to be made is that between mission and missionary work. While the missionary character
of the Church is generally affirmed, this is not identical, for
the majority of authors examined, with the missionary enterprise.[2] Indeed, apart from certain explicitly missionary
groups and organizations (e.g., a segment of the Lutheran
World Federation), missionary work is decried. Dantine
goes so far as to say that "Judenmission as deliberate enterprise of the Church ... is nonsense." For such missionary
activity effectively robs the Jews of their claim to be Israel,
and invalidates, in principle, their sharing in the one Covenant of God, which is also the basis for the Church's existence ["Kirche als Israel Gottes," Jüdisches Volk, p. 335; emphasis in orig.].

A second distinction can be made between missionary
work and conversion. Even for the majority of those authors who reject Judenmission (e.g., the Schism theologians),
conversion of the Jews to Christ at the end of time remains
part of the vision of the one people of God, the Church. Only then will Israel be truly and perfectly Israel and the
Church be indeed a Church of Jews and gentiles.

In the light of history, this represents progress.
For centuries Christianity, claiming to be the heir of Judaism, had turned against its mother. Today the child, who
has become an adult, recognizes his lineage and even cher-
ishes it. Christianity has not, indeed, "renounced conversion, but has understood that conversion depends upon God"
[Guichard, Les Juifs, p. 9].

Another nuance in the use of the concept of conversion today makes it possible to go one step further. Conversion is seen by some (e.g., Gollwitzer, Thoma) not as
converting the other, but in the Biblical sense of metanoia,
repentance, the reorientation of one's whole being to God,
teshuvah. The call to conversion, which is of the essence
of the prophetic message, is reiterated in the New Testament by Jesus himself. Jesus' call to conversion--to the
Father, it should be noted, not to himself--is part of his
proclamation of the Kingdom of God.

If both Jew and Christian strive for conversion, which
is central to both faiths, the final result will not be the victory of one side over the other, but perhaps, in the words
of Buber, "a reality which today is still inexpressible" [Der
Jude und sein Judentum, quoted in Versuche, p. 165]. Not
only conversion itself, but also the form or "shape" it will
take, are here left entirely in the hands of God.

Let us now depart from the material examined and
consider some natural questions and concerns which have
arisen as a result of this study.

Is it possible to go further? To give greater urgency
to this question, is it necessary for the Church to go further,
in an age of religious pluralism? It would seem that this
question is posed for Christianity by its encounter with other
great religious traditions--not only Judaism, but Islam
and the Eastern religions also. This experience challenges the view that it is Christianity's mission to convert
the world to Christ, draw all men and women into the

Church--or extend the Church to all men--and hasten
Christ's return through missionary efforts. It gives rise to
the question whether the already widespread and constantly
growing religious pluralism of today's world can be interpreted, not as a threat and obstacle, or temporary and un-
desirable necessity, but as bearing within itself a positive
religious meaning. To put it more bluntly, Can we still affirm that God intends, through the Church, to bring everyone to one faith? Do other traditions have their own unique
contributions to make to man's religious quest? Is religious
pluralism part of the very stuff of salvation?

     An affirmative answer to these questions does not
necessarily imply the negation of Christianity's mission, although it implies a different view of it. The Christian will
still go out to others; not "to bring them the truth," but to
share with them something that is precious to him, while he
in turn will receive something of their wealth. Such an approach maintains the uniqueness of Christianity, but not its
superiority or absolutist claim to truth. It accepts the fact
that no one tradition can hold all of revealed truth or lay
claim to be the only and full revelation. For God encompasses and is greater than the whole of man's religious
quest. "My ways are not your ways, and my thoughts are
not your thoughts" (Is. 55:8-9). [3]

     The Living God is accessible in different ways and
reaches us through different channels. If certain historical
events have universal significance, as both Christians and
Jews believe, why should not these archetypal experiences
be available to every man, through his own history and tradition of faith?

     At this point the initial premise is returned to: that
the Church's relationship to Israel is in some sense a test,
touchstone, for its wider relationship to the world. The
Church's dialogue with Israel is important for its own life,
since it shares with Israel a common faith and tradition. At
the same time, out of this common ground there have arisen
over the centuries profound differences in interpreting and
living this faith. Thus, through recognizing Israel, in all
its uniqueness and difference, as well as similarity and relatedness, the Christian is forced to confront the non-Christian and recognize his uniqueness. This encounter is a direct challenge to any absolutist claim to truth and to the traditional concept of unity through sameness. Instead, it suggests the possibility that the depth and richness of humanity

are revealed in the diversity and differences among men, at
least as much as through what they hold in common.

One is reminded here of Luther's interpretation of a
verse of Psalm 103: "You send forth springs into the val-
leys." This text suggests to him two mountains standing
side by side, arising out of one and the same valley, so that
they can be said to be united "at their roots" even though
the peaks are separate. He depicts them as carrying on a
friendly conversation, the one saying to the other, "My valley is your valley and your valley is my valley, because we
have one and the same valley" [WA; 179, 32ff.; Luther uses
the Vulgate numbering of the psalms in his Dictata super
psalterium].

Israel's faith, the faith of Abraham, in the God of
Abraham, is also the faith of the Church. Yet it comes to
the Church differently: through Jesus, Son of Abraham. In
this perspective Christianity's "mission" to Israel is reversed. It is transformed into the effort to live in greater
fidelity the faith it has received from Israel, in the specific
way of the Jew called Jesus, whom Christians acclaim as
the Christ. No one can tell where the quest will end--or,
to return to Luther's image, how many peaks arise out of
the one valley. All we know, in faith, is that one day God
will be all in all. Perhaps the quest itself--which requires
a constant letting go of certainties and formulations in order
to make room for a new vision--is the movement of faith,
not only for Jew and Christian, but for everyone.

2.   TOWARD A CONTINUATION OF DIALOGUE

Certain things need to be done if the evolution in
Christian theology regarding Israel (which despite some real
achievements is at present only in its beginnings) is to continue and bear fruit. They are of a practical rather than
theoretical nature, at least in their implications.

Ending the Teaching of Contempt

Christians must do everything in their power to put
an end to the incalculable harm and injustice which traditional Christian teaching has done to the Jewish people. One
hopes the day will come when Christians will take for their
own what Emil Fackenheim has called the new Commandment

for Jews since Auschwitz, "No posthumous victories to Hitler. Never again another Auschwitz!"

Despite some undeniable progress already made in
this area, the demise of the Teaching of Contempt may still
be far in the future. Not only does a great deal of work remain to be done at the theological level, but even the gains
that have been made so far will remain the preserve of a
small elite unless they are implemented at the liturgical,
pastoral, and catechetical levels. Here there are some hope-
ful signs.

Progress in Roman Catholic Liturgy. Several notable
liturgical changes have taken place in Roman Catholicism over the past fifteen years. The best-known of these is the
deletion, by John XXIII, of the phrase "faithless Jews" from
the Good Friday liturgy, and the reformulation of the Prayer
for the Jews.[4] It is instructive to note the various stages
which this prayer has undergone; the different versions are
supplied below. The first two texts date from before Pope
John's intervention in 1959; the third and fourth versions
were revised under the impact of Vatican II (source for these
texts is Oesterreicher, "Introduction," Brothers in Hope, pp.
25-26).

1. Let us pray also for the unbelieving Jews. May
the Lord our God remove the veil from their hearts
so that they, too, may acknowledge our Lord Jesus
Christ.

Almighty and everlasting God, you do not refuse your
mercy even to Jewish unbelief. Hear the prayers we
offer for the blindness of that people. May they acknowledge the light of your truth which is Christ, and
may they be brought out of darkness. Through the
same our Lord Jesus Christ. Amen.

2. Let us pray also for the Jews.

May the Lord our God remove the veil from their
hearts so that they, too, may acknowledge our Lord
Jesus Christ.

Almighty and everlasting God, you do not refuse your
mercy to the Jews. Hear the prayers we offer for
that people. May they acknowledge the light of your
truth which is Christ, and may they be brought out of
darkness. Through the same our Lord Jesus Christ.
Amen.

3.   Let us pray also for the Jews.

May the Lord our God let His countenance shine upon
them so that they, too, may know the Redeemer of
all, our Lord Jesus Christ.

Almighty and everlasting God, You made Abraham and
his descendants bearers of your promise. In your lov-
ing kindness hear the prayers of your Church so that
the people you made your own in olden days attain the
fullness of salvation. Through Christ our Lord.

4.   Let us pray also for the Jews, to whom God spoke
first.   May He grant that they advance in the understanding of His word and love.

[Here follows the same prayer as in No. 3.]

While it would seem that the third and fourth versions can be interpreted as praying for the conversion of the
Jews, the progress in thought between the first and last of
these prayers is nevertheless striking and unmistakable.
Christians, who for centuries had prayed, at the holiest time
of their liturgical year, that the "veil might be taken away"
from the hearts of the "faithless" and "blind" Jews, are now
reminded that this people is the bearer of God's promises
for mankind.

Another recent liturgical change has attracted less
notice: the eucharistic prayer over the gifts, in which the
old offertory has been replaced by a blessing that follows
the traditional Jewish form:

Blessed are you, Lord, God of all creation. Through
your goodness we have this bread to offer which
earth has given and human hands have made. It will
become for us the bread of life.

The Jewish grace before meals is as follows:

Blessed are you, Lord our God, King of the Universe. You bring forth bread from the earth.

A third example is taken from a collection of masses
for special themes and occasions, published in Germany as
a result of the liturgical renewal.[5] One of these masses,
entitled "The Jew--Our Brothers," illustrates the kind of effort that is needed in order to translate new theological insights into liturgical and popular piety. We give excerpts

from the Introduction, and some of the Mass texts, below.[6]
First, from the author's Introduction:

> National Socialism exterminated five to six million
> Jews. Not only through their silence do Christians
> share in this crime. One of the most dangerous
> sources of anti-Semitism has always been a certain
> 'folk piety.' The name 'Jew' has served Christians
> as a term of abuse; even children used it, children
> who had never met a Jew, who had never been
> harmed by a Jew.
>
> They knew the Jew only from the Bible, and even
> the Biblical Jew only as a caricature; as the dread-
> ful man who had wronged the Lord Jesus, who had
> sold Him and spit upon Him, scourged Him and
> nailed Him to the Cross.
>
> "It's about time that we recall, that we learn again,
> that Jews are brothers who implore the same heaven-
> ly Father for His blessing. Catholics, Protestants,
> and Jews dwell on the same river, even though each
> of them draws a different measure from the everlast-
> ing wells.
>
> Respect for any people must begin thus: That we no
> longer see it as a label, but as the sum of individu-
> al men and women, each one of whom bringing his
> own face to his fellows. We will then discover how
> much the things written in the faces of men resem-
> ble one another, across all our divisions [Schilling,
> Motivmessen, p. 62].

The text of the prayers is as follows:

> Father in Heaven,
> Your Son, our Lord Jesus Christ was born a Jew.
> He came to bring peace to the earth.
> We thank you
> For Him who became our brother
> And for the people through whose instrumentality
> You have given Him to us.
>
> Most merciful Father,
> On the Cross your Son forgave
> The members of His people
> Who were drawn into the web of guilt against Him.
> At this meal may he forgive us, too,
> For whatever we have done to offend this people.

Lord most holy,
This meal is able to bind together men and nations
because it brings forgiveness and grants friendship.
Therefore help us to learn to love this people again--
In Jesus Christ, You call it to the service of reconcili-
ation [p. 63].

The Gospel pericope is Jesus' encounter with the Sa-
maritan woman. To the Lord's words, "Salvation is from
the Jews," Schilling adds his own paraphrase: "They are
indeed God's instruments for the happiness of men" [p. 65].

The psalm suggested for the Mass is Psalm 129.
Msgr. Oesterreicher has rendered the German as follows:

Much have they oppressed me from my youth,
So Israel can say.
Much have they oppressed me . . .
Upon my back the ploughers ploughed
Long did they make their furrows.
Our God is just.
He severs the rope of the tormentors,
He puts them to shame,
And--oh wonder!--they all vanish from the face of the
    earth,
All those
Who hate Zion.

Some Catechetical Developments. In the catechetical
field the task is no less urgent, although a good beginning
has been made. Only two years after the end of World War
II, in 1947, ten Catechetical "theses" were published, the
"Seelisberger Thesen." In 1950 a revised version was published jointly at Schwalbach by Protestant and Catholic theologians.[7]

Here is an example of progress from a more recent
project, the Catechetical Guidelines produced by the Christlich-jüdische Koordinierungsausschuss of Vienna ["Darstellung des Judentums in der Katechese, Memorandum,"
Christlich-jüdisches Forum, No. 40 (June 1968), pp. 49-64].
The Guidelines make concrete suggestions for a radical overhauling of catechetical teaching on Judaism. Only two points
will be singled out here, both of which deal with topics
treated earlier in our study: the first-century rift between
Judaism and Christianity, and Jesus' Messiahship.

First-century rift. --The Guidelines point out that the
first apostolic proclamation was made by Jews to Jews. The
gentile Christians, influenced by the already existing pagan
anti-Judaism, came to interpret the polemical words of the
intra-Jewish debate about Jesus' Messiahship in such a manner as to justify their own rejection of Judaism. Thus,
Jesus' woes against the Pharisees, or other polemical say-
ings against contemporary Jewish groups, became the basis
of an anti-Jewish polemic that lasted down the centuries.
Already in St. John's Gospel the Jews have become the representatives of the world that rejected Christ's message.
From the Old Testament, Christianity also took over the
claim to absolute truth, and applied this not only to the gentiles, but also to the Old Testament people themselves, the
Jews ["Darstellung des Judentums," pp. 57-58].

Jesus' Messiahship. --This is the first point dealt with
in the third section of the Guidelines, "Practical Suggestions." In response to the question, Why do the Jews not
recognize Jesus as Christ even though they know the Old
Testament?, the following answer is given:

Judaism was waiting for a Messiah who would estab-
lish a reign of peace over the whole world. There are
many different Messianic concepts in the Old Testament.
Basic to Jewish Messianic expectation, however, is the belief that the Messianic kingdom will bring an end to all the
imperfections and sufferings of this world. As the Jews see
it, this expectation has not been fulfilled by the coming of
Jesus [p. 60]. We have here an effort to teach Judaism to
Christians from the perspective of Jewish self-understanding,
rather than Christian interpretation of Judaism. [8]

Similar efforts are needed in the pastoral field.
Priests must be trained to translate into their preaching
those insights of Biblical scholarship which throw light on
the often difficult and harsh passages about the Jews in the
Gospels. Unless this is done, Christian congregations will
continue to take away with them from many Sunday and Lent-
en services the stereotypes of the hypocritical Pharisees,
of the stubborn, hard-hearted and plotting Jews, etc.

Appreciation of Post-Biblical Judaism

Efforts to end the Teaching of Contempt must not be
limited to "negative" aspects, such as opening Christians'

eyes to the evils of anti-Semitism, or even the Holocaust,
or saying that the Jews are not guilty of deicide, not rejected by God, etc.   The impact of this kind of teaching
may arouse feelings of guilt among Christians. Such feelings
may be long overdue but they will not only not guarantee .a
change of heart but may reinforce anti-Semitism if they are
not transformed into genuine contrition.   But such teaching,
by itself, will not lead to respect for Jews and Judaism,
let alone love.   (Yet nothing less will do, if the future is
to be brighter than the past has been.)

Respect for and appreciation of Judaism can come
about only through knowledge of the Jewish tradition and its
richness.   While the starting point for this would be familiarity with the Old Testament, it must be emphasized that
such familiarity is just that and no more--the starting point.
This is still all too little realized by Christians, who tend
by and large to identify Israel with the Old Testament
Jews. [9]   Such a mentality ignores the fact that Judaism no
less than Christianity has undergone 1900 years of evolution
and development since Biblical times and that, while there
is continuity, there is also much that is different about
post-Biblical or rabbinic Judaism.

How great the difference was, already by the second
century, is illustrated by a Midrash of Rabbi Akiba [from
The Babylonian Talmud, ed. Rabbi I. Epstein (London:
Soncino Press, 1948), Seder Kodashim, vol. I, Pt. 2, p.
190; footnotes a-e are part of orig. text].

> Rab Judah said in the name of Rab, When Moses as-
> cended on high he found the Holy One, blessed be He,
> engaged in affixing coronets to the letters. [a] Said
> Moses, 'Lord of the Universe, Who stays Thy
> hand?'[b] He answered, 'There will arise a man, at
> the end of many generations, Akiba b. Joseph by
> name, who will expound upon each tittle heaps and
> heaps of laws.' 'Lord of the Universe,' said Moses,
> 'permit me to see him.' He replied, 'Turn thee
> around.' Moses went and sat down behind eight
> rows[c] (and listened to the discourses upon the law).

---

[a]These are the Taggin, i. e., three small strokes written
on top of the letters ץ ז ר נ ט ע ש in the form of a crown.
[b]I. e., is there anything wanting in the Torah that
these additions are necessary? [c]Of R. Akiba's disciples.

Not being able to follow their arguments he was ill at
ease, but when they came to a certain subject and the
disciples said to the master 'Whence do you know it?'
and the latter replied 'It is a law given unto Moses at
Sinai' he was comforted. Thereupon he returned to
the Holy One, blessed be he, and said, 'Lord of the
Universe, Thou hast such a man and Thou givest the
Torah by me!' He replied, 'Be silent, for such is
My decree.[d] Then said Moses, 'Lord of the Universe,
Thou hast shown me His Torah, show me his reward.'
'Turn thee round,' said He; and Moses turned around
and saw them weighing out his flesh at the market-
stalls.[e] 'Lord of the Universe,' cried Moses, 'such
Torah, and such a reward!' He replied, 'Be silent,
for such is My decree.'

If the Moses of this Midrash had difficulty in identifying
second-century Judaism with his teaching, how much more
difficult is it for the 20th-century Christian to perceive the
continuity between the contemporary Jew and the Jew of Biblical times! Without an understanding of post-Biblical Judaism, which is largely rabbinic Judaism, he will know very
little of Judaism. Hence the need for Christians to engage
in Jewish studies. The Jew of today is the product of a
2000-year-old post-Biblical history at least as much as of
the Biblical times alone. It follows that the Christian must
have some insight into this development if the Jew is to be
seen in even a small measure as he sees himself.

This history, more ancient and at the same time more
new than that of any other people, stretches from the Exo-
dus, through the Exile and Return, the destruction of the
Second Temple, the diaspora, ghettos and Emancipation, to
the Holocaust and the rebirth of the State of Israel in modern times. The Jew living today is not only the descendant
of the Old Testament people, or Rabbinic Judaism, or any of
the other movements to which Judaism has given birth over
the centuries. He has experienced, along with all this and
in his own flesh, the destruction of his people in this generation, and their subsequent survival and resurrection.

We believe that Jewish experience and history are
paradigmatic, reflecting as in a microcosm human experience

---

[d] Lit., "so it has come to My mind."   [e] R. Akiba died a
martyr's death at the hands of the Romans during the Hadri-
anic persecution. V. Ber. 61b.

in general, and that Elie Wiesel's interpretation of the current wave of protest is correct:

> Its vocabulary takes one back a quarter of a century.
> Factories and university buildings are 'occupied.'
> The Blacks rise up in the 'ghettos.' Prague is in the
> headlines and so is Munich. The police use 'gas' to
> disperse demonstrators. Concentration camps in
> Egypt and Greece. The Watts and Harlem riots are
> compared to the Warsaw Ghetto uprising. Biafra is
> referred to as another Auschwitz. Political analysts
> talk of nuclear 'holocaust" ["To a Young Jew of To-
> day," One Generation After, p. 172].

What the Jewish people have lived in the mid-20th century may well prove to be, in compressed and extreme form, the misery and grandeur of mankind. Behind the face of the Jew at Auschwitz can be discerned the face of the suffering Servant of Second Isaiah--a figure which Christians have perhaps too facilely made their own, even as they have taken so many of Israel's prerogatives. Through his outcries can be heard the relentless answers of Job to his well-intentioned interlocutors, and the cry of the psalmist, "Eli, Eli, lama sabbacthani?" If Christians open themselves to this cry of the Jew at Auschwitz, they may perhaps hope to attain a deeper understanding of the word which the Jewish scriptures have given to the world, the word "redemption."

There are some Jews who feel it is too late; that the message of Auschwitz has fallen on deaf ears, and that those who tried to break the silences did so in vain.[10] Yet these same men continue to speak and write, and exercise a profound impact on a small but growing number of Christians. Perhaps, as Jews, they cannot do otherwise but speak, if "to be a Jew is to testify" [Wiesel, One Generation After, p. 174]. If that is indeed their task, the task of Christians is to try and hear their testimony, and respond.

CHAPTER NOTES

INTRODUCTION

1. I follow Elie Wiesel in rejecting a cause-and-effect relationship between the two which is sometimes made: "Actually, the two experiences have in common only those who lived through them. Thence, their relationship on the level of conscience and sensitivity, perhaps even of memory, but not in any pattern of history. To impose a logical sequence on Auschwitz and Jerusalem, or a design other than dialectical, would be to diminish both. Israel, an answer to the holocaust? It is too convenient, too scandalous a solution...." Elie Wiesel, "Postwar: 1948," One Generation After, p. 128.

2. In a class of freshmen college students taught by the writer in 1969, not one out of 180 students was familiar with the term.

3. "... Adornos Wort, nach Auschwitz könne man keine Gedichte mehr schreiben, hat so viele Missverständnisse provoziert, dass ihm zumindestens versuchsweise die Interpretation nachgeliefert werden muss: Gedichte, die nach Auschwitz geschrieben worden sind, werden sich den Masstab Auschwitz gefallen lassen müssen.
    "Spätestens hier zögere ich, höre ich dem Wort Auschwitz nach und versuche ich, das Wort Auschwitz in seiner Echowirkung zu messen.
    "Wir kennen die trivialste Resonanz: Schon wieder Auschwitz! Immer noch Auschwitz? Wird das nich aufhören? Will das nicht aufhören?
    "Ich hoffe: nein. Ich widerspreche gleichfalls dem verhalten-vornehmen Echo: Die Antwort auf Auschwitz könne nur Schweigen, dürfe nur Scham und Verstummen sein. Denn Auschwitz war kein Mysterium, dem Scheu distanzierte und verinnerlichte Betrachtung befiehlt, sondern Realität, also zu untersuchendes Menschenwerk.
    "Seit Auschwitz folgt zwar der Kalender nich einer neuen Zeitrechnung, wohl aber hat sich in unserem Denken--selten bewusst, doch unvermeidbar unterbewusst--so etwas wie eine neue Zeitrechnung niedergeschlagen. Seit Auschwitz denkt sich der Mensch anders, zwingen wir uns, anders zu denken, und wird überall dort, wo

Auschwitz sich fortsetzt, der einmal gesetzte Massstab mitgedacht werden müssen.

"Was vor Auschwitz sich ereignete, unterliegt anderen Kategorien, sofern es beurteilt wird; obgleich es den Vernichtungsmechanismus schon immer gegeben hat: erst die Perfektion liess ihn zur Kategorie werden. Nicht die namentliche Grausamkeit enzelner Personen, sondern die anonyme Reibungslosigkeit fleissig zu nennender Schreibtischarbeit war das Neue und noch nicht Dagewesene in seiner menschlichen Blässe, die wir, uns distanzierend, unmenschlich nennen.

"Die Reduzierung der Realität Auschwitz zum zeitlichen Wendepunkt hat dem ehemaligen Konzentrations- und Vernichtungslager Symbolgehalt gegeben: Auschwitz steht stellvertretend für Treblinka und Mauthausen, für eine Vielzahl ehemaliger Konzentrations- und Vernichtungslager. Diese Symbolisierung erschwert die Aufgabe, den alltäglichen Mechanismus in Auschwitz zu erklären, weil gleichzeitig mit der Ortsbezeichnung das Schlüsselwort für jeglichen Völkermord mitgesprochen wird.

"... Es gilt, Auschwitz in seiner geschichtlichen Vergangenheit zu begreifen, in seiner Gegenwart zu erkennen und in Zukunft nicht blindlings auszuschliessen. Auschwitz liegt nicht nur hinter uns." Günther Grass, "Schwierigkeit eines Vaters, seinen Kindern Auschwitz zu erklären," Frankfurter Allgemeine Zeitung, Tuesday, June 2, 1970, No. 124, p. 24.

4. Emil Fackenheim, for example, wrote in 1968: "Men shun the scandal of the particularity of Auschwitz. Germans link it with Dresden; American liberals with Hiroshima; Christians deplore anti-Semitism in general, while Communists erect monuments of victims-of-Fascism-in-general, depriving the dead of Auschwitz of their Jewish identity even in death. Rather than face Auschwitz, men everywhere seek refuge in generalities, comfortable precisely because they are generalities. And such is the extent to which reality is shunned that no cries of protest are heard even when in the world community's own forum obscene comparisons are made between Israeli soldiers and Nazi murderers." Emil Fackenheim, "Jewish Faith and the Holocaust, a Fragment," Commentary, Vol. 64, No. 2 (August 1968), p. 30.

5. Jules Isaac, The Teaching of Contempt: Christian Roots of Anti-Semitism (New York: Holt, Rinehart and Winston, 1964). The original edition appeared in Paris in 1962 under the title, L'Enseignement du Mépris.

6. The phrase, "traditional Christian teaching," is used deliberately. There is no dogmatic treatise on Israel in Catholic theology. Among Protestant theologians, Karl Barth was the first to give Israel an integral part in his theological system. Cf. especially his Church Dogmatics, II/2, No. 34; also W. F. Marquardt, Die Entdeckung des Judentums für die christliche Theologie: Israel im Denken Karl Barths (Munich: Kaiser Verlag, 1967). The absence of any official Christian dogma concerning Israel may prove

a happy accident, since it leaves the doors wide open for new theological endeavors. At the same time, one should not underestimate the impact of "traditional Christian teaching," embodied chiefly in preaching and catechetical instruction. It generally has a far greater effect in shaping the religious mentality and attitude of people than dogmatic pronouncements. On this subject, cf. "Der Prozess Jesu im Religionsunterricht," in Judenhass--Schuld der Christen?! ed. by W. P. Eckert and E. L. Ehrlich (Essen: Hans Driewer Verlag, 1964), pp. 111-138; Joseph Solzbacher, "Die Juden in der katechetischen Unterweisung," Ibid., pp. 191-211; Gerhard Teske, "Die Juden in der christlichen Verkündigung. Versäumnisse und Verzeichnungen--Aufgaben und Möglichkeiten," Ibid., pp. 212-284.

7. For example, the editors of Judenhass--Schuld der Christen?! ["Jew Hatred: A Christian Sin?"], W. P. Eckert and E. L. Ehrlich express reservations about linking anti-Judaism with modern anti-Semitism; cf. p. 11; and Eckert, Ibid., pp. 70-72.

8. At the same time, one must be on guard against too great an optimism. The "teaching of contempt" is not a thing of the past even in the post-Holocaust era, not even in Germany. This is graphically illustrated by the following passage, written in 1949 by Michael Schmaus, one of Germany's leading Catholic dogmatic theologians: "God has ... great plans for the people chosen by him.... God's purpose in his judgments upon the chosen people is not destruction, but salvation. The resisting part of Israel, by being cast from its former height through all its visitations, is meant to come to its senses. Only because God cannot forget his people, only because he is unwilling to let it be lost, does he punish it hard and frequently." "Das Verhältnis der Christen und Juden," Judaica V, 1949, p. 189; quoted by Greive, Ideologie, p. 226.
Greive comments: "Thus it was not the Nazis, ultimately, who killed the Jews, nor was it the Christians who contributed their share actively and passively; above all it was not he, Michael Schmaus himself, who had once said that the Jewish people must 'atone for the madness of its rejection' ... it was, rather, God, who carried out all these punishments" (Ibid.).

9. The admission of guilt, however, leaves something to be desired: Rabbi Henry Siegman writes, with reference to Vatican II: "What was called for was an act of contrition; what occurred was an act of charity." Quoted by J. Coert Rylaarsdam, "The Christian and the Holocaust" (unpublished paper), 1969.

10. Both remarks are in H. Berkhof, "Israel as a Theological Problem," Journal of Ecumenical Studies, Vol. 6, No. 3 (Summer 1969), p. 345.

11. Criterion, Divinity School of the University of Chicago, Vol. II, No. 1 (Winter 1963), pp. 23ff.; quoted by Jakob J. Petuchowski in "A Jewish Response to 'Israel as a Theological Problem in the Christian Church'," Journal of Ecumenical Studies Vol. 6, No. 3 (Summer 1969), p. 349.

12. Berkhof [note 10], p. 345.

13. See Leo Katcher, Post-Mortem: The Jews in Germany Today (New York: Delacorte Press, 1968); also Neher, "Dimensions et limites du dialogue Judéo-allemand depuis 1945," in L'Existence Juive, pp. 184-211. Neher's account is helpful in pinpointing the ambiguity facing Jews who decided to return to Germany, as well as that involved in the German government's efforts to make reparation.

14. An exception is the Jewish Community of West Berlin, which numbers about 6000 members and is in close contact with Christian theologians such as Helmut Gollwitzer, Günther Harder, and W. F. Marquardt.

15. A somewhat more optimistic assessment of the situation is given by Eckert: "The Jewish communities in Germany have become very small, many no longer exist. And yet there are Jews in Germany today who, despite everything that has happened, are still willing to forgive, and who welcome dialogue between Jews and Christians. There are young people from Israel who study in Germany and who, not burdened by the past, are able to begin a dialogue. After the war, Dr. Gertrud Luckner, who freely spent several hard years in the concentration camp because she had felt compelled as a Christian to help her Jewish fellowmen, started with other likeminded men and women the Freiburger Rundbrief, intended to serve the reconciliation between the old and new people of God. In many German cities, societies for Christian-Jewish cooperation have been started, which seek to give Christians a knowledge of Judaism, and Jews a knowledge of Christianity. The annual meetings, in March, of the "Brotherhood Week" challenge every German to examine his conscience and determine how ready he is to leave behind old and deeply rooted prejudices, and to enter into a brotherly dialogue. Numerous study weeks are concerned with the task of Christian-Jewish encounter. Thus, Germany is given an unexpected opportunity, perhaps for the last time, to carry on Christian-Jewish dialogue." Eckert, "Verpasste Chancen," in Judenhass, pp. 78-79. On the Freiburger Rundbrief, see Note 30.

16. See Heinz Kremers, "Die reflexion engagée in der politischen Bildung," Erfahrungen einer Israelexkursion. Pädagogische Rundschau, Vol. 15 (1961), pp. 297 ff.

17. In considering this general statement one should be aware of individual German Jews who also make their mark on the theological scene, such as Robert Rafael Geis. Among the younger generation, Rabbi Nathan Peter Levinsohn of Heidelberg, together with the Dominican W. P. Eckert and the Lutheran pastor Martin Stöhr, has formed the "Deutsche Koordinierungsrat der Gesellschaften für christlich-jüdische Zusammenarbeit." This Committee has organized study days at Arnoldshain since 1966.

18. The Institute Germania Judaica, founded in Cologne in

1958 by non-Jews (among them Heinrich Böll), attempts to make up for this lack and to keep Judaism before the German conscience. Through seminars, lectures, an excellent library and series of publications, the Institute tries to restore a permanent Jewish presence to Germany today. It represents one of the most significant and successful efforts in this regard since World War II. See Schochow, Deutsch-jüdische Geschichtswissenshaft, pp. 246-48. The Leo Baeck Institute, founded in 1955 in honor of Leo Baeck, the dean of German Jewry who survived Theresienstadt, has as its task the recording of the history of the Jews of Germany through 1933. It is significant that its headquarters and branches are located outside Germany--in Jerusalem, New York and London.

19. Greive, Theologie und Ideologie, p. 224. This book is helpful not only as background documentation, but also in providing a point of comparison for the evolution--whether genuine or opportune--of the views about Judaism of such prominent German Catholic theologians as Augustin Bea and Michael Schmaus. While it deals only with Catholic authors, the passages quoted here are typical and could be matched by texts from Protestant sources.

20. "Sieht man von einigen ersten Begegnungsversuchen im Zeitalter der Aufklärung und vorsichtigen Gesprächen 'über die Mauer' im neunzehnten Jahrhundert ab, so verdient die Tatsache Beachtung, dass in den Jahren nach dem ersten Weltkrieg zum ersten Mal ein Dialog beginnt, in dem beide Gesprächspartner wirklich einander gegenüberstehen, aufeinander zuhören und einander zu verstehen sich anschicken." Versuche des Verstehens, ed. by Robert Raphael Geis and Hans-Joachim Kraus, Dokumente jüdisch-christlicher Begegnung 1918-1933 (Munich: Kaiser, 1966), p. 173.

21. H. J. Schoeps, The Jewish-Christian Argument, A History of Theologies in Conflict. (New York: Holt, Rinehart and Winston, 1963), pp. 146-58. This debate, and other documents by Jewish and Christian authors from this period, are collected and edited by Geis and Kraus in Versuche des Verstehens. The editors point out in the Preface that, regrettably, none of the Christian theologians represented are Catholic, because no Catholics engaged in Christian-Jewish dialogue prior to World War II. Their assessment of the abiding impact upon history of these discussions is tentative and modest: "Es waren Versuche. Mühsam rangen sie sich aus einem in Jahrhunderten hoch aufgeschichteten Wust der Vorurteile heraus. Kam as wirklich zu einer Begegnung oder zog man aneinander vorbei, sah man einander kaum? Hier und da blitzte es auf: Ein Ahnen, ein Erkennen, ein liebevolles Suchen und Finden. Doch das Gewölk war dicht, oft undurchdringlich." Preface, Versuche.

22. See Karl Heinrich Rengstorf, "Begegnung statt Bekehrung," in Juden, Christen, Deutsche, ed. by H. J. Schultz (Stuttgart: Kreuz-Verlag, 1961), p. 266.

23. Der Ungekündigte Bund, ed. by Dietrich Goldschmidt

and H. J. Kraus (Stuttgart: Kreuz-Verlag, 1962), pp. 251-54.

24. "Fortdauer der Ratlosigkeit," in Ungekündigte Bund, p. 248.

25. A new feature in the Elenchus Bibliographicus of Biblica, ed. by Peter Nober, S.J., bears out the growing interest in Judaism about this time, not only in Germany, but in Western countries in general. Beginning with 1947, Vol. 28, the Elenchus added a new section, XX, to its contents under the title "Judaismus postbiblicus," with the following subdivisions: 1. Fontes: (a) Semitici, (b) Philo et Josephus. 2. Historia Judaeorum. 3. Litteratura iudaica posterior. 4. Res religiosae, sociales, morales. 5. Questiones Judaismi moderni. (This treats a variety of subjects, including, on occasion, mission and Jewish-Christian relations. Only in 1949 and 1950 is section 5 omitted, resuming again in the following year.)

26. This is particularly striking in the case of the original members of the "Arbeitsgruppe Juden und Christen"--see pp. 70 ff. Thus Helmut Gollwitzer, whose concern with Judaism goes back to at least 1938, has in recent years become so actively involved with "Ostpolitik" that he found himself the object of a smear campaign which accused him of being a Communist, and effectively thwarted Karl Barth's wish that Gollwitzer succeed him in his chair at Basel. Neither Gollwitzer nor Kraus have lost their interest in Judaism. For both men, as for a number of other theologians, Judaism seems to have served as a catalyst, sensitizing them to human injustice and threat to freedom in any form, anywhere.

27. Among recent publications in Germany, cf. the following: W. F. Marquardt, Die Bedeutung der biblischen Landverheissung für die Christen, Theologische Existenz heute, NF, No. 116 (Munich: Kaiser, 1964); ibid., "Christentum und Zionismus," Evangelische Theologie 23 (1968) 12, 629-59. Clemens Thoma, ed., Auf den Trümmern des Tempels (Vienna: Herder, 1968). Waldemar Molinski, ed., Unwiderrufliche Verheissung. Die religiöse Bedeutung des Staates Israel (Recklinghausen: Paulus Verlag, 1968). W. P. Eckert, N. P. Levinson and M. Stöhr, eds., Jüdisches Volk--Gelobtes Land (Munich: Kaiser, 1970), the third volume in the series edited by Gollwitzer, Abhandlungen zum christlich-jüdischen Dialog.

28. From an article by Seymor Martin Lipset of Harvard, "The Socialism of Fools": "The New Left Calls it 'anti-Zionism,' but It's No Different from the Anti-Semitism of the Old Right," in The New York Times Magazine, January 3, 1971, p. 6f. See also Elie Wiesel, "To a Young German of the New Left," in One Generation After (New York: Random House, 1970), pp. 156-72.

29. This accounts for the inclusion of some little-known names, such as the critics of the 1961 Kirchentag, and the authors of Das Zeugnis der Kirche für Israel, Reinhardt Dobbert and Horst

Becker; see pp. 114-18 and 187-90.

30. The lack of Catholic theologians dealing with Israel in post-war Germany is compensated for, on another level, by the publication of the Freiburger Rundbrief. Published by the late Karl Thieme and his friend and collaborator, Gertrud Luckner, who has continued to edit the Rundbrief since Thieme's death, this periodical is generally considered the most outstanding of all religious or theological journals dealing with Judaism and Christianity. The editors are Catholic, but the Rundbrief is in no way limited to Catholic circles. It publishes comprehensive bibliographies, reports of Jewish-Christian meetings, and gives an excellent survey of the field in general. It is also one of the best sources for the questions and discussions that surrounded and have followed the Vatican II Declaration on the Jews. Freiburger Rundbrief. Beiträge zur Beiträge zur Förderung der Freundschaft zwischen dem Alten und dem Neuen Gottesvolk im Geiste beider Testamente. Freiburg im Breisgau, 1948 - . Originally published under the title, Rundbrief zur Förderung...., 22 volumes have appeared so far. For a more detailed appraisal of the Rundbrief, see Werner Schochow, Deutsch-jüdische Geschichtswissenschaft. Einzelveröffentlichungen der Historischen Kommission zu Berlin, Vol. 3 (Berlin: Colloquium Verlag, 1969), pp. 242, 243, 245.

31. This opinion, while debatable, is presented with great cogency by Arthur Cohen, in The Myth of the Judaeo-Christian Tradition (New York: Harper & Row, 1970).

32. A Jewish philosopher formulates the problem as follows: "What is a religious recognition which does not recognize the other in terms of his own self-understanding? The heart of dialogue, it seems to me, is to refuse to give an abstract answer to this question, and instead risk self-exposure. If Jew and Christian are both witnesses, they must speak from where they are. But unless they presume to be on the throne of divine judgment, they must listen as well as speak, risking self-exposure just because they are witnesses." --Emil Fackenheim, Quest for Past and Future (Bloomington: Indiana University Press, 1970), p. 22.

33. It should be pointed out that there is a subtle difference between the German word "Judentum" and the English "Judaism": "Judentum" is less exclusively religious and encompasses sociological and cultural aspects of the Jewish reality as well. "Israel" in German has a meaning equivalent to its English counterpart.

34. Cf. H. Küng, The Church, p. 114f. on the meaning of "Israel." Also R. Mayer, "Israel, Jude, Hebräer," Theologisches Begriffslexikon zum Neuen Testament (Wuppertal: Theologischer Verlag Rolf Brockhaus, 1969), Vol. II, 1, pp. 742-752.

35. The name Israel is applied to the new people of God only once in the New Testament: "the Israel of God" (Gal. 6:16).

Cf. H. Küng, The Church, p. 115. On the "Israel of God," see also W. Dantine, "Kirche als Israel Gottes und das Problem der Judenmission," Jüdisches Volk--gelobtes Land, ed. by Eckert, Levinson and Stöhr, Abhandlungen zum christlich-jüdischen Dialog, Vol. 3 (Munich: Kaiser, 1970), pp. 323-335; and Reinhold Mayer, "Das Israel Gottes," Christlich-jüdisches Forum, November 1962, No. 29, pp. 1-8.

36. See Werner Schochow, Deutsch-jüdische Geschichtswissenschaft. Einzelveröffentlichungen der Historischen Kommission zu Berlin beim Friedrich-Meinecke-Institut der Freien Universität Berlin, Vol. 3 (Berlin: Colloquium Verlag, 1969), p. 151, n. 69.

37. Thus, for instance, Paul Tillich, Die Judenfrage, ein christliches und deutsches Problem. Schriftenreihe der Deutschen Hochschule für Politik, Berlin (Berlin, 1953); also Helmut Gollwitzer, "Die Judenfrage--eine Christenfrage," Christen und Juden, pp. 284-92. The common usage of the term is further attested to by the following text: "Instead of the usual terms 'Jewish problem' and 'Jewish question' we shall use the terms 'relation to Jews' or 'relation to Judaism'." --Heinz David Leuner, "From Mission to Dialog--Rethinking the Relation of Christians and Jews," Lutheran World X, No. 4 (October 1963), p. 385.

CHAPTER I

1. See Otto Michel, "Opferbereitschaft für Israel," In Memoriam Ernst Lohmeyer (Stuttgart, 1951), pp. 94-100.

2. Thus Thomas Aquinas: "Infidelesqui numquam susceperunt fidem, sicut gentiles et judaei, nullo modo sunt ad fiden compellendi ut ipsi credant, qui credere voluntatis est." ST II:II, Q. 10, Art. 8.

3. Cf. W. P. Eckert, "Geehrte und geschändete Synagogue. Das kirchliche Mittelalter vor der Judenfrage," Christen und Juden, p. 111; also, Eckert, "Hoch-und Spätmittelalter. Katholischer Humanismus," Kirche und Synagoge, ed. by Karl Heinrich Rengstorf and Siegfried von Kortzfleisch, I, pp. 235-265.

4. K. H. Rengstorf, "Begegnung statt Bekehrung," in Juden, Christen, Deutsche, ed. by H. J. Schulz (Stuttgart: Kreuz Verlag, 1961), p. 268.

5. Von den Juden und ihren Lügen, 1543, WA 53, 412-552.

6. See, for example, Kraus, Versuche des Verstehens, pp. 173-74.

7. Adolf von Harnack, Marcion, 2d ed., 1924, pp. 127 and 222; quoted in Kraus, Versuche, p. 176.

8. See Kraus, Versuche, pp. 174-75.

9. Kraus, Ibid., p. 175.

10. "Jedes Volk, das sich in seiner Eigentümlichkeit und Würde zu behaupten und zu entwickeln wünscht, muss alle fremdartigen Teile, die es nicht innig und ganz in such aufnehmen kann, zu entfernen und auszuscheiden suchen, dies ist der Fall mit den Juden." F. Rühs, Über die Ansprüche der Juden an das deutsche Bürgerrecht (Berlin 1816), pp. 23ff., quoted in Christen und Juden, p. 172.

11. "Die Juden als Juden passen nicht in diese Welt und in diese Staaten hinein, und darum will ich nicht, dass sie auf eine ungebührliche Weise in Deutschland vermehrt werden. Ich will es aber auch deswegen nicht, weil sie ein durchaus fremdes Volk sind, und weil ich den germanischen Stamm so sehr als möglich von fremdartigen Bestandteilen rein zu erhalten wünsche." E. M. Arndt, Ein Blick aus der Zeit auf die Zeit, 1814, quoted in Kraus, Versuche, p. 175.

12. "... Wichtig endlich ist es, den Juden den Übertritt zum Christentum zu erleichtern; hier ist offenbar von den Christen zu wenig geschehen, und das ist der Punkt, wo wir uns die grössten und verdientesten Vorwürfe machen können: Unmenschlich ist es, den Juden einen Vorwurf zu machen, dass sie Juden sind; nur darin liegt ihre Schuld, dass sie es bleiben, selbst wenn sie Gelegenheit haben, von ihren Irrtümern und den Ursachen ihres traurigen Zustandes sich zu überzeugen." F. Rühs, Ansprüche, pp. 23 ff., quoted in Ehrlich, Christen und Juden, p. 172.

13. J. Philippson, Allgemeine Zeitung des Judentums, 25, No. 37 (1861), pp. 527 ff., quoted in Ehrlich, ibid., p. 149.

14. Quoted in Hans-Joachim Barkenings, "Die Stimme der Anderen," Christen und Juden, p. 210. Delitzsch here uses the term "Synagogue" in a non-derogatory way, as do some contemporary wirters also.

15. See the references in Karl Heinrich Rengstorf, Das Institutum Judaicum Delitzschianum 1886-1961 (Münster 1963), pp. 11-12, especially the article on Delitzsch in Encyclopedia Hebraica, XII (Jerusalem 1959), col. 646 f.

16. See Barkenings, "Die Stimme," p. 211, n. 30.

17. See Rengstorf, Institutum Judaicum, p. 13, n. 19.

18. Saat auf Hoffnung. Vierteljahrschrift für das Gespräch zwischen Christentum und Judentum. Forced out of publication by the Nazis in 1935, it reappeared anew in the summer of 1950. Publication ended for good later that year, however, when this periodical was replaced by Friede über Israel.

19. Closed down by the Nazis in 1935, it moved to Vienna under its new director, Hans Kosmala. The reprieve was of short duration. In 1939 the Institute closed once more, its valuable library was confiscated--never to be recovered--and Kosmala went into exile in England. A new beginning was made by Rengstorf as early as 1945, and in 1947 the Delitzschianum officially re-opened in Münster, affiliated with the Protestant Faculty of the Kaiser-Wilhelms-Universität, where Rengstorf was Professor of New Testament at the time. Under his direction the Delitzschianum built up a valuable research library and competent staff, which includes at present two Jewish scholars, and trains foreign as well as German students in Judaica. The major scholarly undertaking at present is a critical edition of the works of Flavius Josephus.

20. See Schochow, Deutsch-jüdische Geschichtswissenschaft, pp. 64 f., 235-38.

21. No one acquainted with Grüber's heroic work under the Nazis, or his efforts to help Jews after the war--both in Germany and the State of Israel--would deny him their profound admiration. At the same time, one is confronted with the ambiguous phenomenon that several of Germany's leading Christian Hebraicists, also products of the 19th-century interest in Judaism, became Nazis and anti-Semites. The most outstanding example is probably Gerhard Kittel, son of Rudolf Kittel. His Judenfrage, published in 1934, is a grotesque mixture of apparent love of the Jews and the desire to be done with them--a precursor, in its own way, of Hitler's "Final Solution." The book is unfortunately out of print; it throws much light on the complex and perverse elements present in German Christian anti-Semitism.

22. See Vorträge des Institutum Judaicum an der Universität Berlin, Vol. I, 1925-1926 (1927), p. 1, quoted in Kraus, op. cit. p. 179.

23. The phrase is Heinrich Heine's, probably the most famous of German Jews to have accepted baptism in the hope of gaining acceptance in society at large. This hope proved vain for him --as it did for many others. In 1826, shortly after his baptism, Heine wrote to his friend Moses Moser: "Now I am hated by Christian and Jew alike. I greatly regret that I had myself baptized, I see no evidence that things have been easier for me since; on the contrary, I know nothing but misery now.... What a crazy business: no sooner am I baptized than I am maligned as a Jew...." Quoted in Ehrlich, "Emanzipation," p. 165. Thus Heine and many others found themselves in the tragic position of having repudiated their own people and heritage, only to be repudiated in turn by the German people to which they so desperately wanted to belong. This led to severe guilt feelings on the part of some baptized Jews. It is at least possible that, in the famous words Heine spoke on his deathbed--"Dieu me pardonnera, c'est son métier,"--he referred, although in irony, to his "sin" of having left his people.

24. See Rengstorf, Institutum Judaicum, p. 15, n. 23.
One is reminded in some ways of Johannes Reuchlin, also a lover
of Judaism and first-rate Hebraicist in his time, and of his battle
with the Dominican Pfefferkorn. For an account of the controversy,
see Eckert, "Verpasste Chancen," Judenhass, pp. 53-54.

25. Sind die Juden wirklich das auswerwählte Volk? Leipzig 1889, p. 8, quoted in Barkenings, "Die Stimme der Anderen,"
p. 215.

26. Saat auf Hoffnung, Vol. 18, p. 227, quoted in Barkenings, ibid., p. 216.

27. Even though, for Delitzsch, Israel continues to have
meaning and plays a role in God's plan, one is reminded here of
Martin Noth's statement that, with A.D. 135 Israel's history has
come to an end. That some theological evolution has taken place
in recent years in this respect is illustrated by a catechetical document published in 1960. It stresses the importance of post-Biblical
Judaism--not only in its heilsgeschichtliche aspect, but as a living
and ever growing tradition: "Die christlichen Religionsbücher lassen
zumeist jüdische Lehre und Geschichte mit dem Jahre 70 enden.
Damit aber wird die wirkliche jüdische Geschichte ignoriert; dadurch
kann man auch zu keinem echten und wirklichen Verständnis des
heutigen Judentums kommen. Die Pharisäer haben über die Zerstör-
ung des Tempels hinaus Leben und Lehre des Judentums hindurch-
gerettet und vielfach auch das Einstehen für ihren Glauben mit ihrem
Blut besiegelt ... Hier beschwört Jules Isaac (Jesus and Israel) den
Religionslehrer: 'Auf Grund der wertvollsten historischen Forschun-
gen anzuerkennen und loyal auszusprechen, dass das Christentum
nicht aus einem degenerierten, sondern aus einem lebendign Judentum entstanden ist....' " From Sechs Thesen für die Gestaltung
der Religionsbücher und des Religionsunterrichts, Bergneustadt,
June 4, 1960.

28. Thus the historian of Judenmission, J. F. de la Roi, at
times supported Stoecker; see Barkenings, op. cit., p. 206.

29. It also failed quantitatively. Despite the supposed advantages to be gained by becoming a Christian, a relatively small
number of Jews, out of the total, were baptized--see Ehrlich,
"Emanzipation," p. 156. Whether one considers this a tragic or
"blessed failure"--in the words of Otto Michel--depends on one's
theological outlook.

CHAPTER II

1. See L. Goppelt, Christentum und Judentum im ersten und
zweiten Jahrhundert. Ein Aufriss der Urgeschichte der Kirche.
Beiträge zur Förderung der christlichen Theologie, 2. Reihe, Vol.
55, Gütersloh, 1954; H. Cazelles, Naissance de l'Eglise, Secte
Juive rejetée? (Paris: Cerf, 1968); C. Thomas, "Judentum und

Christentum im ersten Jahrhundert," Judentum und christlicher Glaube (Klosterneuburg, 1965), pp. 47-69; K. Schubert, Die Religion des nachbiblischen Judentums (Vienna: Herder, 1955), pp. 69-80.

2. Krister Stendahl, "Judaism and Christianity: A Plea for a New Relationship," Harvard Divinity Bulletin (Fall 1967); reprinted in Cross Currents 17 (1967), pp. 445-58; this quotation is taken from the Cross Currents reprint, p. 452. Stendahl adds his own commentary on this process: "The Christian Church has no 'right' to the use of these prophetic statements, once it has lost its identification with Judaism. Even if we repeated the actual words of Jesus, preserved by tape-recordings, these very words of Jesus would mean something else, something contrary to his intention, once they were uttered from without instead of from within the Jewish communities." Ibid.

3. H. L. Ellison, "The Church and the Hebrew Christian," The Church and the Jewish People, ed. by G. Hedenquist (London: Edinburgh House Press, 1954), pp. 149-50.

4. Hans Ehrenberg, "72 Leitsätze zur judenchristlichen Frage," 1933; excerpts appear in Ungekündigte Bund, pp. 199-203.

5. Leuner, "Bezeichnung," p. 378.

6. The same point has been well made by Heinz Kremers: "One often hears and reads that Gal. 3:28 proves that Jewish Christians could no longer remain Jews.... But Paul's phrase, "for you are all one in Jesus Christ,' proves precisely the contrary. We are all one in Christ as Jews and non-Jews, as men and women, as employers and workers--or are Christians angels or eunuchs, and no longer men and women?" "Römer 9-11," p. 155.

7. Elwyn Smith, Journal of Ecumenical Studies, 1, No. 3 (Fall 1964), p. 506; quoted in Leuner, "Bezeichnung," p. 374. Again, Heinz Kremers makes the point succinctly: "The Church since the second century made of Judenmission a legalistic religion. She imposed upon those Jews who wished to become Christians the Law that they must become pagan in order to be Christian, by forbidding them to remain Jews as Christians, to live as Jews among the Jewish people." "Römer 9-11," p. 155.

8. Thus, the IHCA has as the second of its stated aims the bearing witness to Christ among Jews. At the same time, some national groups belonging to the IHCA disavow any missionary purpose. H. D. Leuner wrote the author a letter (London, June 16, 1971): "I can officially inform you that there are at least three national alliances of Hebrew Christians in Europe whose members have excluded any missionary element explicitly from their constitutions: Holland, Germany and Switzerland. These three alliances actively support a number of Israeli institutions and organizations and are on the best of terms with the respective Jewish groups."

9. See Rengstorf, "Die eine Kirche aus Juden und Heiden."
Also, Ira O. Glick, "The Hebrew Christian: a Marginal Religious
Group," in The Jews, ed. by Marshall Sklare (New York: The
Free Press, 1957), pp. 415-31.

10. In this context attention should be directed to the extraordinary life of Aimé Pallière (1875-1949), "marked by the double
seal of the Synagogue and the Church" [Alain Guichard, Les Juifs
(Paris: Grasset, 1969), p. 196]. Born a Catholic, intending to
become a priest, Pallière entered a synagogue on the Day of Atone-
ment, at the age of 16. Henceforth his life was torn between Judaism and Catholicism. He converted to Judaism in 1900, and for
years took an active part in Jewish affairs. In 1942 he was re-
conciled with the Church, yet did not break with the Synagogue.
He died a Christian on December 24, 1949, in a Benedictine abbey,
and asked that the Kaddish be prayed over him. His main work,
Le Sanctuaire inconnu, was published in 1950 by Editions de Minuit.

11. "For Jews, the conviction that conversion is the Christian intent behind every discussion of religious matters, as was
openly the case in the compulsory debates sponsored by the Church
in the Middle Ages, has stifled dialogue before it could begin." D.
N. Freedman, Journal of Ecumenical Studies, Vol. 6 (Winter 1969),
No. 1, p. 82.

12. This question was raised by H. Gollwitzer, in an unpublished interview in Berlin, in May 1970. It seems also to be
implied when P. Démann expresses doubts as to the Christian's
"right" to separate the Jew from his people--see Chapter IV.

13. See his article "Judenchristentum heute," Saat auf Hoffnung 73 (1950), pp. 156-57.

14. C. E. Florival, "Divided Christendom in Relation to
Judaism," SIDIC (Service international de documentation judéo-
chretienne), Vol. III, No. 3 (1970), p. 17.

15. See Werner Schochow, Deutsch-jüdische Geschichtwiss-
enschaft, p. 65.

CHAPTER III

1. Renate Maria Heydenreich, "Fortdauer der Ratlosigkeit
1945-1950," Ungekündigte Bund, pp. 248-71. On the resumption
of contact between Jews and Christians, see also Günther Harder,
"Christen vor dem Problem der Judenfrage. Evangelische-
jüdisches Gegenüber seit 1945," Christen und Juden, pp. 251-69.

2. Quoted by Ruth Rouse, "Voluntary Movements and the

Changing Ecumenical Climate," in A History of the Ecumenical Movement, 1517-1948, ed. by Ruth Rouse and Stephen Charles Neill (Philadelphia: Westminster Press, 1967, 2d & rev. ed.), p. 314.

3. The same scholarliness and thoroughness characterize a companion volume, Das Gespaltene Gottesvolk, ed. by Helmut Gollwitzer and Eleonore Sterling (Stuttgart: Kreuz-Verlag, 1966), which grew out of the DEK held in Dortmund in 1963, and in Cologne in 1965. Both volumes are invaluable tools for a study of Judaism and the Church in post-war Germany.

4. A comprehensive summary of the main criticisms, as well as some .of the replies, is provided by Hansgeorg Schroth, "Auseinandersetzung mit der Pressekritik," Ungekündigte Bund, pp. 161-81.

5. This is a free rendering of the German, "man möchte den Pelz waschen, ohne ihn nass zu machen," Ungekündigte Bund, p. 13.

6. The most negatively critical articles were the following: C. Hummel, in Christ und Welt, July 28 (1961); Paul Reinhardt and Kurt Wendlandt, in Lutherische Monatshefte, I, No. 2 (1962) and I, No. 7 (1962); J. K. Mehl, "Kirche und Synagoge," in Gottesdienst und Kirchenmusik, 5, No. 61. See also Paul Reinhardt, "Zur gegenwärtigen Diskussion des Verhältnisses von Kirche und Judentum," Friede über Israel (1963) No. 4, pp. 99-111.

7. Respectively, in: Christ und Welt (quoted in Ungekündigte Bund, p. 161); Paul Reinhardt in Lutherische Monatshefte, I, No. 2, (1962), p. 77; Kurt Wendlandt, ibid., p. 82; Ibid., p. 83.

8. Lutherische Monatshefte, I, No. 2 (1962), p. 83.

9. Ibid., p. 76.

10. "Kirche und Synagoge," p. 19. In a 1963 article, in which he reviews the Kirchentag, Reinhardt gives even stronger emphasis to what he considers a serious failure: "It probably was no mere coincidence that in the detailed bibliography of the Ungekündigte Bund Judenmission is, for all practical purposes, not mentioned. Even the Institutum Judaicum Delitzschianum is not mentioned as a missonary institute, although several of its publications are mentioned.... Nor is it surprising that during the 1961 Kirchentag itself Judenmission was mentioned only with negative accents.... This negative evaluation of Judenmission seems no accident to me, but rather to result from an attitude which is un-

willing to give to Israel that unequivocal witness of its Messiah, Jesus Christ, which the New Testament lays upon us." Paul Reinhardt, "Zur gegenwärtigen Diskussion," p. 105.

11. Lutherische Monatshefte, I, No. 2 (1962), p. 77; and No. 7 (1962), p. 327.

12. "Nicht Mission, sondern Gespräch," Ungekündigte Bund, pp. 138-41.

13. Established in 1960, the Institute carries on important research work under Harder's assistant, Dr. Ursula Bohn. A bulletin, Institut Kirche und Judentum, makes this work available to pastors and religious educators.

14. Not only Harder, but most theologians treating of Israel and the Church, pay special attention today to Romans 9-11. It was not always so. Indeed, until Barth used this text for his theology of election (KD II/2, No. 34, 1942), these chapters were almost totally ignored with regard to Israel in the history of Christianity. And yet, today they have become the New Testament locus theologicus for any Christian theology of Israel, and no serious study of this subject can fail to take them into account. The decision not to devote a section of the present work to contemporary commentaries grew out of the realization that, because Paul is not at all concerned in this text with the question of Christianity's mission to Israel, these commentaries shed little light on the question of Judenmission. As Krister Stendahl writes in his Introduction to J. Munck's Christ and Israel, "At no point does Paul urge the gentiles to carry on a mission for the purpose of converting Jews" (Philadelphia: Fortress Press, 1967), p. ix.

15. Reinhardt, Lutherische Monatshefte, I, No. 2 (1962), pp. 76-81.

16. Lutherische Monatshefte, I, No. 7 (1962), p. 325. A passage by Franz Rosenzweig illustrates the gap that still exists today between the Christian view of the Jew and Jewish self-understanding, even in the case of Christian theologians who are sympathetically inclined toward Judaism: "Christianity acknowledges the God of the Jews, not as God but as 'The Father of Jesus Christ.' Christianity itself cleaves to the 'Lord' for all time, until the end of the world, but then he will cease to be the Lord, and he too will be subject to the Father who will, on this day, be all in all .... No one can reach the Father! But the situation is quite different for one who does not have to reach the Father because he is already with him. And this is true of the people of Israel (though not of individual Jews). Chosen by the Father, the people of Israel gazes fixedly across the world and history, over to that last, most distant time when the Father, the One and Only, will be 'all

in all.' Then, when Christ ceases to be the Lord, Israel will cease
to be the chosen people.... But until that day dawns, the lifework
of Israel is to anticipate the eternal day, in profession and in action, to be its living presage, to hallow the name of God through
its, Israel's, own holiness and with its Law as a people of priests."
Franz Rosenzweig, from a letter written to Rudolf Ehrenberg,
cited in Nahum N. Glatzer, Franz Rosenzweig, His Life and
Thought (New York, 1953), pp. 341-42 (emphasis added).

17.   The paper appears in Ungekündigte Bund, pp. 145-59,
under the title, "Das christlich-jüdische Gespräch im Verhältnis
zum christlichen Zeugnis an Israel." Although no explicit reference
is made to the Kirchentag controversy, Harder is obviously concerned to alleviate fears that his views imply "Judaization" or a betrayal of the Gospel. Even though the articles in Lutherische Monatshefte began to appear only in January 1962, those by Mehl and
Hummel had been published during the summer of 1961; nor could
Harder have been unaware by this time of the mounting criticism
that was about to appear in the press.

18.   "Allerdings kann das Zeugnis in seiner Ausschliesslich-
keit (Acts 4:12, "No other name is given to men for salvation")
dem Judentum nicht einräumen, dass es als solches vollgültiger
Weg zu Gott ist. Es spricht ihm seine Sonderstellung und Erwähl-
ung nicht ab, aber es kann ihm als solchem das Heil, die endzeit-
liche Errettung, nicht zusprechen." Ungekündigte Bund, p. 146.

19.   Given the contradictions in this statement, one might
ask in what way the scriptures are still "the book of the Jews."

20.   Four years later, at the 1965 Kirchentag in Cologne,
in his commentary on Romans 11:16-24, Harder seems to attribute
a lesser place to Judenmission. Looking forward to the day when
the natural olive branches will be grafted back on, he maintains
that this will happen, "not through the efforts of Christian missionary work, but solely through God's power." Das Gespaltene
Gottesvolk, pp. 110-11.

21.   Paul Reinhardt is of the opinion that the "excitement
which was so rightly aroused by AG VI" should have come about
much earlier: after the Evanston Conference of the WCC in 1954,
"at the least." For on that occasion, the recommendation that the
theme of the Conference, "Christ, the Hope of the World," include
a statement about "Christ, the hope of Israel," was rejected by a
majority, which feared that the missionary implications of such a
statement would alienate Jews. P. Reinhardt, "Zur gegenwärtigen
Diskussion," p. 109. It is Reinhardt's view, in other words, that
the General Assembly gravely failed in one of its central obliga-
tions.

22.   These ambiguities are well brought out by Reinhardt in
his article, "Zur gegenwärtigen Diskussion." Reinhardt represents,
of course, the position of the critics of the Kirchentag and the

advocates of Judenmission. While one may disagree with his premises, his pinpointing of theological questions seems accurate.

CHAPTER IV

1. Das Gespaltene Gottesvolk. Im Auftrag der Arbeitsgemeinschaft Juden und Christen beim Deutschen Evangelischen Kirchentag, ed. by H. Gollwitzer and E. Sterling (Stuttgart: Kreuz-Verlag, 1966).

2. See Willem Adolf Visser 't Hofft, "The Word 'Ecumenical'--History and Use," A History of the Ecumenical Movement, 1517-1948, pp. 735-40. For a fuller treatment, cf. Visser 't Hofft, The Meaning of Ecumenical (The Burge Memorial Lecture, 1953), London, 1953. The third edition of RGG, 1960, lists seven different meanings of the term, only the last two of which pertain to Christian unity; see RGG³ Vol. IV, col. 1569.

3. Quoted by Alan T. Davies, Antisemitism and the Christian Mind. The Crisis of Conscience after Auschwitz (New York: Herder and Herder, 1969), p. 155. Frequent use will be made of Davies in this section; much of his interpretation is highly plausible.

4. John Thomas McNeill, "The Ecumenical Idea and Efforts to Realize It, 1517-1618," in A History of the Ecumenical Movement, p. 27.

5. Neill, "Epilogue," ibid., p. 725.

6. Brown, The Ecumenical Revolution. An Interpretation of the Catholic-Protestant Dialogue (New York: Doubleday, 1967), pp. 247-48.

7. Respectively, in "Introduction," The Church and the Jewish People, pp. 11-25; and "Introduction," Ecumenical Movement, p. 6.

8. It may also be pointed out that, whereas this approach takes the divisions within the people of God back from the Great Schism of the 16th century to the first, another "variant" goes yet further back, and considers the schism between Israel and the Church as only one in a series of schisms that began with the separation between the Northern and Southern Kingdoms in the eighth century B.C. This is the view of Skydsgaard, "Israel, the Church and the Unity," Lutheran World, X, no. 4 (October 1963), p. 349f. Karl Thieme speaks of the break between Christianity and Judaism as neither the first nor the last schism in salvation history. Freiburger Rundbrief, VIII, 1955, quoted in Davies, p. 95.

9. "Le schisme dans le cadre de l'économie divine," Irénikon, Vol. 21, 1st Quarter, (1948), pp. 6-31. A section from

this article appears on pp. 263-66 of Gespaltene Gottesvolk. References here are to the French original. According to Davies, there is some doubt whether Oehmen's ideas originated with him or with the Protestant Jean Louis Leuba--cf. Antisemitism [note 3], p. 92. Is is this article and his use of the schism concept that make Oehmen important theologically with regard to Judaism and Christianity.

10. Although a Frenchman, formerly editor of Les Cahiers Sioniens, Démann's writings are widely known in Germany and translated, as are those of his fellow countrymen, Bernard Lambert, and Kurt Hruby; the latter is his successor as editor of Cahiers Sioniens.

11. "Israel et l'unité de l'Eglise," Cahiers Sioniens VII, No. 1, (March 1953), pp. 17-24. Excerpts from this article appeared under the title, "Jüdisch-christliche und innerkirchliche Komplimentarität," Gespaltene Gottesvolk, pp. 256-60; our references are to the latter.

12. Gespaltene Gottesvolk, p. 258. The concepts "reintegration," "restoration of unity," "reunion," etc., seem to us to raise a basic question with regard to the ecumenical movement in general, and the schism proponents in particular. What was the nature of that original "unity" in the early days of Christianity, before the official break with Judaism? Was there not a far greater diversity and plurality, both of life and belief, than is often assumed? While there is no denying a perennial nostalgia for a once-existing and subsequently lost unity--see Neill, Ecumenical Movement, p. 24--one wonders whether it corresponds to historical reality, and whether the achievement of true unity is not exclusively reserved for the future, in a "shape" that cannot be determined.

13. It seems to us that this goes back to much earlier times. Take, for instance, the following statement by Luther, quoted approvingly by Wendlandt in Lutherische Monatshefte, February 1962, p. 82: "For whatever is outside Christendom, whether it be pagans, Turks, Jews or false Christians and hypocrites, even if they believe in and worship only one God, they do not know what he intends for them ... hence they remain in eternal wrath and damnation. For they do not have the Lord Christ, nor are they graced and enlightened with gifts through the Holy Spirit."

14. Davies speaks of them as Catholic "radical theologians" with regard to Judaism; see Antisemitism, pp. 91-107.

15. Without wishing to lessen the importance of Romans, does not the Old Testament itself give ample evidence of God's unshakeable love for and fidelity to his people? Cf. only these few texts: Ex. 17:7; Hos. 2:19-21; Jer. 31:3; Ps. 105:8; Ps. 148:14.

16. "Israel und die Kirche," p. 279. This would seem to be an ambiguous formulation, for it lends itself to the interpretation

that, ideally, Israel should be absorbed by the Church. It brings us back to the question raised earlier (note 12), What kind of unity is envisaged? Restoration, reunion, sameness, uniformity, or something that has never yet existed and the nature of which cannot be predicted?

17. The vehemence of the 1961 Kirchentag controversy, where all the chief critics were Lutherans--not surprisingly, since the DEK is a Lutheran Church meeting--as well as the 19th-century Judenmission, carried on largely by Lutherans, seem to bear this out, at least for Germany. What, however, of the "Catholic liability" of having for centuries claimed to be the sole possessor of absolute truth?

18. Démann points out that the increased missionary activity during the 19th century, while undoubtedly leading to some sincere conversions, on the whole--and understandably--increased Jewish mistrust of Christians; ibid., pp. 275-76.

19. Baptism invariably, throughout Jewish history, was--and still is--considered a radical separation and betrayal of the Jewish people. See Chapter II.

20. "Israel und die Kirche," p. 280. One might question this argument on at least two counts. First, must Romans 9-11 be made into an absolute? Secondly, it is based on a Christian interpretation of Jewish history. The Jew finds ample meaning in his history over the past 19 centuries apart from Paul and the Church.

21. An essay by Spaemann, "Die Christen und das Volk der Juden. Gedanken zur kommenden Konzilserklärung über die Juden," first appeared in Hochland LVII, June 1965. An excerpt was reprinted under the title, "Gnadenaustausch zwischen alt-und neubundlichem Gottesvolk," in Gespaltene Gottesvolk, pp. 261-62. These pages later became, with some slight changes, the concluding chapter to Spaemann's book, Die Christen und das Volk der Juden (Münich: Kösel, 1966). The quotations in this section are from the latter, unless otherwise indicated.

22. Ibid., p. 28. The phrase, "die Fortexistenz der Synagoge," recurs on p. 40 in a similar context. The impression it conveys is that the continued existence of the Synagogue is something that ought not to be--a mishap, due to Christian lack of brotherly love.

23. Ibid., p. 49 (emphasis in original). It is interesting to compare this text with one by Abbé Henri Grégoire, an 18th-century Churchman and champion of equal citizenship rights for Jews. He too exhorts Christians to show love to their Jewish brothers. But his conclusion is totally free from that "ulterior motive" one so often detects in Christian theologians, including Spaemann: that greater Christian charity will make possible the Jews' recognition of Christ, a view that was already propounded by Luther in the mildest

of his "Judenschriften," Dass Jesus Christus ein geborener Jude sei.
Here is the pertinent passage from Grégoire: "Give them homes
where they may rest their heads in peace and dry their tears.
Then the Jew will return tenderness to the Christian and embrace
in me his fellow citizen and his friend." Essai sur la régénération
physique, morale et politique des Juifs (Metz, 1789), p. 194; quoted
in John M. Oesterreicher, The Rediscovery of Judaism: A Re-Examination of the Conciliar Statement on the Jews (Seton Hall University, N.J.: The Institute of Judaeo-Christian Studies, 1971), p. 44.

24. See Rosenzweig's "We are already with the Father,"
Chapter III, note 16.

25. "Kirche aus Heiden ohne Juden"--a probable reference
to Erik Peterson's now classic Kirche aus Juden und Heiden.

26. "Kirche und Israel," pp. 77-78.

27. Ibid., p. 78.

28. Ibid., p. 19.

29. Jacob B. Agus, in Jean Daniélou, Dialogue with Israel
(Baltimore: Helicon, 1968), pp. 123-24. Agus goes on to suggest
that we need each other "to breathe freely and grow straight. Does
the Divine 'mystery,' perhaps consist in this very need?" Ibid.,
p. 124.

30. See the detailed commentary of the Declaration's history by John M. Oesterreicher, "Erklärung über das Verhältnis der
Kirche zu den nichtchristlichen Religionen," Lexikon für Theologie
und Kirche (Freiburg: Herder, 1967), 426-67.

31. "Israel, the Church, and the Unity of the People of God,"
Lutheran World X, No. 4 (October, 1963), p. 351.

32. "Kirche und Synagoge," p. 11. The word "pagan" is
used here, since it reflects Mehl's attitude accurately.

33. A report of this meeting appeared in Israelitisches
Wochenblatt für die Schweiz, No. 15, (1950), p. 26f. and, based upon this, in Freiburger Rundbrief, 7 (1950), p. 20. The source here
is the latter.

34. "Judenmission und Heidenmission," first published in
Lutherische Monatshefte, II, No. 1 (1963). It was reprinted, with
some additions, in Judaica 19 (1963), pp. 113-126; references here
are to the latter.

35. Ernst Ludwig Ehrlich, "Der Stand des Gespräches
zwischen Christen und Juden," Christlich-judisches Forum, No. 24,
(October 1960), pp. 1-5.

36. Walter Holsten, "Ökumenische Probleme in der zweiten Jahrhunderthälfte, III; Das Problem Israel?, Lutherische Monatshefte, III, No. 11, (1964), pp. 506-17.

37. Ibid., p. 517. Gollwitzer expresses a similar view. Election is for the sake of mission, of service. Those to whom we are sent are not "object of mission," we go out to serve them ("Adressaten des Dienstes"). Helmut Gollwitzer, "Ausser Christus kein Heil? (Johannes 14:6)," Antijudaismus im Neuen Testament?, ed. by W. Eckert, N. P. Levinson, and M. Stöhr (Munich: Kaiser, 1967), pp. 185-86.

38. See Jaspers, "Gibt es für die Kirche heute einen Sendungsauftrag an Israel?" Judaica 17 (1961), p. 136.

CHAPTER V

1. See Jakob J. Petuchowski, "The Christian-Jewish Dialog: A Jewish View," Lutheran World X, No. 4 (October 1963), p. 273.

2. See Eckert, "Geehrte und geschändete Synagoge," Christen und Juden, pp. 98-103.

3. See Rengstorf, "Begegnung statt Bekehrung," p. 266, on this epoch-making event; also Leonhard Goppelt, "Israel and the Church in Today's Discussion and in Paul," Lutheran World X, No. 4 (October 1963), p. 355.

4. On the various attitudes within the Jewish community, cf. Henry Siegman, "Dialogue with Christians: a Jewish Dilemma," Judaism, Vol. 20, No. 1 (Winter 1971), pp. 93-103.

5. Cohen, The Myth of the Judeo-Christian Tradition, p. 52. Manfred Vogel also discusses the importance to dialogue of both "kinship" and difference, in "The Problem of Dialogue between Judaism and Christianity," Journal of Ecumenical Studies IV, No. 4, (Winter 1967), pp. 684-99.

6. E.g., the Statement issued in 1964 at Løgumkloster by the Consultation for "The Church and the Jewish People," which had been established by the Lutheran World Federation.

7. Becker, "Gibt es ein Zeugnis der Kirche für die Juden?," Das Zeugnis der Kirche für die Juden, ed. by Reinhard Dobbert (Berlin: Lutherisches Verlagshaus, 1968), "... nicht überredet, sondern überzeugt." It is not clear precisely wherein the distinction lies. Moreover, even if this was the Church's concept of mission "in theory," the gap between theory and practice is too glaring to enable one to take this view seriously. See the remarks about the history of enforced conversion, at the beginning of Chapter I.

8. See Anker Gjerding, "Kirche und Judentum in der

Ökumene," in Die Hoffnung der Kirche und die Zukunft Israels, Sondernummer, Summer 1969, p. 50.

9. "Judenmission oder Gespräch?", in Der Zeuge, 3. Folge, No. 32, Jg. 15 (January 1965), p. 9, although Grolle, as shall be seen, also advocates dialogue on theological grounds.

10. "Ist nicht der jüdische Weg der Theologie, der Weg des ständigen Fragens und Infragestellens, der Einbeziehung der gesamten, auch widersprüchlichen Tradition, das Verzichtes auf eine Systematisierung, ja auf eine Einheit oder gar ein Material-prinzip der Heiligen Schrift, der Geschichtlichkeit der Offenbarung Gottes angemessener als die christliche dogmatische Tradition?" Stöhr, Diskussionsbericht," in Antijudaismus im Neuen Testament?, p. 196.

CHAPTER VI

1. It should be noted that such a view is not found in the New Testament texts. In the Synoptic Gospels, and more rarely in John, "Israel" refers to the Jewish people, as people of God, and is not yet applied to the Christian community. The same is true of Paul. However, his phrase, "the Israel of God" (Gal. 6:16) approaches the usage that was later to become common.

2. This phrase is used with an awareness that a distinction must be made between "Church" and "People of God." As Küng points out, "the concept of the Church can rightly be applied to the Christian Churches which compose a community of baptized Christians united by the message of the New Testament, believing in Christ the Lord, celebrating the Lord's Supper, trying to live according to the gospels and wishing to be regarded by the world as a Church. It seems mistaken, however, to extend the concept of the Church to people who do not belong to a community believing in and publicly acknowledging Christ...." Küng, The Church, p. 317.

3. See H. Cazelles, Naissance de l'Eglise, secte juive rejetée? Paris 1968; see also Krister Stendahl, "Judaism and Christianity: a Plea for a new Relationship," Harvard Divinity Bulletin (Fall 1967), reprinted in Cross Currents 17 (1967) 445-458.

4. The Viennese Lutheran theologian, Wilhelm Dantine, also argues against the Church's seeing itself "also" as people of God on two counts. Either, this will lead the Church to seeing itself as the "true" and "better" Israel, or, it will make it into a "Jewish variant, a Jewish sect, a kind of Reform Judaism...." "Kirche als Israel Gottes und das Problem der Judenmission, Jüdisches Volk--gelobtes Land, p. 324; see also Küng, The Church, pp. 107-113.

5. H. Diem, "Predigt über Römer 11:33-36," originally published in Predigten aus Ebersbach (Stuttgart: Kohlhammer, 1948), and reprinted in Das Rätsel des Antisemitismus,

Theologische Existenz heute, No. 80 (Münich: Kaiser, 1960), pp. 18-22; the quotation is taken from the latter.

6. Kraus, "Von der Eigenart des hebräischen Denkens," Begegnung mit dem Judentum, pp. 28-52; also "Treue und Hoffnung der Juden," ibid., pp. 52-70. Spaemann's assessment of the Church's impoverishment through the loss of Judaism has already been mentioned--see Chapter IV, "Israel's Return."

7. This view, by a Christian, of Israel's role is echoed thirty years later by Elie Wiesel: "I think we Jews are the question mark of mankind, and that in creating us God chose thus to question mankind. Which is the reason, perhaps, why we seem to be the center of so many tales, often not our own." Elie Wiesel, Jewish Legends: The Image of the Jew in Literature. New York, Catholic Archdiocese of New York and the Anti-Defamation League of B'nai B'rith, Teachers' Study Guide, p. 10.

8. The phrase is the title of an article by J. Coert Rylaarsdam: "Common Ground and Difference," The Journal of Religion, Vol. 43, No. 4 (October 1968), pp. 261-70.

9. Josef Klausner, Jesus of Nazareth, His Life, Times and Teachings (New York: Macmillan, 1929). David Flusser, Jesus (New York: Herder and Herder, 1969). Robert Aron, The Jewish Jesus (Maryknoll, N.Y.: Orbis Books, 1971). H. J. Schoeps, Jewish Christianity (Philadelphia: Fortress Press, 1969). Jules Isaac, Jesus and Israel (New York: Holt, Rinehart and Winston, 1969).

10. It should be pointed out that interest among Jewish scholars today is not confined to Jesus, but extends even to Paul-- long considered the arch-enemy of Judaism and source of many of its problems with Christianity. See, e.g., H. J. Schoeps, Paul, The Theology of the Apostle in the Light of Jewish Religious History (Philadelphia: Westminster, 1961).

11. M. Buber, Christus, Chassidismus, Gnosis, quoted in Versuche des Verstehens, p. 129. See also Donald J. Moore, "Martin Buber on Jesus: a Jewish Reading," America Magazine, June 13, 1970.

12. The German word is "Heimholung." After tracing the change among Jews toward Jesus, from hatred to appreciation, Hug labels this arrogant usurpation, and useless to boot: for how can we hope to paint a picture of Jesus? All we know is that "Jesus is Christ, King of the Jews, Savior of the world." The Jews reject this confession of the Church, seeking to put into its place something of their own making. H. Hug, Das Volk Gottes: Der Kirche Bekenntnis zur Judenfrage (Zürich: Zollikon, 1942, pp. 47ff.). Despite the author's good intentions, the book, in the present author's opinion, only perpetuates the old stereotypes.

13. A striking exception to this, and one of the most fascinating episodes in Jewish history, is the case of Sabbatai Zevi in 17th-century Poland. After proclaiming himself as Messiah and being hailed as such by the Jews of his time, Sabbatai Zevi went over to Islam, thus committing apostasy. While the mainstream of rabbinic Judaism disclaimed him from that moment on, belief in his mission and role lived on among a not inconsiderable number of his followers, and gave rise to two heretical sects within Judaism, the Sabbatians and the Frankists, who survived into the 19th century. New light has recently been shed on this obscure chapter in Jewish history by Gershom Scholem, in "The Holiness of Sin," Commentary, Vol. 51 No. 1 (January 1971), pp. 41-70. This is the first English translation of the author's essay written originally in Hebrew in the mid-thirties. It is reprinted in the Messianic Idea in Judaism (New York: Schocken Books, 1971).

14. See Gollwitzer, "Ausser Christus kein Heil? (Johannes 14:6)," Antijudaismus im Neuen Testament?, pp. 171-72.

15. "Geht es nicht um eine völlige Neurorientierung der Christologie in der Dimension der Geschichte, um ein viel konzentrierteres und klareres Bezugnehemen auf das Alte Testament?"

16. Another persuasive school of thought believes that the early Creeds were formulated by the Church as a safeguard against Greek speculation. Thus, Jaroslav Pelikan, The Emergence of the Catholic Tradition (100-600).

17. Once again, however, too much optimism must be cautioned against. The positions just described are by no means those of a majority. Thus, for Gerhard Jaspers, the reconsideration of Christology forced upon Christians by their encounter with Judaism means something quite different. It will help Christians realize that, all too often, they profess "only the first article of the Creed. This cannot attract Jews, since they themselves subscribe to an 'ethical monotheism'." For Jaspers, Christians will be driven to a recommitment to and reaffirmation of classical Christological creedal formulations. Gerhard Jaspers, "Gibt es für die Kirche heute einen Sendungsauftrag an Israel?" Judaica, 17 (1961), p. 138.

18. H. J. Schoeps, "Probleme der christlich-jüdischen Verständigung," in Welt ohne Hass (Berlin: Christian Verlag, 1950), pp. 70-80. Schoeps' essay originally appeared in the form of a letter in 1939 and is quoted as such--disapprovingly--by H. Hug, Das Volk Gottes, p. 151.

CONCLUDING REMARKS

1. These words were spoken by Heschel during the early debates of Vatican II, when the Declaration on the Jews included--or seemed to Heschel to include--reference to the Jews' conversion; quoted by Robert McAfee Brown, The Ecumenical Revolution, p. 269.

2. John M. Oesterreicher distinguishes between what he
calls the "inner mission" of the Church, whereby it bears witness
to Christ by its very presence and even without preaching, and organized missionary activity. Speaking for the Roman Catholic
Church he states, "There is in the Church today no drive, no organized effort to proselytize Jews, and none is contemplated for to-
morrow." Rediscovery of Judaism, p. 39.

3. See also Romans 11:33-34, where Paul, after wrestling
with the destiny of Israel for three chapters, gives up and exclaims:
"O the depth of the riches and wisdom and knowledge of God! How
unsearchable are his judgments and how inscrutable his ways! For
who has known the mind of the Lord, or who has been his counsel-
or?' "

4. Prior to this, on November 16, 1955, the Sacred Congregation of Rites ordered that the invitation to kneel ("flectamus
genua") be used with all the Good Friday prayers of intercession.
It had previously been omitted from the Prayer for the Jews. On
the history of this rubric, see John M. Oesterreicher, "Pro perfidis
Judaeis, Theological Studies, Vol. VIII, No. 1 (March 1947), pp.
87-95.

5. Alfred Schilling, Motivmessen I. Thematische Messformulare für jeden Tag (Essen: Verlag Hans Driewer, 1970).

6. We are indebted to Msgr. John Oesterreicher not only for
calling our attention to this mass, but also for supplying us with his
translation of the texts. H. Spaemann had pleaded for such a "vot-
ive mass" in 1966, and made some suggestions for the texts that
could be used. See his Die Christen und das Volk der Juden, pp.
50-51.

7. See Freiburger Rundbrief, August 1950, 8/9, pp. 5-12,
for an annotated text and history of the "Seelisberger" and "Schwal-
bacher Thesen."

8. The catechetical work of the Pedagogical Institute at Duisburg should also be mentioned. Under the direction of Prof. Kremers, the program is specifically aimed at educating teachers in a
new attitude toward Israel and influencing textbooks. The most recent addition to the program is a research seminar on the topic,
"Judaism in Religious Education."

9. This writer is not likely ever to forget her first meeting
with Rabbi X. Asked whether she knew anything at all about Judaism,
she replied, "I have a fairly good knowledge of scripture." Rabbi
X responded, with some exasperation, "I wish you Christians would
stop thinking of us as the people of the Bible!"

10. Thus, e.g., Elie Wiesel, One Generation After, and
Emil Fackenheim, "Jewish Faith and the Holocaust," Commentary
August 1968, pp. 30-36.

SELECTED BIBLIOGRAPHY

1. Collections of works by several authors are listed
alphabetically by titles. The same works appear in
Section 2 of the Bibliography, under the editor's name.

Antijudaismus im Neuen Testament? Exegetische und systematische
Beiträge. Edited by Willehad Paul Eckert, Nathan Peter Levinson, and Martin Stöhr. (Vol. 2 of Abhandlungen zum christlich-jüdischen Dialog, edited by Helmut Gollwitzer.) Munich:
Kaiser, 1967.

Auf den Trümmern des Tempels: Land und Bund Israels in Dialog
zwischen Christen und Juden. Edited by Clemens Thoma.
Vienna: Herder, 1968.

Brothers in Hope; Vol. V, The Bridge. (Judaeo-Christian Studies)
Edited by John Oesterreicher. New York: Herder and Herder, 1970.

The Church and the Jewish People. Edited by Göte Hedenquist.
London: Edinburgh House Press, 1954.

Christen und Juden: Ihr Gegenüber vom Apostelkonzil bis heute.
Edited by Wolf-Dieter Marsch and Karl Thieme. Mainz:
Matthias-Grünewald Verlag, 1961.

Entscheidungsjahr 1932: Zur Judenfrage in der Endphase der Weimarer Republik. Ein Sammelband. Edited by Werner E.
Mosse. Tübingen: Mohr, 1965.

Das Gespaltene Gottesvolk: Im Auftrag der Arbeitsgemeinschaft
Juden und Christen beim deutschen evangelischen Kirchentag.
Edited by Helmut Gollwitzer and Elenore Sterling. Stuttgart:
Kreuz-Verlag, 1966.

A History of the Ecumenical Movement, 1517-1948. Edited by Ruth
Rouse and Stephen Charles Neill. Philadelphia: Westminster,
1967 (1st ed. 1954).

Die Hoffnung der Kirche und die Zukunft Israels: Sonderheft der
Handreichung des Evangeliumsdienstes. Hrsg. von Reinhard
Dobbert, im Auftrag des Arbeitskreises "Kirche und Judentum:
der VELKD." Neuendettelsau: Freimund-Druckerei, 1969.

Israel und die Kirche: Eine Studie, im Auftrag der Generalsynode
der Niederländischen Reformierten Kirche, zusammengestellt
von dem Rat für das Verhältnis zwischen Kirche und Israel.
Zürich: EVZ-Verlag, 1961 (orig. Dutch ed. 1959).

Juden, Christen, Deutsche. Edited by Hans-Jürgen Schulz. Stuttgart: Kreuz-Verlag, 1961.

Judenhass--Schuld der Christen?! Versuch eines Gesprächs. Edited by W. P. Eckert and Emil-Ludwig Ehrlich. Essen: Hans
Driewer Verlag, 1964.

Jüdisches Volk--gelobtes Land: Die biblischen Landverheissungen
als Problem des jüdischen Selbstverständnisses und der christlichen Theologie. Edited by W. P. Eckert, N. P. Levinson,
and Martin Stöhr. (Vol. 3 of Abhandlungen zum christlich-
jüdischen Dialog. Edited by Helmut Gollwitzer.) Munich:
Kaiser, 1970.

Judentum und christlicher Glaube: Zum Dialog zwischen Christen
und Juden. Edited by Clemens Thoma. Klosterneuburg:
Klosterneuburger Buch- und Kunstverlag, 1965.

Kirche und Synagoge. Edited by K. H. Rengstorf and Siegfried von
Kortzfleisch. (Handbuch zur Geschichte von Christen und Ju-
den. Darstellung mit Quellen.) Stuttgart: Ernst Klett Verlag
Vol 1, 1968; Vol 11, 1970.

Der Ungekündigte Bund: Neue Begegnung von Juden und christlicher
Gemeinde. Edited by Dietrich Goldschmidt and Hans-Joachim
Kraus. Stuttgart: Kreuz-Verlag, 1962.

Unwiderrufliche Verheissung: Die religiöse Bedeutung des Staates
Israel. Edited by Waldemar Molinski. Recklinghausen:
Paulus Verlag, 1968.

Versuche des Verstehens. Dokumente jüdisch-christlicher Begegnung aus den Jahren 1918-1933. Edited by Robert Raphael
Geis and Hans-Joachim Kraus. (Theologische Bücherei. Neu-
drucke und Berichte aus dem 20. Jahrhundert; Vol. 33 of
Systematische Theologie.) Munich: Kaiser, 1966.

Viva Vox Evangelii: Festschrift für Hans Meiser. Munich, 1951.

Welt ohne Hass: Aufsätze und Ansprachen zum I. Kongress über
bessere menschliche Beziehungen in München. Berlin: Christian Verlag, 1950.

Das Zeugnis der Kirche für die Juden: Missionierende Gemeinde,
Heft 16. Im Auftrag des Arbeitskreises der Vereinigten
Evangelisch-Lutherischen Kirche Deutschlands für Kirche und
Judentum. Edited by Reinhard Dobbert. Berlin and Hamburg:
Lutherisches Verlagshaus, 1968.

2. Works listed by Author and/or Editor. Citations to title only appear in full in Section 1 of the Bibliography.

Aron, Robert. The Jewish Jesus. New York: Maryknoll, 1971. (French ed. Ainsi priait Jésus enfant. Paris: Grasset, 1968.)

Baeck, Leo, "Das Judentum auf alten und neuen Wegen." Judaica, Vol. 6 (1950).

_____. "Some Questions to the Christian Church from the Jewish Point of View," in The Church and the Jewish People.

Barkenings, Hans-Joachim. "Die Stimme der Anderen. Der heilsgeschichtliche Beruf Israels in der Sicht evangelischer Theologen des 19. Jahrhunderts," in Christen und Juden.

Barth, Karl. Church Dogmatics. 11/2, #34.

_____. "Die Judenfrage und ihre christliche Beantwortung." Judaica, Vol. 6 (1952), pp. 67-72.

Becker, Horst. "Gibt es ein Zeugnis der Kirche für die Juden?," in Das Zeugnis der Kirche für die Juden.

Ben Chorin, Schalom. "Jüdische Fragen um Christus," in Juden, Christen, Deutsche.

Berkhof, H. "Israel as a Theological Problem." Journal of Ecumenical Studies, Vol. 6, No. 3 (Summer 1969), pp. 329-47.

Bokser, Ben Zion. Judaism and the Christian Predicament. New York: Knopf, 1967.

Bonhoeffer, Dietrich. No Rusty Swords. Letters, Lectures and Notes, 1928-1936. Vol 1 of The Collected Works of Dietrich Bonhoeffer, edited by Edwin H. Robertson. New York: Harper & Row, 1965.

Brown, Robert McAfee. The Ecumenical Revolution: An Interpretation of the Catholic-Protestant Dialogue. New York: Doubleday, 1967.

Buber, Martin. Two Types of Faith. New York: Macmillan, 1951 (Harper Torchbooks, 1961).

Cazelles, Henri. La Naissance de l'Eglise, Secte Juive rejetée? Paris: Editions du Cerf, 1968.

Cohen, Arthur A. The Myth of the Judeo-Christian Tradition. New York: Harper & Row, 1970 (Schocken paperback, 1971).

Daniélou, Jean, S. J. Dialogue with Israel. Baltimore: Helicon, 1968.

Dantine, Wilhelm. "Kirche als Israel Gottes und das Problem der Judenmission," in Jüdisches Volk--gelobtes Land.

"Darstellung des Judentums in der Katechese; Memorandum." Christlich-jüdisches Forum. No. 40 (June 1968), pp. 49-64.

Démann, Paul. "Israel et l'unité de l'Eglise." Cahiers Sioniens, vol. 7, No. 1 (1953), pp. 1-24.

_____. "Kirche und Israel in ökumenischer Sicht. Katholische Besinnung auf Israel seit 1945," in Christen und Juden.

Diem, Hermann. Das Rätsel des Antisemitismus. Vol. 80 of Theologische Existenz heute. Munich: Kaiser, 1960.

Dobbert, Reinhard. "Das Zeugnis der Kirche für die Juden," in Das Zeugnis der Kirche für die Juden.

Dulles, Avery, S. J. "Dogma as an Ecumenical Problem." Theological Studies, Vol. 29, No. 3 (September 1968), pp. 397-416.

Eckert, Willehad Paul. "Geehrte und geschändete Synagoge," in Christen und Juden.

_____, and Ehrlich Ernst-Ludwig, eds. Judenhass--Schuld der Christen?! Versuch eines Gesprächs. Essen: Hans Driewer Verlag, 1964.

_____, Levinson, Nathan Peter, and Stöhr, Martin, eds. Jüdisches Volk--gelobtes Land.

Ehrlich, Ernst-Ludwig. "Emanzipation and christlicher Staat," in Christen und Juden.

_____. "Der Stand des Gespräches zwischen Christen und Juden." Christlich-jüdisches Forum, No. 24 (October 1960), pp. 1-5.

Elenchus Bibliographicus. Edited by Peter Nober, S. J. Biblica. Rome. Pontificum Institutum Biblicum.

Ellison, H. L. "The Church and the Hebrew Christian," in The Church and the Jewish People.

Fackenheim, Emil. "Jewish Faith and the Holocaust, a Fragment." Commentary, Vol. 64, No. 2 (August 1968), pp. 30-36.

_____. Quest for Past and Future: Essays in Jewish Theology. Bloomington: Indiana University Press, 1970.

Florival, Claude E. "Divided Christendom in Relation to Judaism." SIDIC, Vol. 111, No. 3 (1970), pp. 12-18.

Flusser, David. Jesus. New York: Herder and Herder, 1969.

Geis, Robert Raphael, and Kraus, Hans-Joachim, eds. Versuche des Verstehens: Dokumente jüdisch-christlicher Begegnung aus den Jahren 1918-1933. Munich: Kaiser, 1966.

Gjerding, Anker. "Kirche und Judentum in der Ökumene," in Die Hoffnung der Kirche und die Zukunft Israels.

Glatzer, Nahum N. Franz Rosenzweig, His Life and Thought. New York: 1953.

Glick, Ira O. "The Hebrew Christian: A Marginal Religious Group," in The Jews, edited by Marshall Sklare. New York: The Free Press, 1958.

Goldschmidt, Dietrich, and Kraus, Hans-Joachim, eds. Der Ungekündigte Bund.

Gollwitzer, Helmut. "Ausser Christus kein Heil? (Johannes 14:6)," in Antijudaismus im Neuen Testament?

_____, and Sterling, Elenore. Das Gespaltene Gottesvolk.

_____. "Die Judenfrage--eine Christenfrage," in Christen und Juden. Originally as a lecture at the Free University of Berlin, January 29, 1960, and published in "Die Diskussion." Blätter der Deutsch-Israelischen Studiengruppe an der Freien Universitat Berlin, Vol. 1 (December 1960), pp. 1-7.

Goppelt, Leonhard. Christentum und Judentum im zweiten Jahrhundert: Ein Aufriss der Urgeschichte der Kirche. Beiträge zur Förderung der christlichen Theologie. 2. Reihe, Vol. 55. Gütersloh, 1954.

_____. "Israel and the Church in Today's Discussion and in Paul." Lutheran World, X, No. 4 (October 1963), pp. 352-72.

Grass, Günter. "Schwierigkeiten eines Vaters, seinen Kindern Auschwitz zu erklären." Frankfurter Allgemeine Zeitung, Tuesday, June 12, 1970, No. 124, p. 24.

Greive, Hermann. Theologie und Ideologie: Katholizismus und Judentum in Deutschland und Osterreich, 1918-1935. Heidelberg: Lambert Schneider Verlag, 1969.

Grolle, Johan Hendrik. "Judenmission oder Gespräch?" Der Zeuge. 3. Folge, Vol. 15, No. 32 (January, 1965), pp. 4-11.

_____. "Verwandlung, nicht Verwerfung. Dialog statt Mission. Das Wirken des Heiligen Geistes in der Synagoge," in Das Gespaltene Gottesvolk.

Guichard, Alain. Les Juifs. Paris: Grasset, 1969.

Harder, Günther. "Christen vor dem Problem der Judenfrage; Evangelisch-jüdisches Gegenüber seit 1945," in Christen und Juden.

_____. "Das christlich-jüdische Gespräch im Verhältnis zum christlichen Zeugnis an Israel," in Der Ungekündigte Bund.

_____. "Nicht Mission, sondern Gespräch," in Der Ungekündigte Bund.

_____. "Nochmals: Zum Verhältnis von Judentum und Kirche." Lutherische Monatshefte, Vol. 1, No. 7 (1962), pp. 325-26.

Hedenquist, Göte, editor. The Church and the Jewish People. London: Edinburgh House Press, 1954.

Holsten, Walter. "Judenmission und Heidenmission." Judaica, Vol. 19 (1963), pp. 113-126. Also in Lutherische Monatshefte, 11, No. 1 (1963)

_____. Ökumenische Probleme in der zweiten Jahrhunderthälfte, 111; Das Problem Israel." Lutherische Monatshefte, Vol. 111, No. 11 (1964), pp. 506-17.

Hruby, Kurt. "Reflections on Dialogue," in Brothers in Hope, Vol. V: The Bridge.

Hug, Herbert. Das Volk Gottes: Der Kirche Bekenntnis zur Judenfrage. Zürich: Evangelischer Verlag Zollikon, 1942.

Isaac, Jules. Jesus and Israel. New York: Holt, Rinehart and Winston, 1971 (orig. French ed. 1959).

_____. The Teaching of Contempt: Christian Roots of Anti-Semitism. New York: Holt, Rinehart and Winston, 1964 (orig. French ed., 1962).

Jaspers, Gerhard. "Gibt es für die Kirche heute einen Sendungsauftrag an Israel?" Fragen der Judenmission. Judaica, 17 (1961), pp. 129-40

Katcher, Leo. Post-Mortem: The Jews in Germany Today. New York: Delacorte Press, 1968.

Kittel, Gerhard. Die Judenfrage. Stuttgart: Kohlhammer Verlag, 1933.

Klausner, Josef. Jesus of Nazareth: His Life, Times and Teachings. New York: Macmillan, 1929 (Beacon paperback, 1964).

Kraus, Hans-Joachim. Begegnung mit dem Judentum: Das Erbe Israels und die Christenheit. Hamburg: Furche Verlag, 1963.

Kremers, Heinz. "Die réflexion engagée in der politischen Bildung." Pädagogische Rundschau, Vol. 15 (1961), pp. 297 ff.

_____. "Römer 9-11 in Predigt und Unterricht," in Dienst für Schule, Kirche und Staat, Gedenkschrift für Arthur Bach. Heidelberg, 1970.

_____. Das Verhältnis der Kirche zu Israel. Düsseldorf: Presseverband der Evangelischen Kirche im Rheinland, 1965.

Küng, Hans. The Church. New York: Sheed and Ward, 1967.

Leuner, Heinz David. "From Mission to Dialog--Rethinking the Relation of Christians and Jews." Lutheran World, X, No. 4 (October 1963), pp. 385-99.

_____. "Ist die Bezeichnung 'Judenchrist' theologisch richtig?" Pastoraltheologie: Wissenschaft und Praxis. Vol. 55, No. 9 (September 1966), pp. 372-79. Göttingen: Vandenhoeck & Ruprecht.

Lipset, Seymor Martin. "The Socialism of Fools: The New Left calls it 'anti-Zionism,' but it's no different from the anti-Semitism of the Old Right." The New York Times Magazine, January 3, 1971.

Luther, Martin. Dass Jesus Christus ein geborener Jude sei. WA 11; 307-36.

_____. Von den Juden und ihren Lügen. WA 53; 412-52.

Marquardt, Friedrich-Wilhelm. Die Bedeutung der biblischen Landverheissung für die Christen. (Theologische Existenz heute, NF, No. 116.) Munich: Kaiser, 1964.

_____. Die Entdeckung des Judentums für die christliche Theologie: Israel im Denken Karl Barths. Vol. 1 of Abhandlungen zum christlich-jüdischen Dialog, edited by Helmut Gollwitzer. Munich: Kaiser, 1967.

Marsch, Wolf-Dieter, and Thieme, Karl, eds. Christen und Juden.

Mayer, Reinhold. "Das Israel Gottes." Christlich-jüdisches Forum, No. 29 (November 1962), pp. 1-8.

_____. "Israel, Jude, Hebraer," in Theologisches Begriffslexi-

kon zum Neuen Testament, Vol. II. Wuppertal: Theologischer Verlag Brockhaus, 1969.

_____. "Zum Gespräch mit Israel." Arbeiten zur Theologie,
No. 9, edited by Theodor Schlatter, with Alfred Jepsen and
Otto Michel. Stuttgart: Calwer Verlag, 1962.

McNeill, John Thomas. "The Ecumenical Idea and Efforts to Realize It, 1517-1618," in A History of the Ecumenical Movement.

Mehl, Johannes G. "Kirche und Synagoge." Gottesdienst und
Kirchenmusik, No. 5 (1961), pp. 155-71.

Michel, Otto. "Jüdischer und christlicher Erlösungsglaube," in
Juden, Christen, Deutsche.

_____. "Opferbereitschaft für Israel," in In Memoriam Ernst
Lohmeyer. Stuttgart, 1951.

Miskotte, Kornelis Heiko. Das Judentum als Frage an die Kirche.
Vol. 5 of Schriftenreihe für christlich-jüdische Begegnung,
edited by G. Harder and H. H. Esser. Wuppertal: Theologischer Verlag Brockhaus, 1970.

Molinski, Waldemar, ed. Unwilderrufliche Verheissung.

Moore, Donald J. "Martin Buber on Jesus: A Jewish Reading."
America Magazine, Vol. 122. June 13 (1970).

Mosse, Werner Ed., editor. Entscheidungsjahr 1932: Zur Judenfrage in der Endphase der Weimarer Republik. Ein Sammelband. Herausgegeben von Werner E. Mosse, unter Mitwirk-
ung von Arnold Paucker. Tübingen: Mohr, 1965.

Munck, Johannes. Christ and Israel: An Interpretation of Romans 9-11. Philadelphia: Fortress Press, 1967.

Neher, André. L'Existence juive: Solitude et affrontements.
(Collection Esprit.) Paris: Editions du Seuil, 1962.

Oehmen, N. "Le schisme dans le cadre de l'économie divine."
Irénikon, Vol. 21, 1st quarter (1948), pp. 6-31.

Oesterreicher, John M., ed. Brothers in Hope: Vol. V, The
Bridge.

_____. "Declaration on the Relationship of the Church to Non-
Christian Religions, Introduction and Commentary." Com-
mentary on the Documents of Vatican 11. New York: Herder
& Herder, 1968, pp. 1-136. (Published in German; Lexikon
für Theologie und Kirche; Das zweite Vatikanische Konzil,
Dokumente und Kommentare. Edited by Herbert Vorgrimler.

Freiburg: Herder, 1967.)

_____. "Pro perfidis Judaeis," Theological Studies, Vol. 8, No. 1 (March 1947), pp. 87-95.

_____. The Rediscovery of Judaism: A Re-Examination of the Conciliar Statement on the Jews. Institute of Judaeo-Christian Studies: Seton Hall University, 1971.

Pallière, Aimé. Le Sanctuaire inconnu. Paris: Editions de Minuit, 1950.

Petuchowski, Jakob J. "The Christian-Jewish Dialogue: A Jewish View. Lutheran World, 10, No. 4 (October 1963), pp. 273-84.

Rahner, Karl. "Bekenntnis zu Jesus Christus," in Juden, Christen, Deutsche.

Reinhardt, Paul. "Zum Verhältnis von Judentum und Kirche: Synagoge oder Altes Testament?" Lutherische Monatshefte, 1, No. 2 (1964), pp. 76-81.

_____. "Zur gegenwärtigen Diskussion des Verhältnisses von Kirche und Judentum." Friede über Israel, No. 4 (1963), pp. 99-111.

Rengstorf, Karl Heinrich. "Begegnung statt Bekehrung: welchen Sinn kann das jüdisch-christliche Gespräch für Christen haben?," in Juden, Christen, Deutsche.

_____. "Die eine Kirche aus Juden und Heiden," in Viva Vox Evangelii.

_____. Das Institutum Judaicum Delitzschianum 1886-1961. Münster, 1963.

_____, and Kortzfleisch, Siegfried von. Kirche und Synagoge.

Rouse, Ruth, and Neill, Stephen Charles, eds. A History of the Ecumenical Movement, 1517-1948. Philadelphia: Westminster, 1967 (1st ed., 1954).

Rylaardsdam, J. Coert. "The Christian and the Holocaust." New York, 1970 (unpublished paper).

Schilling, Alfred. Motivmessen 1: Thematische Messformulare für jeden Tag. Essen: Hans Driewer Verlag, 1970.

Schmidt, Karl Ludwig. Die Judenfrage im Lichte der Kapital 9-11 des Römerbriefs. (Theologische Studien No. 13.) Zürich: Zollikon, 1943 (2d ed., 1946).

Schochow, Werner. Deutsch-jüdische Geschichtswissenschaft: Eine Geschichte ihrer Organisationsformen unter besonderer Berücksichtigung der Fachbibliographie. Mit einem Geleitwort von Guido Kisch. Vol. 3 of Einzelveröffentlichungen der Historischen Kommission zu Berlin beim Friedrich-Meinecke Institut der Freien Universität Berlin. Berlin: Colloquium Verlag, 1969.

Schoeps, Hans-Joachim. The Jewish-Christian Argument. New York: Holt, Rinehart and Winston, 1963 (Ger. ed.: Israel und die Christenheit, Munich and Frankfurt, 1961).

_____. Jewish Christianity: Factional Disputes in the Early Church. Philadelphia: Fortress Press, 1969 (orig. Ger. ed.: Das Judenchristentum, 1964).

_____. Paul: The Theology of the Apostle in the Light of Jewish Religious History. Philadelphia: Westminster, 1961.

_____. Rückblicke: Die letzten dreissig Jahre (1925-1955) und danach. Berlin: Hande und Spenersche Verlagsbuchhandlung, 1956.

Scholem, Gerschom. "The Holiness of Sin." Commentary, Vol. 51, No. 1 (January 1971), pp. 41-80.

Schroth, Hansgeorg. "Ausverkauf der Kirchengeschichte? Auseinandersetzung mit der evangelischen Pressekritik," in Der Ungekündigte Bund.

Schubert, Kurt. Die Religion des Nachbiblischen Judentums. Freiburg: Herder, 1955.

Schulz, Hans-Jürgen, ed. Juden, Christen, Deutsche.

Sechs Thesen für die Gestaltung der Religionsbücher und des Religionsunterrichts. Bergneustadt, June 4, 1960.

Siegman, Henry. "Dialogue with Christians: A Jewish Dilemma." Judaism, Vol. 20, No. 1 (Winter 1971), pp. 92-103.

Sklare, Marshall, ed. The Jews: Social Patterns of an American Group. New York: The Free Press, 1958.

Skydsgaard, K. E. "Israel, the Church, and the Unity of the People of God." Lutheran World, X, No. 4 (October 1963), pp. 345-51.

Spaemann, Heinrich. Die Christen und das Volk der Juden. Munich: Kösel, 1966.

Stendahl, Krister. "Judaism and Christianity: A Plea for a New Relationship." Harvard Divinity Bulletin, Fall (1967); reprinted in Cross Currents, 17 (1967), pp. 445-58.

Stöhr, Martin. "Diskussionsbericht," in Antijudaismus im Neuen
Testament?

Thoma, Clemens, ed. Auf den Trümmern des Tempels. Vienna:
Herder, 1968.

_____, ed. Judentum und christlicher Glaube.

_____. "Points of Departure," in Brothers in Hope, Vol. V:
The Bridge.

Tillich, Paul. Die Judenfrage: Ein christliches und deutsches
Problem. (Schriftenreihe der Deutschen Hochschule für Politik.) Berlin, 1953.

Wendlandt, Kurt. "Zum Verhältnis von Judentum und Kirche.:
Fragen zur Kirchentagsthese 'Juden und Christen sind unlösbar
verbunden.'" Lutherische Monatshefte, 1, No. 2 (1962),
pp. 81-83.

Wiesel, Elie. Jewish Legends (The Image of the Jew in Literature).
Teachers' Study Guide. New York: Catholic Archdiocese of
New York and Anti-Defamation League of B'nai Brith,   .
[Note: This study guide for a film series should not be con-
fused with Wiesel's Legends of Our Time (New York: Holt,
Rinehart and Winston, 1968).]

_____. One Generation After. New York: Random House,
1970.

Wirth, Wolfgang. "Der ökumenische Aspekt der Begegnung mit den
Juden," in Judentum und christlicher Glaube.

3. Periodicals used in this study, as well as a selection of other journals dealing with Judaism and Christianity, are listed here.

Cahiers Sioniens, Paris.

Criterion. Divinity School of the University of Chicago, Vol. II, No.
1 (Winter 1963).

Emuna Horizonte. Zur Diskussion über Israel und das Judentum.
Deutsche Koordinierungsrat der Gesellschaften für christlich-
jüdische Zusammenarbeit und der deutsch-israelischen Gesell-
schaft. Frankfurt/Main: Emuna-Verlags-Verein; published
every two months.

Encounter Today: Judaism and Christianity in the Contemporary
World. Paris.

192 / Bibliography

Freiburger Rundbrief. Beiträge zur Förderung der Freundschaft
zwischen dem alten und dem neuen Gottesvolk im Geiste
beider Testamente. 1948 -

Friede über Israel. Zeitschrift für Kirche und Judentum. Eine
Zeitschrift des Evangelisch-Lutherischen Zentralvereins für
Mission unter Israel.

Irénikon. Chevetogne, Belgium. Quarterly.

Journal of Ecumenical Studies. Philadelphia, Temple University.

Judaica. Beiträge zum Verständnis des judischen Schicksals in
Vergangenheit und Gegenwart. Zürich.

Kairos. Zeitschrift für Religionswissenschaft und Theologie. Salz-
burg.

Leo Baeck Institute of Jews from Germany. Year-Book. Publications. London, East and West Library, 1956- .

Lutheran World. Publication of the Lutheran World Federation,
Geneva (published simultaneously in German: Lutherische
Rundschau). See especially Vol. X, No. 4 (October 1963),
special issue on "The Church and the Jews;" Vol. XI, No. 3
(July 1964), "Christians, Jews and the Mission of the Church;"
and Vol. XIII, No. 1 (1966), pp. 66-67, "The Use of the
Term 'Hebrew Christian'."

Lutherische Monatshefte. Hamburg.

Saat auf Hoffnung. Vierteljahrschrift für das Gespräch zwischen
Christentum und Judentum. 1863-1935; 1950.

SIDIC. Service international de documentation judéo-chrétienne.
Rome.

INDEX

193